Basic Psychotherapy

To E., C. & M.

'. . . . whatever fortune brings,
Don't be afraid of doing things,'
(Especially, of course, for Kings.)

Basic Psychotherapy

Richard Parry
MB FRCP FRCPsych DPM

Consultant Psychiatrist, Royal Edinburgh Hospital.
Honorary Senior Lecturer, Department of Psychiatry,
University of Edinburgh

SECOND EDITION

CHURCHILL LIVINGSTONE
EDINBURGH LONDON MELBOURNE AND NEW YORK 1983

CHURCHILL LIVINGSTONE
Medical Division of Longman Group Limited

Distributed in the United States of America by
Churchill Livingstone Inc., 19 West 44th Street, New
York, N.Y. 10036, and by associated companies,
branches and representatives throughout the world.

First edition 1975
    Published under title *A Guide to Counselling and Basic
    Psychotherapy*
Second edition 1983

ISBN 0 443 02616 5

British Library Cataloguing in Publication Data
Parry, Richard
    Basic psychotherapy — 2nd ed.
    1. Psychotherapy
    I. Title   II. Parry, Richard, Guide to
    counselling and basic psychotherapy
    616.89'14   RC480

Library of Congress Cataloging in Publication Data
Parry, Richard Albert.
    Basic psychotherapy
    Rev. ed. of: A guide to counselling and basic
psychotherapy. 1975.
    Bibliography: p.
    Includes index.
    1. Psychotherapy. 2. Counselling. I. Parry, Richard
    Albert. Guide to counselling and basic
    psychotherapy. 1975.
    [DNLM: 1. Counselling. 2. Psychotherapy.
WM 420 P265g]
    RC480.P36   1983   616.89'14   82–4118
                                    AACR2

Printed in Singapore by Selector Printing Co Pte Ltd

Preface to Second Edition

'Lord Emsworth ... was wondering, like all authors who have sent their stuff off, if it could not have been polished a bit and given those last little touches which make all the difference. However, again like all authors, he knew that what he had written, even without a final brush-up, was simply terrific ...'*

We first-time authors know exactly how he felt. 'What purity of thought,' we say, 'What elegance of expression!' However, there is a second phase, when the warts become apparent, and I was very relieved to have the opportunity of preparing a second edition.

The title has been changed, the text rewritten, and new material added. In response to several requests, one (one!) new chapter, on 'Schools of medical psychology' has been included, and a short list of suggestions for further reading has been added.

I am very grateful to everyone who made comments and criticisms of the first edition. One wrote that I had obviously enjoyed writing it. I hope it will be equally obvious that I have enjoyed re-writing it.

Edinburgh, 1983   R.A.P.

* Wodehouse P G 1974 Pigs have wings. Barrie & Jenkins, London

Preface to First Edition

My undergraduate interest in psychiatry evaporated during my clinical years, as it does for many medical students, when I encountered psychiatrists and psychiatric patients. It was re-awakened during six years of general practice during which I had the opportunity of attending one of the seminars for general practitioners organised by the late Dr Michael Balint and his colleagues at the Tavistock Clinic.

This had the unexpected but not absolutely unique consequence of leading me to suppose that I was a better psychiatrist than the psychiatrists, and I decided to specialise. Perhaps psychiatry's loss has been general practice's gain. In consequence I have fallen into many of the pitfalls of psychotherapy and have sometimes seen others fall in after me. I decided, therefore, to introduce some order into my own practice, partly in the hope that others as well as myself might learn something from my mistakes.

This book is, therefore, really an account of some of the guidelines used by one man in his psychotherapeutic work. They are certainly not the only guidelines, neither are they necessarily the best ones. It is not easy always to adhere to them, and it may be a comfort to the reader, as it is to the author, to know that in their time, some of the greatest therapists have strayed from the ideal.

It is hoped that the book may be of value to the medical student, particularly during his clinical years. It would best be studied during his course on psychiatry, as a supplement to his standard textbook, for at this stage, he may be interested in acquiring some psychotherapeutic skills. Perhaps too it will be of value to other doctors, especially to general practitioners, to psychiatrists at the beginning of their training, and to members of other professions which run parallel to medicine and especially psychiatry: nurses, social workers, occupational therapists and clinical psychologists.

I have another important group in mind. This comprises the increasing number of people who offer some sort of counselling, either as part of their own profession (clergymen, welfare officers, etc.) or in a voluntary capacity (Marriage Guidance Counsellors, Samaritans, etc.). These people often use skills which are similar to those employed by the psychotherapist, just as physiotherapists and osteopaths may use techniques which were developed by specialists in physical medicine.

It may be surprising to learn that the book has no clearly stated theoretical basis. I have in fact used only those concepts which are acceptable to most theoretical schools. I assume the existence of unconscious mechanisms, that there is a part of the personality which is called the conscience, and that some people may have incestuous thoughts and feelings.

Only very limited use has been made of case histories, and these are fictional or apocryphal. I have not used the experience of specific patients known to me, but because patients may have rather similar experiences, some may think that they recognise themselves or others. The only non-fictional character is the author himself, and he has been considerably romanticised.

It must be conceded that psychotherapy is not in the high regard of many psychiatrists at the present time — indeed, many take a great deal of trouble to demonstrate that, not only is it of no value, but that in some cases it may actually be harmful. These criticisms must be taken very seriously, but unfortunately, it is not always clear what is meant by the word 'psychotherapy'. Until the subject can be defined more precisely, the criticisms can neither be confirmed nor corrected. I hope that this book may add one small straw to the wind of definition.

Many people have helped me in the preparation of this work — albeit unknowingly. They include my friends, my foes, my family; my professors, my pupils, my patients and my publishers. They are really so numerous that it would be invidious to pick out a few in particular. They all have my sincere thanks.

Edinburgh, 1975   R.A.P.

Acknowledgements

The author wishes to express his gratitude to the following authors and publishers, for permission to quote from copyright material:

Ernest Benn Ltd., for an extract from *Psychopathology of Everyday Life* by Sigmund Freud, Ed. James Strachey.

Michael Flanders, Esq., for 'The Spider'; words by Michael Flanders. Recorded in 'The Bestiary of Flanders and Swann', Parlophone PCS 3026.

W. H. Freeman and Co., and the Editor of *Scientific American*, for the dialogue from 'Doctor-Patient Communication' by Barbara M. Korsch and Vida Francis Negrete.

Hutchinson and Co. Ltd., for an extract from *The Prince who Hiccupped* by Anthony Armstrong.

The Editor of the *Lancet*, for the definition of *Le Bovarysme* by Forfar and Benhaman.

Methuen's Children's Books and Mr C. R. Milne, for 'Happiness', from *When We Were Very Young* by A. A. Milne.

Frederick Muller Ltd., for an extract from *Maybe You're Just Inferior* by Herald Froy.

Sigmund Freud Copyrights Ltd., for the letter from Freud quoted in *Life and Work of Sigmund Freud* by Ernest Jones.

The Society of Authors on behalf of the Bernard Shaw Estate, for two extracts from *Pygmalion* by Bernard Shaw.

Acknowledgements

The author wishes to express his gratitude to the following authors and publishers, for permission to quote from copyright material:

Ernest Benn Ltd., for an extract from *Psychopathology of Everyday Life* by Sigmund Freud, (ed. James Strachey)

Michael Lambton, Esq., for 'The Stance', words by Michael Flan... first Recorded in 'The History of Planthres and Swarth'. Tele-phone P65-2020

W. H. Freeman and Co., and the Editor of *Scientific American*, for the dialogue from 'Doctor-Patient Communication' by Barbara M. Korsch and Vida Francis Negrete.

Hutchinson and Co. Ltd., for an extract from *The Front case Dr...* inqui by Anthony Armstrong.

The Editor of the *Lancet*, for the definition of the Doctorate by Peter Jag and Reutianan.

Methuen's Children's Books and Mr. C. R. Milne, for Happiness, from 'When We Were Very Young' by A. A. Milne.

Frederick Muller Ltd., for an extract from *Maybe You're Just In...?* Jerome by Harold Evans.

Sigmund Freud Copyrights Ltd., for the text from Freud quoted in *Life and Work of Sigmund Freud* by Ernest Jones.

The Society of Authors on behalf of the Bernard Shaw Estate, for two extracts from 'Pygmalion' by Bernard Shaw

Contents

Introduction   1
 1. 'The talking cure'   3
 2. Patient and therapist   21
 3. What does the therapist do?   40
 4. What does the therapist say?   51
 5. Some psychological mechanisms   71
 6. The mechanical details   98
 7. Problems for the therapist   114
 8. Patients with difficult problems   133
 9. Problems with difficult patients   152
10. Some schools of medical psychology   169
11. Termination   191
Suggestions for further reading   199
Index   201

Introduction

'Psychotherapy is, above all, not theoretical knowledge, but a personal skill,' Michael Balint. *The doctor, his patient and the illness*.

The high ambition of this book is to teach the student nothing that he does not already know. This became the author's intention when, at the end of the course on which it is based, a member of the class said 'You have not told me anything new, but you have made me think about it'.

'Thinking about it' is the first stage of the 'limited but considerable change in the doctor's personality' which Balint considered to be an essential in the acquisition of psychotherapeutic skill. The development of the skill requires practice, and whilst a book can offer some guidelines and indicate the pitfalls, it cannot replace actual experience. In his 'Introductory lectures on psycho-analysis' Freud reminded his audience that by listening to him they would not learn 'how to set about a psycho-analytic investigation or how to carry the treatment through'. Operative surgery provides a suitable parallel. No book can teach the surgeon how to proceed in an individual case, but it may supplement his own experience and the examples of his teachers.

The medical student's first contact with patients occurs when he learns to take a case history. It is then that he begins to observe the patient — and to be aware of the patient's observation of him. The art of careful history taking is without doubt a matter of prime importance. There are few diseases in which a careful history does not reveal the diagnosis. It is confirmed subsequently by physical examination. Symptoms are seldom preceded by physical signs. As a result of history taking, the student will, for example, learn to differentiate between organic heart disease and a neurotic preoccupation with cardiac function. It is a matter of regret that history taking frequently ceases at this point. Many investigations might be avoided and much anxiety alleviated if, as the result of a few more questions, the reasons for the neurotic preoccupation could be elicited.

The influence of a doctor upon his patient is tolerated in these days of scientific medicine as an inevitable but regrettable distraction. Ingenious methods are devised in an attempt to eliminate it from therapeutic trials or at least to neutralise it. Doctors often feel slightly dishonest when they use their relationship with him for the benefit of the patient and prefer to ascribe the credit to a placebo reaction. But the influence of the 'bedside manner' cannot be denied.

Balint formulated the useful proposition that the doctor himself could be thought of as a potent drug which may be used for good or ill. He emphasised the care with which the doctor must be 'dispensed'. The aim of this book is partly to help the reader define the nature of this 'drug' and to use it in a way which will be helpful to himself and beneficial to his patients. There is no wish to define it for him.

So far, we have spoken about the relationship between a doctor and his patient, but others also relate to patients. Furthermore, not everyone who needs the assistance of a helpful relationship is a patient. Nurses, social workers, occupational therapists, clinical psychologists and other members of the para-medical professions may exert a powerful influence on their patients and they must learn to employ this influence to its maximum effect. Other people, too sometimes counsel: they may be church workers, welfare officers or members of one of the voluntary organisations such as the Marriage Counselling Service or the Samaritans. It is hoped that the methods described here may be of value to them also.

Lest it should be questioned that a book designed primarily for doctors should be offered also to non-medical workers, it may be pleaded that treatment is not the exclusive prerogative of doctors. The same general methods may be used by workers in other fields as well as the medical one. For example, simple therapy for colds, coughs and constipation may be suggested by pharmacists and herbalists as well as by doctors. It is, however, hoped that if the non-medical or voluntary worker finds that he has undertaken something which appears to be beyond his capacity, he will seek the help of a professional adviser.

1

'The talking cure'

CARDINAL PRINCIPLE: There is nothing so obvious that it can be accepted without question.

If you agree with everything you read in this book, it will have failed in its purpose. For it is not a dissertation. It is an account of some of the techniques which have been evolved to cope with the problems which arise in medical (not exclusively in psychiatric) practice. Some have been adopted by the author because they suit his personality, his way of working, his profession and his speciality. He sometimes finds it is necessary to modify them.

He does not suppose that his approach will suit everyone who reads about it. However, he hopes that others, whether psychiatrists, general practitioners, specialists in other branches of medicine or members of allied professions, will be encouraged to compare their own techniques, to criticise, modify or adopt, those which may be useful, and to think carefully about those they reject. At the same time, the reader who is learning his craft should take the opportunity of observing his colleagues and teachers, criticising, modifying and, where appropriate, adapting the techniques used by them. He should also watch and compare the techniques used by all those who interview others, particularly on the radio and television. The intention is to help him to develop the most appropriate approach for his professional needs.

Although written primarily for doctors and nurses, many of the problems to be discussed here will be familiar to others who are concerned with helping people. It is possible that they too will find something of value.

Talking with patients is not concerned merely with gathering information about them. If this were so, doctors could one day be replaced by computers. Talking is also the means by which a diagnosis is achieved, a course of treatment planned, and a prognosis assessed. It has a further function. We will try to show that whatever the disorder, whether psychological or organic, there is something about talking with patients which is itself therapeutic. The matter is, therefore, of the greatest clinical importance.

Some of the problems we will discuss are very complicated. Let us begin with one which appears to be simple. By what name should one address a patient?

In the 1940s and 1950s, male patients were often called simply by their surname. The nurse would say, 'Here are your tablets, Smith.' In still earlier times, patients were often called by the number of the bed which they occupied. The doctor might ask, 'Let me see your tongue, Number 22.' What is appropriate to the 1980s?

It is acceptable to call children by their first names, but at what point does a child become an adult? Adolescents, in their struggle towards maturity, sometimes resent being called by their first names. They feel that people who do so are treating them like children. At the other extreme, some adults plead to be called by their first names. It is as though they still yearn to be treated as children. Which is correct?

In some centres, the problem is solved by calling every patient, whatever his age, by his first name. This is a simple solution, and may seem suitable to the times. Elsewhere, some patients are called by their first names and others by their surnames. Unfortunately, the therapist sometimes forgets who is called which. When he discovers that he is called John on one occasion and Mr Smith on the next, the patient may wonder what has happened: and whether he has offended. Such inconsistency is clearly undesirable.

Some therapists choose age as the criterion. They call patients who are younger than themselves by their first names, and older patients by their surnames. This solution may be satisfactory when the therapist is in his 20s. But the years pass by quickly, and if he sticks to his principle, he will soon find himself calling people in their 50s by their first names, by which time, it may be less appropriate.

Other therapists deal with the problem by presenting it to the patient. They ask him to choose how he wishes to be addressed. Usually the patient asks the therapist to call him by his first name. It sounds more friendly. In turn, and for the same reason, the patient may ask the therapist for permission to call him by his first name. It sounds more friendly. This raises a fresh problem. What is the nature of the relationship between the patient and his therapist? Is it one of friendship? In the view of the author, a relationship of friendship is not appropriate in psychotherapy. The relationship is a professional one, of great complexity. In friendship, confidences are exchanged, favours granted and pleasures shared. Such things never happen in psychotherapy. The relationship can be a kindly one, without being friendly.

Thus, we find that the problem is not simple, after all. There is neither a right nor a wrong answer. Each raises problems of its own. None is too trivial to be dismissed. The reader may, and should, make his own decision.

It is the author's practice to call all his patients by their appropriate title — Mr, Mrs, Miss, Doctor, Professor, Ayatollah, Your Majesty, and so on. He expects his patients to address him by his formal title. He tries to be consistent, and adopts the same approach, even with young people. Many of his colleagues disagree with him.

Problems in medicine may arise out of things which appear to be very simple, from the moment of the first contact between doctor and patient. In fact, there is little that is simple.

Now we will describe a common but rather surprising phenomenon. We will use as an illustration, an experience which recurred frequently in the author's early years in medicine, which were spent in general practice.

Appointments systems were then unusual. Provided that the patient came during advertised hours and was prepared to wait long enough, he would eventually be seen. The doctor saw everyone — however many there were. This was often an arduous task, but he tried to perform it as skilfully and as speedily as possible.

Sometimes the patient — more often a woman than a man — came with a rather vague complaint, and whilst the doctor was gathering his thoughts, she offered her own explanation. It usually involved her husband, her children, her parents, her brothers and sisters, her in-laws, her friends, her neighbours, her husbands' colleagues, other doctors, shopkeepers, the clergy, the Government, the Opposition, the Communists, the Trade Unions and the Russians. The interminable story was interpersed by a variety of emotions. Sometimes the patient was angry, sometimes she laughed, sometimes she cried, sometimes she looked embarrassed, sometimes she shouted, sometimes she whispered.

The doctor tried to listen attentively to this torrent of words, but to tell the truth, he was completely bewildered. To add to his problems, he could hear more and more patients coming into the waiting room. Eventually the patient stopped for breath, and the doctor did the thing which, as a medical student, he had been taught never to do. He prescribed a hurried tonic and told the patient to return in a week.

She usually did so, and her opening words were nearly always the same. She said, 'Doctor, I want to thank you for all the advice you gave me last week. I did exactly as you suggested and my symptoms have completely disappeared.' Then she would add, 'I didn't need your prescription', and give it back. The doctor was always very puzzled. He could not remember giving any advice. He could remember only his increasing impatience with her garrulity, and his inability to understand what she was talking about. Yet now she was reporting that she was cured.

This sequence of events recurred many times, but the doctor remained perplexed. What was happening? If the patient had *taken* the tonic, he would have ascribed her recovery to its placebo effect. He would have concluded that an inert but rather disagreeable medicine had been invested with magical powers and that her recovery was due to simple faith. But she had not taken it. Anyway, what is a 'placebo effect'? Is it real or imaginary, good or bad? If it makes the patient better, we should surely pay more attention to it.

And how can one explain her recovery when she did *not* take the tonic? Was it because the doctor had a 'placebo effect'? Did the patient look upon him as a witch doctor, with magical powers of cure? If this were so, we are still no further forward. In fact, she herself would have rejected the idea as nonsense. She would have insisted that she merely did as the doctor advised. She disagreed that the doctor had given her no advice.

As time went by, the author was to discover that experiences such as these were very common. Many of the doctors who worked with Balint (1961) encountered similar phenomena.

A century previously, a Viennese neurologist, Josef Breuer, who is still remembered for his work in respiratory physiology and particularly for his part in the description of the Hering-Breuer reflex, had a similar experience.

He was responsible for the treatment of a young and attractive patient named Bertha Pappenheim. Fraulein Pappenheim complained of a variety of physical symptoms. Excluding only her left arm, she had lost the power of all her limbs. She was unable to speak her own language, although she could communicate in English. She had alternating states of consciousness, tunnel vision, and sometimes suffered from terrifying visual hallucinations. There was no organic cause for any of her symptoms, and nowadays a diagnosis of conversion hysteria would probably have been made.

Breuer discovered that if the patient could remember the circumstances which existed when the symptoms started, they disappeared.

Unfortunately, however, she was seldom able to recall the circumstances. Breuer therefore adopted a technique which had been employed by Charcot in Paris in the course of his investigations into post-hypnotic suggestion. Charcot had observed that patients could often remember things that they had 'completely forgotten' whilst under the influence of an hypnotic trance. This observation played an important part in the renewal of interest in the 'unconscious'. Fraulein Pappenheim was a good subject for hypnosis, and Breuer used the technique to help her recall the origin of her symptoms. When he did so, she was freed of them.

He quotes several examples. In the heat of the Viennese summer, and although she suffered greatly from thirst, the patient was unable to drink any fluid for about six weeks. Under hypnosis, she recalled that this symptom had originated when she walked unexpectedly into a room used by her companion — an English girl whom she disliked. There she found her companion's dog lapping from a glass. The patient was angry and very disgusted, but she had been carefully brought up to believe that it is not ladylike to express vulgar emotions. She concealed her revulsion and left the room without speaking.

When, under hypnosis, she recalled the incident, the patient gave vent to her disgust, asked for a glass of water, immediately drank a large quantity, and wakened with the glass at her lips. The symptoms never returned. Fraulein Pappenheim herself nicknamed the process, 'The talking cure'.

Nowadays, such extreme cases of conversion hysteria are rare. Nevertheless, we are still taught that it is not always polite to express our feelings. The events which puzzled the author when he was in general practice occurred when his patients gave vent to their true feelings. Although he neither used, nor thought of using, hypnosis in order to obtain their 'confessions', he had, without realising it, been using a technique which was very similar to that of Breuer. Frequently, it resulted in recovery.

'Just talking'

When someone is overwhelmed by a psychological problem, his friends often ask, derisively, how 'just talking' can be of help. We have made a first attempt to answer this question. There is something about 'just talking' that encourages us to remove the pejorative word 'just'. Whatever the disorder, psychological or organic, talking seems to help patients.

Our intention, therefore, is to help the reader to develop his technique in interviewing: to assist him in helping his patients to 'talk' in the way which is most beneficial. We do so in the belief that *talking* is helpful to them. It is not our intention to demonstrate how the reader can amaze his friends, psychoanalyse his enemies, and discover the hidden weaknesses of his seniors.

A patient

When a patient asks for help, she does so with the natural expectation that her problems will be solved.

Here is such a patient. She is a good looking woman in her early 30s, with long, straight hair, very dark, with a few streaks of grey. Her figure is trim and she dresses well. She has arrived 30 minutes early. The previous patient has cancelled his appointment, and consequently she is seen immediately. She appears slightly disconcerted when she is ushered straight into the consulting room, and enquires, with a hint of anxiety, 'I'm not late, am I? My appointment was for 3 o'clock! The doctor explains what has happened and shows her to a chair. The reader will notice that he does not leave the choice to her. When both are seated, he says, 'Tell me what problem is.' The exact form of his opening question is still evolving.

The patient speaks in a pleasant and well-modulated voice. She tells her story very concisely and it sounds as though she has rehearsed it carefully. Briefly, it is this. Her husband, who, is an executive a little older than herself, has started to drink heavily. She fears that he is becoming an alcoholic. She says that she cannot stand it any longer. Unless he does something she will leave him. He does nothing. What should she do?

Well, what should she do? Here are some of the suggestions made to the many patients of whom she is compounded:

Get a job.
Find a hobby.
Do voluntary work.
Flirt with other men to make him jealous.
Ask your doctor for a tranquilliser.
Start drinking with him.
Make sure that he is never alone.
Ask a friend to speak to him.
Remember that many husbands who drink have lost their job, and
   he still has his.
Buy some provocative underwear.
Think positively.
Think of all the good things.
Think of all the people who are worse off than you.
Pull yourself together.

Make yourself attractive.

Wait until he gets worse.

Wait for him to do something for himself.

Be thankful for small mercies.

You have to expect that sort of thing when they get to the male menopause.

The reader is invited to comment on each of these suggestions.

The patient's question was a simple one. What should she do? As she told her story, she herself provided a *logical* solution. She said, 'Unless he does something, I will leave him.' The *logical* answer is that she should leave him.

However, when this is pointed out to her, she bursts into tears. She says, 'I can't possibly do that. I love him. Besides, there are the children. Can't you do something?' The *logical* solution has been of no help.

It is improbable that the reader will find words to solve the problems of his patients in a book. Emotional problems are not solved by words, however elegant, well-intentioned, passionate or eloquent they may be. Neither are they solved by logic.

One well-meaning person suggested that our patient should think of all the people who are worse off than she. The reader should reflect upon this fatuous but common cliché. If I have toothache, it is not alleviated by the contemplation of someone else's toothache. Pain is not relieved by thinking about the pain from which others are suffering. Patients are not cured by being told to think of something else, to find a hobby, to snap out of it or to appreciate that 'You have to accept that sort of thing at your age.' Clichés have no part to play in psychotherapy.

There is no 'technique' by which a husband can be prevented from drinking. No therapist would expect a loving wife to accept her drunken husband without complaint. However, the therapist can — and will — ask, 'How has this situation come about? Why has it persisted? Why has it not been possible to find a solution? What avenues must be explored if we are to make progress?' Some of the questions to be asked may seem trivial to the point of insult. However, there may be great difficulty in obtaining the answers, even to the most simple.

An obvious question is, *why* does the husband drink? Is he someone who cannot cope with the demands that are made upon him? Perhaps drinking is part of his job. There may be many matters of which we know nothing. Does he have a troubled conscience? Does he dislike the atmosphere at home? Is he trying to get rid of his wife? Does he hope that she will keep her promise, and leave him if he continues to drink? Does he look for some sort of revenge upon her? Has she herself contributed to the problem? Does she *want* him to get better?

His wife will almost certainly say that she will do anything to improve matters. She must therefore consider the unwelcome possibility that she herself has played a part in creating the problem. Could it be that she herself derives some sort of masochistic satisfaction from his behaviour? Is she someone who needs a 'burden' to carry through life?

Such ideas may seem to be so absurd that it is an impertinence to present them. But nothing is so absurd that it can be rejected without consideration. Nothing is so obvious that it can be accepted without question.

Very soon, it is time for the patient to leave. The therapist has asked a few questions, but has said very little. He has silently limited himself to a few, rather wild speculations. He has given her no hope, and nothing to work on. The reader may feel that she has derived very little benefit from her interview. He may wonder if she feels as demoralised as he does.

The therapist does not set out to design a cliché-ridden blueprint which enable his patients to solve their problems. He seldom makes suggestions and rarely gives advice. This often surprises beginners, and it certainly puzzles their patients. How can they recover if the doctor does not tell them what to do? It is alleged that in other branches of medicine, the doctor always does something active. He prescribes a drug, makes an incision or applies a dressing. As a result of this expectation, and although deplored by purists, much of medical treatment is symptomatic. Someone who complains of indigestion is likely, in the first instance, to be treated with an antacid. Even psychiatrists, who should know better, treat headaches with paracetamol, insomnia with hypnotics and constipation with laxatives. Why does the psychotherapist do nothing?

In medicine and surgery, cure is *not* achieved by what the *doctor* does. Most diseases and many injuries would get better *without* medical intervention. Antibiotics do not *cure* infected tissues; plaster casts do not heal fractures. In medicine, the aim is to provide the patient's body with an environment which gives it the best possible opportunity to heal itself. When regarded from this point of view, it is clear that psychotherapy is similar to most other forms of medical treatment in its mode of operation. Psychotherapy is not something which is totally different.

Those who are prepared to pay close and unbiassed attention will see and hear many things. The reader must listen carefully to what he is told. He will observe not merely through the medium of words, but of emotions, subtleties of behaviour, apparently minor errors, variations in emphasis, and trivial omissions.

A paediatric case

We do not propose to examine individual cases in detail. However, here is the verbatim transcript of a short interview in which a paediatrician tries to reassure two very worried parents. The case, which is not a psychiatric one, illustrates how easy it is, with the best of intentions, to confuse, frighten and mislead people.*

Father: How does his heart sound?

Doctor: Sounds pretty good. He's got a little murmur there. I'm not sure what it is. It's...it er...could just be a little hole in his heart.

Mother: Is that very dangerous, when you have a hole in your heart?

Doctor: No, because I think it's the upper chamber, and if it's the upper chamber then it means nothing,

Mother: Oh.

Doctor: Otherwise they just grow up and they repair them.

Mother: What would cause the hole in his heart?

Doctor: H'm?

Mother: What was it that caused the hole in his heart?

Doctor: Its cause...er...just developmental, when their er...

Mother: M-h'm.

Doctor: There's a little membrane that comes down, one from each direction. And sometimes they don't quite meet, and so there's either a hole at the top or a hole at the bottom and then... It's really...er ...almost never causes any trouble.

Mother: Oh.

Doctor: It's er...one thing that they never get S.B.E. from...it's the only heart lesion in which they don't.

* from 'Doctor-Patient Communication', © Korsch and Negrete, Scientific American, August 1972. 227:2 p.68.

Mother: Uh-huh.

Doctor: And er...they grow up to be normal.

Mother: Oh, good.

Doctor: And er . . . if anything happens, they can always catheterise them and make sure that's what it is, or do heart surgery.

Mother: Yes...

Doctor: Really no problem with it. They almost never get into trouble, so . . .

Mother: Do you think that he might have developed the murmur being that my husband and I both have a murmur?

Doctor: No.

Mother: No? Oh, it's not hereditary, then?

Doctor: No.

Mother: Oh, I see.

Doctor: It's true that certain people . . . tendency to rheumatic fever, for instance.

Mother: M'mm?

Doctor: There is a tendency for the abnormal antigen – antibody reactions to be inherited, and therefore they can sometimes be more susceptible.

Mother: Oh, I see. That wouldn't mean anything if er . . . I would . . . I'm Rh negative and he's positive. It wouldn't mean anything in that line, would it?

Doctor: No.

Mother: No? Good.

Doctor: No. The only thing you have to worry about is other babies.

Mother: M-h'm?

Doctor: Watch your Coombs and things.

Mother: Watch my what?

Doctor: Your titres... Coombs titres.

Mother: Oh, yes.

Before we discuss this interview, it will be helpful if the reader will read the transcript for a second time. He should take particular note of the occasions on which things go wrong. How would *he* have managed these occasions?

We may assume that the doctor is competent and well-informed, and that he wishes to help the parents to the best of his ability. Nevertheless, it will scarcely be disputed that he conducts the interview badly. Probably this is as clear to him as it is to everyone else.

We might begin by imagining the state of mind of the parents *before* they meet the paediatrician. Physicians seldom give thought to how patients feel before the consultation. In the present case, the parents are naturally concerned for the health of their son. He is certainly very precious to them. Before the meeting, they may have had several anxious sleepless nights. Will the news be good or bad? What will they be asked? What will they be told? Will there be something for which they will blame themselves? Will the doctor be harsh or gentle, sympathetic or critical? They will assume that he is wise and knowledgeable, but may already wonder whether there is someone else who is even more wise and knowledgeable.

The father speaks first and his question sets the tone for the whole interview:

'*How does his heart sound?*' This question is not to be taken literally. It is an example of what we shall later call a 'verbal non-verbal communication'. The father is using one question to ask another. He is really asking, 'Is his heart healthy?' Many people think of the heart as the most important organ in the body. If it is healthy, all is well. A psychotherapist might immediately have commented on the father's *unspoken* anxiety. Perhaps he would have said, 'It sounds as though you were worried that your son had some form of heart disease.' However, the paediatrician is reassuring. He says:

'*Sounds pretty good.*' The psychotherapist will not object to this reply. The paediatrician is a specialist in paediatrics, not in psychotherapy. The parents are seeking a paediatric opinion. They will be pleased to hear the good news. However, the reassurance is immediately qualified:

'*He's got a little murmur there*'. Now, to the parents, what does this mean? Doctors recognise things called 'benign' murmurs. Often, in order to avoid unnecessary alarm, they do not mention them to their patients. Unfortunately, without further investigations, it may not be possible to confirm that the murmur is a benign one. Perhaps the paediatrician felt that his reassurance was too immediate and too absolute. He forgets that patients quickly make mountains out of mole-hills. The parents will have heard about heart murmurs. They may even have heard of people dying from such things. What is a murmur anyway? To the paediatrician it is probably something very trivial: a tiny variation in a familiar tune. To the parents it may portend disaster.

'*I'm not sure what it is.*' The expert is baffled. We may guess that he does not consider it to be of any great importance. However, the parents will not guess anything of the sort. To them, it sounds very frightening. The doctor realises that he may have caused unnecessary alarm. He hazards an explanation:

'*It's . . . it er . . . could just be a little hole in his heart.*'

The parents may find this even more alarming. A hole in any part of the body sounds frightening. A hole in an organ as vital as the heart sounds terrifying. It is likely that the parents have read about children with holes in their hearts, and of some of the operations which are undertaken. Heart operations are surely very dangerous. We may try to think of the fantasies which the parents might have. Could their son die during an operation for a hole in his heart? The mother begins to express her anxiety:

'*Is that very dangerous when you have a hole in your heart?*'

And the paediatrician hastens to reassure her:

'*No, because I think it's the upper chamber, and if it's the upper chamber, then it means nothing.*'

A psychotherapist might have evaded the question by replying, 'I see I have alarmed you. You must have been very frightened by what I said.' The paediatrician's reassurance involves a new concept: that of an 'upper chamber'. If the parents do not understand him, they may be reluctant to confess their ignorance, and their uncertainty will be increased.

'*Otherwise they just grow up and they repair them.*' The paediatrician amplifies and extends his reassurance, but the effect is to make matters worse. Who just grow up? Who repair them? How do they repair them? Who repair what? Is it bad if they don't repair them? The mother looks for enlightenment. Her question is very specific:

'*What was it that caused the hole in his heart?*' A complete answer to this question might be very complicated. The paediatrician is unlikely to be in possession of sufficient information to give an accurate reply. Furtheremore, he is not even certain that the child has a hole in the heart. He makes a fumbling attempt to reply:

'*Its cause . . . er . . . just developmental, when their er . . .*'

It is instantly obvious that the mother does not understand. She may even be wondering if the doctor understands. It is evident to the paediatrician that things are getting out of hand. Defensively, he becomes technical:

'There's a little membrane that comes down, one from each direction. And sometimes they don't quite meet, and so there's either a hole at the top or a hole at the bottom and then . . . it's really . . . er . . . almost never causes any trouble.'

The parents must be completely overwhelmed. What does the doctor mean when he says that if they don't meet there is a hole at the top or the bottom? The top or the bottom of what? What does he mean by the word 'membrane'? Some people speak of old people getting a membrane in their eyes. The paediatrician tries to find a few words of comfort:

'It's er . . . one thing that they never get S.B.E. from . . . it's the only heart lesion in which they don't.'

What will the parents make of that? The doctor has mentioned yet another condition: a strange disease of which they have probably never heard. It sounds something like Espie. He also indicates that their child has a heart lesion. What does 'lesion' mean? Is it good or bad? Is a lesion safer or more dangerous because their child will not get Espie? Will it make him better or worse? They will look it up in the medical dictionary when they get home.

The paediatrician continues to reassure:

'And er . . . they grow up to be normal.'

And spoils it again:

'And er . . . if anything happens, they can always catheterise them and make sure that's what it is, or do heart surgery.'

Now he seems to be condemning the parents to years of uncertainty. Will their child require heart surgery when he grows up? Isn't catheterisation something to do with the bladder?

'Really no problem with it. They almost never get into trouble, so . . .'

But the mother is very worried. She fears that her child may be gravely ill. Is it her fault? She asks:

'Do you think that he might have developed the murmur being that my husband and I both have a murmur?'

In addition to her concern for her child, we may wonder how long she has been worrying about the murmurs in her heart and in her husband's. Are they to blame for the fact that their son has a murmur? The doctor reassures her again:

'No.'

Then, for no obvious reason, he adds:

'It is true that certain people . . . tendency to rheumatic fever, for instance.'

Is he now trying to tell them that their child has a tendency to rheumatic fever? What is rheumatic fever? Is it anything to do with rheumatism?

The doctor sees that he is increasing their confusion and embarks upon another technical explanation. It is probably incomprehensible to the parents and is too brief to be completely accurate:

'*There is a tendency for the abnormal antigen–antibody reactions to be inherited and therefore they can sometimes be more susceptible.*'

Her next question illustrates the mother's total failure to understand. She asks about the Rhesus status of her husband and herself. Is it something in that line? This too may be something that has worried her in the past. The doctor gives a perfect answer. It is brief, precise, clear, simple, dogmatic, informed and helpful. He says:

'*No.*'

Then he spoils it again:

'*The only thing you have to worry about is other babies.*'

It is, of course, entirely proper to tell parents something about the possible consequences of conflicting Rhesus blood groups on unborn children. But this is not an appropriate time to do so. Once again the parents are out of their depth, and once again the doctor tries to help:

'*Watch your Coombs and things ... your titres ... Coombs titres.*'

What will the parents have made of that? Did they hear one word or two? Kumsteaters? What is a Kum? What are Steaters?

The reader may feel that the author has been excessively critical of the doctor in this discussion. Surely he will acknowledge that he was doing his best? The circumstances may have been difficult. The doctor may have been distracted by the fact that the interview was being recorded. There may have been other matters to be taken into consideration. The author should have been more sympathetic. Already, therefore, the reader may find himself disagreeing with the author. He is reminded that his disagreement is welcomed.

We will frequently remind the reader that nothing in psychotherapy may be ignored, and nothing should escape observation, examination and analysis. Detailed scrutiny may be painful for the patient and may appear cruel to the onlooker. But if it is agreed that there is nothing so trivial that it may be ignored, and nothing so obvious that it can be accepted without question, there is no escape. As he develops his skills, the beginner will always be very critical of himself. He must also be free to criticize his colleagues, both senior and junior. What is the correct thing to say? Why was that phrase used? Could it have been worded better? What were the precise words used by the patient in his reply? What information does he seek when he asks a question? (We have already noted that the question, 'How does his heart sound?' was not meant to be taken literally. It was a way of saying, 'Is his heart healthy?').

The reader should now read the whole transcript for a third time. Does he notice anything else? For example, has he observed that, apart from the opening question, the father does not speak?

Terminology

Throughout the book, we will refer to doctors, patients, therapists, and psychotherapy. These names may not always be appropriate. The reader may be a nurse, a clinical psychologist, a social worker, an occupational therapist, or a member of one of the other helping professions. The words 'client' and 'counselling' might be more suitable for people who are members of voluntary counselling organisations.

The reader may wonder about the differences between psychotherapy and counselling. Sometimes they seem very similar. How do they differ? The brief answer is, sometimes very little. Both the psychotherapist and the counsellor deal with people who have encountered certain problems. The problems themselves may be very similar and the choice of helper is sometimes quite arbitrary. Doctors may refer 'patients' to counsellors: counsellors sometimes refer 'clients' to doctors. The decision may depend on how each sees his ability to cope with the problems which are presented. In addition, there may be more specious considerations, such as the amount of space available in the appointment book. Therapists deal with 'disease'; identical situations may be dealt with by counsellors as 'problems'.

This blurring of roles may be confusing. When both are faced with a marital problem, how does the approach of a doctor differ from for example, that of a marriage counsellor? The answer is one of some subtlety. The difference lies in the *roles* allocated by society to the people who are involved. Doctors are professionals who are trained to treat *disease*. They look upon the people who consult them as patients. Patients often regard their doctor as a wise and knowledgeable man, who has undertaken a prodigious amount of training, enabling him to take upon himself the cares of the world. Counsellors sometimes think of themselves, quite erroneously, as amateurs, whose training is substantially less than that of doctors. In fact, the opposite is sometimes true. Clients expect their counsellors to be trained and knowledgeable people — an expectation which some counsellors find very difficult to tolerate. 'After all,' they protest, 'we are just ordinary people.' But by their protest they demonstrate their failure to appreciate that it is sometimes impossible, and may not be desirable, to set aside the role which is allocated to them by the people who seek their help. An experienced counsellor who has learned to be gentle, tolerant and observant, may have much to teach doctors. The author hopes that the converse is also true.

A different problem arises because of the attitude which the patient — or client — adopts towards *himself*. The person who thinks of himself as a patient may expect to be treated with the consideration and compassion to which invalids are entitled. He may hope that there are tablets, injections or even operations which will relieve him of his difficulties. He may be willing to submit passively to everything that is done to him, but expect to do very little for himself. The *client* may see himself in a much more active role. He hopes that his counsellor will make suggestions, and he will expect to carry them through. He may expect to rely less heavily on his counsellor than he would on his doctor.

The reader will appreciate that these are complex matters and include many misconceptions. Later we will return to some of them.

Types of psychotherapy

It is usual to distinguish between intensive psychotherapy and supportive psychotherapy. The aim of intensive psychotherapy is to help the patient to examine those aspects of his behaviour which are irrational, inappropriate or irrelevant and to help him modify his way of life, thereby developing more realistic methods of dealing with his problems. Intensive psychotherapy and intensive counselling are creative endeavours. They seek to identify the maladaptive aspects of the patient's personality so that he can, if he wishes, take steps to change them. Intensive counselling and intensive psychotherapy involve work which is arduous, time consuming but fascinating. For the patient, it involves a degree of self-scrutiny which can be disagreeable, disconcerting and sometimes very distressing. Doctor and patient usually meet frequently and regularly for months or even for years. The therapist spends a *substantial* fraction of his *total* work time with one patient. In consequence, it is possible for most doctors to accept only a few patients for intensive therapy.

Occasionally, intensive psychotherapy is quite brief. A single hour may be sufficient to bring relief to a patient of previously good personality who has encountered a serious problem. The author's experience in general practice, to which reference has already been made, and which concluded with 'thanks for all your help and advice', were examples of brief but effective intensive psychotherapy.

Supportive psychotherapy may be offered to the large number of patients who, for one reason or another, are denied intensive psychotherapy. Perhaps they are of unstable or inadequate personality or have no particular intelligence. They often seem to prefer a neurotic way of life and show no serious wish to alter it. They may derive some benefit by spending a short time with their counsellor or therapist, but no-one really expects them to change, and no great efforts are made to persuade them to do so.

They meet their therapist infrequently and briefly: perhaps for only a few minutes every few months. During the sessions, the patient describes some of the difficulties which he has encountered, whilst the therapist tries to listen attentively — although to tell the truth, his mind sometimes wanders to more agreeable topics. At the end of the session, the therapist draws together a few threads, reassures the patient and dismisses him until their next meeting. No real effort is made to change the status quo. The patient is allowed to maintain the role of a 'sick' person. Later we shall see that this may bring him many advantages.

Everyone involved in counselling and psychotherapy carries a number of 'supportive cases' such as these. They know that they are doing very little to change them. Sometimes they try to refer them to someone else, but most therapists already have a similar burden and it is never easy to find new shoulders. The patients themselves often seem to be grateful for their brief sessions, and there may be details of technique to be learned. Working with them is part of the price that must be paid for the more gratifying intensive work. Here, we will not consider supportive psychotherapy to any extent.

To the patient
It is a fact of medical life that when they have the opportunity, patients read what they can about their illnesses. Even doctors, when they are ill, check up in their textbooks. This is understandable. If there is something wrong with him, the patient wishes to acquire all possible information.

It is generally supposed that doctors do not approve of this practice. Journalists delight in the concept of a medical closed shop. In truth, few doctors seriously disapprove. They are mainly concerned because it is very easy for patients, even if they are medically qualified, to be misled. Some textbooks are seriously out of date. Some contradict others. A few might most charitably be described as eccentric. Many raise questions to which there are no answers.

Many people hope to gain knowledge about themselves and their friends from textbooks of psychiatry and psychology. Who is normal? Who develops psychiatric illness? How does it start? Can it be inherited? Is it really curable? Does it lead to homicidal mania?

It is understandable that some individuals worry about the possibility of developing a serious psychiatric disorder. Most people can recall occasions when they have been muddled or confused. There may have been times when they found themselves indifferent or even antagonistic to those whom they thought they loved. From time to time, they may feel that others look strangely at them. Under certain circumstances, normal people may become hallucinated.

Those readers who are patients may dip into this book, in the hope of discovering something about themselves. In addition, they may hope to learn more about their therapist. What is he doing? Does he know what he is about? Is he doing it properly? Would it not be better to be treated by that nice Dr Parry? Or, conversely, how fortunate it is not to be treated by that frightful Dr Parry!

Whatever the patient's thoughts may be, his therapist would like to know about them. This also applies to the author's patients. Whatever their feelings, whether they are friendly or hostile, he would like to know.

The reader may recall an incident in Jerome K. Jerome's *Three Men in a Boat*. J., glancing idly through a medical dictionary, was horrified to find that he had every disease in the book from ague to zymosis, with the single exception of housemaid's knee. In dire distress, he consulted a medical friend, who gave him the following prescription:

'Rx
1 lb beefsteak, with
1 pt bitter beer every six hours.
1 ten-mile walk every morning.
1 bed at 11 sharp every night.
And don't stuff up your head with things you don't understand.'

'I followed the directions, with the happy result — speaking for myself — that my life was preserved......'.

2

Patient and therapist

CARDINAL PRINCIPLE: People are people

Many laymen have a high expectation of psychotherapy. They see it as a panacea for all the ills to which flesh is heir, a cure for everything which cannot be treated by any other means. Needless to say, such expectations are completely unfounded. Some doctors look upon psychotherapy as a convenient dumping ground for troublesome patients and a handy scapegoat when they do not become trouble-free.

Psychotherapy makes very few claims for itself. It does not aspire to make bad people good, the idle industrious, or to change cowards into heroes. It will not make dullards brainy, short people tall, or turn brunettes into blondes. It does not pretend to turn sows' ears into silk purses. The therapist will try to help the patient to make the best of his assets, but he can give no guarantee of success. If the patient is helped, his therapist knows that many problems will remain when therapy comes to an end. He will anticipate only limited benefit in return for much hard work.

The problems encountered by patients arise from conflicts which occur between them and other people. Problems never arise between people and things. 'People' may be one, two or many. They may be close acquaintances or ill-defined groups. They may be parents, children, husbands or wives. They may be the Reds, the Whites, the Blues, the Russians, the Management, or the Unions. They are people whose needs and perceptions differ from those of the patient.

When problems arise between people and things, the solution is swift and painless. An inanimate object can be discarded, a dress changed, a house sold. But when the thing has a human association, problems may emerge. The dress may have been bought by a loved partner. It may not be the house which is wrong, but the people who live in it.

When problems arise between people, feelings are induced. If they are not, there is no problem. There never was, for they would have drifted apart. Happiness or sadness springs from the interaction between one person and another. Fear, love, anxiety, terror, pleasure: every emotion springs from the relationship between people.

Although we call them by different names, the therapist and his patient are people, and psychotherapy is, at its simplest, people trying to help people. The similarities between the patient and the therapist are considerable, much greater than their differences. They are psychologically similar just as they are physically similar. It is likely that they have similar hopes and fears, similar desires, prejudices and weaknesses. They usually come from the same culture. The things of which they are ashamed will be the same. They will be ambitious for common goals; and will share similar illogicalities.

The patient's expectations

Sherlock Holmes had many of the attributes of the ideal psychotherapist and in this book, we will meet him more than once. Watson described him as 'the most perfect reasoning and observing machine that the world has ever seen'. Although he had astonishing gaps in his education (he did not know that the earth moves round the sun*), he knew everything about his own subject. When confronted with a fresh problem, he was usually able to refer to others like it. He would say, 'You will find parallel cases in Andover in '77 and there was something of the sort at The Hague last year'.

But Holmes is one of the immortals and was created omniscient. Therapists and their patients are people and being only people, their powers are limited. Sam Weller made a similar point although the context was slightly different. During his cross-examination in the trial of Bardell v Pickwick, he was asked by Mrs Bardell's Counsel, 'You were in the passage, and yet saw nothing of what was going forward. Have you a pair of eyes, Mr Weller?' With the most complete simplicity and equanimity of manner, Sam replied, 'Yes, I have a pair of eyes, and that's just it. If they wos a pair o' patent double million magnifyin' gas microscopes of hextra power, p'raps I might be able to see through a flight o' stairs and a deal door; but bein' only eyes, you see, my wision's limited!'

The patient hopes that his problem will be solved speedily and painlessly. He presumes that the therapist, like Sherlock Holmes,

---

* Since Einstein, it seems that no-one else does, either.

is familiar with many similar cases from the past. This expectation may sometimes lead him to complain that the therapist is trying to pigeon-hole him, instead of treating him as a unique human being.

The patient will certainly expect the therapist to tell him what to do, to issue some suggestions as to how to solve his difficulties and to tell him what is wrong with his own behaviour, so that he can make the necessary adjustments. He will often emphasise that he is quite prepared to accept criticism. But the therapist may find little to criticise, because the problem does not exist between the patient and the therapist but between the patient and someone else. The patient's account may sound very reasonable, and his complaints about others often seem justified.

Newly fledged therapists sometimes share the patient's phantasy that they can tell him what to do. In consequence, they often make many suggestions. But even as they do so, they recognise how pointless they are, and what little impact they are making on the patient.

The truth is that the psychotherapist is seldom able to make any suggestions which have not already been examined and rejected by the patient himself. It is rare for there to be any untried secret paths. All the choices seem to be painful, useless or impossible, and most have already been rejected. Sherlock Holmes said, 'When you have eliminated the impossible, whatever remains, *however improbable*, must be the truth'. Applying this aphorism to psychotherapy, when everything that is impracticable has been excluded, whatever remains, however, unpalatable, must be the solution.

At first, the patient may not realise that he will be expected to attend many sessions, many of which will appear to be repetitive and unproductive. There will be times when he doubts the wisdom of having undertaken therapy. To complicate matters, the solution of one problem sometimes reveals others which are even more confusing and alarming. Nevertheless, most patients accept the rules of therapy, its limitations and its disadvantages. They know that the price of success is the risk of failure. Although they may suffer anguish and distress, they will learn to make the most of their assets and may find a fuller life despite its problems.

During their preliminary meetings, it is usual for the therapist to obtain a very full biography from the patient. He will ask many questions, some of which will be delicate, embarrassing or even impertinent. As he becomes more experienced, he will learn to recognise the earliest signs of distress. Sometimes he will draw attention to these signs and may precipitate a violent emotion by doing so. The patient is often impressed by the astuteness of his enquiry and the intuitiveness of his observations.

The therapist is often very satisfied with the early interviews. Sometimes the patient will tell him that no-one else has ever been so kind, helpful, or sympathetic. Privately, the therapist may agree with him, although he does not say so to the patient.

We have noted that problems arise between people. The therapist and the patient are people. It is probable that certain problems will arise between them. The therapist who already knows something of himself will realise that there are certain aspects of his own personality which may cause difficulty, and he will try to take avoiding action. On the other hand, the patient will be very puzzled when problems arise between him and the therapist. The reasons may spring from the very matters which he seeks to relieve. The problems which he encounters with other people are repeated in his relationship with the therapist.

The patient's first favourable impression consequently gives way to a period of disillusionment. The therapist does not seem to be offering any practical advice. At times he appears to have forgotten what was discussed at a previous meeting. Things seem to be getting worse instead of better. The therapist is not as sympathetic as might be expected. He does not show any particular pleasure when success is reported. At first, the patient had looked forward eagerly to their meetings and enjoyed them. Now they are becoming a chore and he wonders why he ever began. There are occasions when he is forced to cancel his appointment. Sometimes he forgets them altogether. The therapist seems sceptical and unsympathetic. He does not seem to realise that everyone makes mistakes.

Things go wrong for the therapist too. The patient becomes critical. Sometimes he speaks warmly of previous therapists. He reads about other forms of treatment and asks if they would be more effective. He points out that he is getting worse rather than better. Privately, the therapist may agree with him, although he does not say so to the patient.

As these difficulties continue, the patient pays careful but largely unconscious attention to the behaviour of the therapist. He was told that he could say anything. Did this include criticism? It is easy to praise a doctor; much more difficult to criticise him. Will the doctor be angry if he does so? It is a great relief to the patient when he discovers that he really can say anything. Treatment is moving forward. The patient begins to appreciate that whilst his therapist cares, is willing to share, and would like to help, he does not have an easy solution.

Self-awareness

A substantial part of psychotherapy is concerned with helping the patient to learn about himself: to modify or come to terms with those aspects of himself which he dislikes. He must learn to recognise his blind spots, to understand how he protects himself from insight by the use of defence mechanisms (q.v.), and find the courage to modify those aspects of his personality which he finds distasteful.

Self-awareness is something which is sought by nearly everyone, not merely by patients. Part of the proof lies in the popularity of such things as astrological character readings, and the questionnaires in popular magazines which promise to tell the enquirer whether he is ambitious, determined, popular with women or a successful lover. Usually, he finds that he is all four, because the most common reason which leads us to seek the 'truth' about ourselves is vanity.

Being himself human, the therapist will wonder what sort of person *he* is. A substantial number of therapists embark upon their career with a conscious, but usually unformulated hope, of learning something about themselves.

It would be valuable for them to do so. The therapist cannot help a patient to recognise blind spots if he himself has the same ones, or help him to overcome a prejudice which he himself shares. A therapist cannot cope with the patient's antagonism if he himself is unable to tolerate criticism. Self-knowledge is as important to the therapist as it is to the patient. How may it be acquired?

The best way of learning about oneself is probably through a personal analysis with a competent analyst. However, this procedure is lengthy and expensive. It requires many hours of hard work, is sometimes tedious and usually expensive. The cost may run to five figures. In the absence of a rich uncle, a training analysis is not really compatible with a wife, a family, a mortgage and a motor car. Some registrars try to solve the problem by marrying their analyst, but this plays havoc with the transference. Others sell their motor car and buy a bicycle. At least they can be assured of good physical health.

Furthermore, and although not everyone will be pleased at the author's presumption, not all analysts are competent. We must, therefore, consider whether it is feasible to develop some self-knowledge without professional help.

Most analysts would say that it is not, even though Sigmund Freud himself embarked upon a long, lonely process of self-discovery. He was assisted in his task by many friends and patients. Karen Horney believed that it is possible to develop a degree of self-awareness as a result of one's own efforts. Whatever may be possible is worth trying, but the reader is warned that it involves much tedious and sometimes disagreeable work, requires great patience and may produce nothing.

A few therapists look upon such private attempts as unwise, potentially dangerous and possibly liable to precipitate insanity or suicide. Adler, however, wrote that 'man knows more than he understands', and few would disagree with him. People often fail to pay attention to what is there to be seen. In the words of Sherlock Holmes, they *see* but they do not *observe*.

In the opinion of the author, it is not possible to know more about oneself than one knows already. The development of self-awareness is a matter of observing what is there to observe. Some of it is unpleasant. Like the eavesdropper, a person who who wishes to learn the truth about himself will find that much of what he is forced to acknowledge is an affront to his vanity.

The author holds to his opinion that there is nothing so absurd that it can be dismissed without consideration. Those who wish, therefore, may try. However, one precaution must be observed. The reader should not undertake such an investigation if anyone from among his family, friends or colleagues has commented that he seems to have changed, that he is not the person he used to be, that he has become 'different', that he has become morose, preoccupied, or unduly suspicious. In such circumstances, the enquirer should first seek professional advice.

There are many components to a training analysis. One of the most important is a a careful examination of the relationship which develops between the trainee and his analyst. Such an examination is denied to anyone who embarks upon a solo investigation. However; he is not denied the opportunity of carefully (though one-sidedly) considering his relationship with the people with whom he works, his seniors, his juniors and his peers. Whom does he like? Whom does he dislike? Whom does he find stimulating and whom does he hold in contempt? Why? It is the author's belief that everyone reminds everyone of someone. If the enquirer agrees, of whom do other people remind him? It is not sufficient to reply 'no-one'. He must think again.

Another component of a training analysis is that in which the trainee is helped to recognise his resistances (q.v). This is difficult for someone who acts alone, but it is not impossible. Everything said and done by the enquirer must be questioned. How, when and why does he take his attitudes? There will be times when an 'instant' answer comes to mind, only to be followed by the thought, 'No, it is not that.' Further thought must then be given. Could it be that? The enquirer should pay attention to everything that is said to him, by whomsoever it is said. We are often told disagreeable truths by people who dislike us and by people who are drunk. Patients also tell us disagreeable truths when they pass through the stage of their negative transference. Friends may tell us the truth, but there are certain truths which our best friends are reluctant to mention. The enquirer must not dismiss something which is said by someone whom he does not like, or by someone who does not like him.

Dreams say many things, although they are difficult to interpret. They are often connected with events of the previous day, although it is not always easy to establish the connection. If it is discovered, it may seem rather trivial. Nevertheless, further thought should be given to it. Dreams constitute a hotchpotch of unfinished business, and one dream may have many different associations.

Dreams are usually forgotten quickly, and some people keep a notebook at the side of their bed, so that they can record them immediately on wakening. However, the dream often disappears, even as it is being noted. It is seldom possible to recapture the 'atmosphere' of a dream from a later reading of a written account, but this may be the crucial element. If the dream is noted on wakening, an immediate attempt should be made to note the atmosphere and the associations.

The enquirer must be prepared to consider any proposition, no matter how unlikely it may seem. Nothing should escape scrutiny, nothing rejected because it seems too absurd. He should remember as much as he can about himself: the good things, the bad things, and the emotions which accompany them. What is he proud of, and of what is he ashamed? Whom does he love; whom does he hate? What are his prejudices?

Quite often, he will remember something which he had 'completely forgotten'. He should write it down at once. What is he sure of? Of what is he less certain? What are his strengths and weaknesses? Are they really weaknesses and strengths? Does he have memories that puzzle him? Are there certain matters of which he is perfectly certain, yet which cannot possibly be true? What are the wicked things, the dangerous things, the puzzling things? What are the extremes of his experience: the worst things, the saddest things, the most humiliating things, the most embarrassing things?

There will be occasions when he makes mistakes, forgets appointments and mislays objects. He may find himself unable to recall a name, although it is on the tip of his tongue. There is something to be said for the proposition that there is no such thing as a mistake.

'Errors' often conceal an unacceptable thought, and provide a guide to its identification.

There will be times when the enquirer is sad and may want to cry. At other times, he will be angry and may want to shout. Naturally, he should express these emotions in privacy. Sometimes he will find himself lying awake at night, his mind a turmoil of thoughts. He should allow them to churn around, pay attention to them and try to follow them through.

We have a natural facility to forget things that we do not want to remember, so it is important to write everything down. The enquirer should compile a detailed autobiography. Adequate time should be allowed for this. He should not say of a dream 'that was so vivid that I cannot possibly forget it'. If he does not record it, he probably will. Writing everything may seem tedious and time wasting: it may be looked upon as equivalent to the time which would otherwise be spent in travelling to the analyst's rooms.

During a training analysis, the trainee will spend up to five hours a week with his analyst. If the only mutually convenient time for this meeting is 5.00 a.m., it will be held at 5.00 a.m. The lone enquirer must be willing to devote a large amount of time to reviewing what he has written. If the only convenient time for such a review is at 5.00 a.m., it should be made at 5.00 a.m.

The whole procedure takes a great deal of time, is very hard work and can become very tedious. Much the same comments could apply to a training analysis.

A pattern will slowly emerge. Like a photograph, it may be oddly familiar yet curiously unfamiliar. The behaviour which is most difficult to recognise is often that associated with aggressive and sexual matters. Sometimes the enquirer will see his own behaviour reflected in that of other people, behaviour which hitherto he had deplored.

Having learned a little about himself, the individual must decide what he is going to do with it. This may require great determination. For example, he may be one of the many people who find it hard to say disagreeable things to people. If he is to do his job as a psychotherapist effectively, it will sometimes be necessary for him to say disagreeable things to his patients. The enquirer who has hitherto found it impossible to do so, must one day take his courage in his hands, even though he runs the risk of causing offence to his patient.

When he encounters something disagreeable in himself, the enquirer will probably feel slightly depressed. Self-knowledge is not always a pleasant experience. The pain which it creates is a necessary preliminary to change.

A change in one aspect of behaviour may cause reciprocal changes in the others. The total personality is a combination of forces, some associated, some collaborative and some which work in opposition. It is seldom possible to change one aspect without affecting the others.

However great their initial enthusiasm, most enquirers become disenchanted with the whole process. Indeed, some come to look upon the notebook in which they keep their thoughts with a distaste analagous to that experienced by a trainee who is passing through a negative transference towards his analyst.

It is very common for the enquirer to abandon the exercise. He concludes that the whole thing is tedious nonsense and that he has more important things to do. This attitude is a healthy and protective one, although it may not be conducive to self-knowledge. It confirms that the disillusioned reader is essentially normal.

Selection of patients

A large number of doctors refer a large number of patients to a large number of psychiatrists. The psychotherapist may spend a substantial proportion of his working time with a selected patient: perhaps as much as two hours every week for at least two years. If, in addition, he has, every week, one hour's supervision on the case, he may spend nearly a twelfth of his working time with a single patient. If he can devote two years exclusively to intensive psychotherapy, the therapist will be able to accept only one new patient every two months. If, as is more likely, he has other calls on his time — patients for supportive psychotherapy, responsibility for long-term wards, ward rounds and case discussions to attend, for example — even this small number is too many.

It follows that patients who are chosen for *intensive* psychotherapy must be selected with very great care. It is unlikely that the average psychiatrist can take on more than two or three cases in the course of a year. His other patients must be content with a pale substitute for what is ideal.

Such limitations are inevitable in any therapeutic regime when the procedure is lengthy and the number of trained personnel is small. It may seem unfair that so many people must be excluded, but this is one of the facts of medical life. The number of patients who might benefit from a heart transplant must be enormous compared with those who actually receive one. Even for comparatively common operations, such as kidney transplants, there is a limit to the number of potential recipients, and many criteria are taken into account before the final selection is made. This may be very unfair, but life is unfair. Many people are denied things for which they yearn. A mental defective might like a university place, but however hard he was prepared to work, he would not be successful.

Motivation

This is the first criterion to be considered. The therapist tries to answer a deceptively simple question: what does this patient really seek when he asks for psychotherapy? We have already stressed that there can be no promise as to the outcome, that treatment is complex, difficult and prolonged. These facts must be assimilated and comprehended by the patient before he can be considered. If it is only possible for him to attend periodically, outside his working hours, provided that there are no other distractions, so long as he is not feeling tired, and on condition that an ambulance is supplied to take him to and fro, he is unlikely to be accepted. A candidate for psychotherapy will have to submit himself to considerable personal inconvenience. Within reason, he will be expected to attend during the therapist's working hours, not during his own free ones. If he has a more attractive engagement, he must forgo it in favour of therapy. He may find therapy unpleasant, disquieting, anxiety provoking, demoralising and extremely depressing. At times it may seem boring, aimless, fruitless, perhaps infuriating. There will be occasions when the therapist will appear obstinate, unsympathetic, offensive, objectionable, hostile, sadistic, excessively pedantic, even impertinent. There are moments when psychotherapy is one of the most painful of all medical procedures. Furthermore, there is no analgesic to relieve the pain.

These obstacles have not been exaggerated. The difficulties of psychotherapy are formidable. It follows that patients must be very highly motivated indeed. Their motivation must be closely scrutinised, and may be put to various tests.

A bland assurance that 'I will do anything to get better' is insufficient. Some people will say anything to free themselves from inconvenience, especially if they have been subjected to external pressure. A man whose wife has finally left him will make any promise if he hopes that by doing so, she will be persuaded to return. An employee who, after many warnings, is finally dismissed, will protest that he has at last recognised the error of his ways, and that he will take all necessary steps to reform — if he is given just one additional chance. A prisoner who has made a sexual assault on a child may 'realise' that he is in urgent need of treatment and will promise to do anything — even to 'go into a mental institution' if, by doing so, he can avoid punishment.

When motivation seems to arise mainly from such external pressures, it should be looked upon with great suspicion. Notwithstanding his passionate pleas, it is usually wise to allow the patient to suffer the dreaded event, and to offer treatment subsequently. Psychotherapy must never be regarded as a soft alternative to punishment. The child molester who truly realises that he requires treatment, will not lose this realisation because of imprisonment. When he has completed his sentence, he may be considered for treatment. Unhappily his motivation is then usually exposed as being totally insincere.

The therapist need have no hesitation in discussing his doubts with the patient when motivation seems to arise from external pressure. If his motivation is sincere, the patient will understand that it must be so, and will be prepared to return when the disaster is behind him. Those who, when their motivation is questioned, respond with virtuous indignation, seeing it as an attack on their probity, will naturally cause serious doubts to arise in the mind of the therapist.

When external pressures do not seem excessive, the therapist will try to gauge the strength of the internal ones. The assessment of internal pressures is based on the psychotherapist's evaluation of the history: and to some extent on his own intuitive appraisal. What has the patient himself done to overcome his difficulties? When his efforts have been limited to asking his doctor for a prescription for sleeping tablets and tranquillisers, a certificate for the local authority requesting a change of accommodation, and one for his employers to enable him to obtain lighter work, he seems to be demonstrating his intention to leave the real work to others, so that he himself can continue a life of cosy convenience. On the other hand, when a patient has embarked upon a difficult task and has done his best to follow it through, he shows a valuable streak of independent purpose. The patient who acknowledges that he himself is partly responsible for his misfortunes, will compare favourably with the grandiose infallibility of the man who can always find a scapegoat. People who always see themselves as the innocent victims of the regrettable behaviour of other people, are not likely to be good subjects for psychotherapy.

The therapist may sometimes set a task as a test of motivation. The heavy drinker may be asked to abstain from alcoholic drinks completely (i.e. completely) for a short period — perhaps a month — and then to report on his progress. Some patients will truly make an effort. They may not be successful, but that does not matter. They have made an attempt. Others will not even try. They say,

'Why should I? I like it. Anyway, I am not an alcoholic.' Patients whose attitude to a test of motivation is 'Why should I?' are demonstrating that they are not prepared to tolerate any personal discomfort or inconvenience. They are not likely to be satisfactory candidates for intensive psychotherapy. It might be suggested to an alcoholic whose motivation is suspect, that he should attend some of the meetings of Alcoholics Anonymous. Again, the patient who refuses, saying perhaps, 'I don't like them' is unlikely to persist with psychotherapy, which will involve a great deal of what he does not like.

Occasionally, a deficiency of motivation becomes evident only after psychotherapy has been started. The patient repeatedly arrives late, or offers trivial or sometimes convincing excuses for failing to attend. ('I forgot'; 'I had to work late'; 'It was my birthday'; 'I was saving a child from a runaway horse', etc). When this happens, the therapist should always discuss his patient's motivation with him. When it is inadequate, the patient may take the opportunity of withdrawing from treatment. He may also try to transfer the responsibility to the therapist. ('Well if you think I don't want to come, I won't...').

There are times when it becomes apparent that a patient is attending only because someone else has told him to do so. In these circumstances, it is natural if he regards his attendance as contrary to his own wishes. Some patients do not seem to know whether or not they are attending of their own free will. If he has doubts, the patient may indicate that he wishes to withdraw from treatment. He should be allowed to do so. When he realises that his attendance was purely voluntary, and that there was no *force majeure*, he is often very willing to return. The seeds of insight may already have been planted. Motivation can develop from them, and time will not necessarily have been wasted.

We have been speaking of motivation as though it were something that is either present or absent. In fact, it rarely shows itself in such a black or white fashion. There are both 'positive' and 'negative' motivating forces. Amongst the positive forces, there is the distress caused by the problem and the desire for relief. Negative forces include such rationalisations as 'If things don't work out, I can blame the therapist'. Certain motivating forces may be scarcely relevant to the problem. Some potential patients are simply curious about what psychotherapy feels like. They may seek the self-indulgent pleasure of a captive, uncritical audience.

The therapist's task is to identify, as precisely as he can, the positive motivating forces, the counteracting ones, the balance between them and their ultimate direction. In this, he may be forced to rely on his intuition. He will also be influenced by his own feelings towards the patient (see counter-transference, p. 96). Some of his assessments will be incorrect, but others may be triumphantly successful. Time and experience will improve his accuracy. He need not feel too dispirited if at first he is wrong more frequently than he would wish.

Intelligence

During therapy, it is necessary for the patient to reflect upon his past experiences; to search for recurrent patterns in his behaviour; to consider their possible significance and to examine the various ways in which he relates to the therapist. For this, a reasonable level of intelligence is required. Psychotherapy is not likely to be successful with people who are dull, even if their I.Q. is within normal limits. Provided that he has had the opportunity of doing so, a prospective patient should have obtained at least three or four 'O' Levels.

To many people it seems a paradox that high intelligence is *not* a particular advantage in psychotherapy, and that patients should *not* be selected solely on this criterion. A high I.Q. may even be an *obstacle* to success. The problems of highly intelligent people sometimes arise directly from their ability to form conclusions well in advance of their fellows. Just as intelligence cannot be increased in those who are dull, it cannot be reduced in those who are bright. Some therapists find it difficult to understand that people of high intelligence do not always form good therapeutic prospects, but the fact remains. If they lack motivation, very intelligent people may take a perverse and destructive delight in running rings round the therapist. We emphasise this point because many therapists suppose that individuals who are very intelligent *should* be able to use their gifts to solve their problems quickly. Experience repeatedly shows that this is not necessarily so.

Age

Many people begin their careers as psychotherapists or counsellors with a desire to work with young people. This is understandable. The young are lively, attractive and enquiring, and it is a pleasure to watch them develop. However, many of their problems arise directly out of their immaturity, and are solved automatically as they grow older. A therapist who accompanies them through this stage of their development may be pleased to take the credit for a success which is really due to nature.

When young people encounter problems, their parents may be more in need of help than they. It is better that the therapist who is beginning his training should practise his craft on older rather than younger people. Considerable experience is required to distinguish between those young people who will improve with maturation, and those who need skilled help. Such experience can be gained only by serving time as a 'bread and butter' therapist.

It is sometimes stated that the 'old' are unsuitable for intensive therapy, and it is true that people who have been settled in a fixed way of life for many years may find it difficult to adjust to new situations. However, such circumstances may be imposed upon them by death, disease or retirement. Limited psychotherapy with older people is sometimes very rewarding, and much may be learned from them. Two precautions should first be taken. The therapist should satisfy himself that the patient is not suffering from a psychotic illness, especially an affective one. Second, he should assure himself that the patient is physically healthy. He himself should make a careful physical examination, whether or not others have already done so. He will not wish to dismiss a physical complaint without good reason. He should also confirm that the patient's previous personality was reasonably stable. People who have been neurotic semi-invalids for the whole of their lives do not usually improve with age.

The distinction between 'young' and 'old' patients requires brief examination of the words 'young' and 'old'. Perhaps they are best considered in comparison with the age of the therapist. When two or more generations separate him from his patient, the therapist should give thought to whether he is 'too old' or 'too young' to undertake the case.

Other factors

The therapist is unlikely to undertake the treatment of someone to whom he takes a profound dislike. He should also be cautious when he finds the patient unusually attractive. In such circumstances, he would be wise to ask someone else to review the case. He should also think about the reason for his feelings (see countertransference, p. 96).

He should never treat someone who is being treated by someone else. If he discovers that he has been doing so inadvertently, he should proceed no further. The patient may protest that he much prefers his present therapist, or that the other therapist does not understand him so well. There are likely to be other indications of disharmony. The therapist should advise the patient to pass this information on to the original therapist. It will be useful if he will write to the other therapist to explain what has happened.

Intensive psychotherapy should not be offered to patients who are suffering from psychotic illnesses. These patients usually respond well to the appropriate physical treatment. Naturally the doctor will show his interest in them, and will wish to support them, but it is not necessary to subject them to analytical dissection. Some people claim that it is harmful to do so. This is not the author's experience, but he finds it neither very fruitful nor a sensible use of limited therapeutic time.

The therapist is unwise to undertake treatment of patients who have serious life-long personality disorders — people who, for example, are habitually dishonest, impulsive, irresponsible and self-centred. Patients who regard themselves as uniquely lovable, or who think that it must be a great privilege for the doctor to be allowed to treat them, are unlikely to change.

It is seldom possible to change the *direction* of the sexual drive. Homosexuals cannot usually be turned into heterosexuals, although, as Freud pointed out in a famous letter (see p. 136), they may need help in dealing with the problems which stem from their sexual orientation.

An inexperienced therapist should avoid psychotherapy when someone whom he respects advises him not to proceed with it. He should also be wary of undertaking psychotherapy simply because he has been asked to do so. He himself knows when he feels able to help a patient and he should usually have the right to make the final decision. His decision will be based on his own view of the case, although he will naturally consider the views of others.

The therapist should not undertake psychotherapy with friends, relatives or neighbours. It is necessary to maintain a professional 'distance' from the patient, and this cannot be achieved when the two are acquainted. The therapist should certainly not undertake the treatment of patients of whom he is in awe, or because he is flattered by a request to do so. Patients should not be accepted for psychotherapy simply because their name appears on the Medical Register.

It is relatively easy to describe patients who should be rejected. It is less easy to describe those who should be accepted. The ideal patient is neither too old nor too young. His adjustment to life is reasonable. His work record is good and domestic relationships are satisfactory. Almost certainly there is no history of criminal activity. The problem will have been precipitated by considerable trauma.

The patient is reasonably intelligent, and is prepared to accept any necessary inconvenience in order to obtain relief. He will already have made attempts to overcome his problem, and will appreciate that much of the final outcome depends on the efforts which he himself is prepared to make. He accepts that he may have to tolerate some discomfort. Thus, the ideal patient is relatively 'healthy', before he comes for treatment.

Selection of the therapist

The first stage in the procedure is when the therapist chooses himself. He thinks, 'I should like to be a psychiatrist', or 'I should like to be a marriage counsellor'. When selection includes a formal interview, he will be asked for reasons. He usually replies with a modest platitude about wishing to help other people, either because of his own supreme happiness, or because of some devastating experience which has given him an understanding which might be of benefit to others.

The would-be therapist should give serious consideration to his choice of career. What does he really seek? In his heart, he will know that there are many reasons, some of which are rather selfish. He will hope to acquire an understanding of the vagaries of his own mind. His curiosity about the secrets of other people will be amply rewarded.

Most people begin their work with great enthusiasm and exalted hopes, but quickly find themselves demoralised and defeated. The work is far more arduous and exacting than can be imagined. Sometimes it is monotonous and sometimes it is frightening. It is common for beginners to feel that they are getting nowhere, and that their mentors have little guidance to offer.

If he is already a member of one of the helping professions, the therapist will already have undertaken a formidable period of training. Still more postgraduate study will be required, and there will be other obstacles to overcome before he is established in his career.

Candidates for membership of one of the counselling organisations are usually subjected to a series of interviews, case discussions, psychological tests and so on, designed to probe their suitability for the work. Most of these organisations enjoy a considerable degree of public esteem and carry a substantial burden of responsibility. They are jealous of their status, and employ a formidable selection process.

Occasionally during his career, the therapist may encounter the most distressing event of all — the death of one of his patients by suicide. Such a thing sometimes happens when the patient can see no other solution. Other patients habitually use suicide '*attempts*' as a means of gaining control of situations, but something sometimes goes wrong, and they die unintentionally.

From the outset, the psychotherapist must face the fact that such a thing can happen to him: that one of his patients may kill himself. Sometimes they warn of their intention, but sometimes it is only in retrospect that the therapist realises that such a warning was given. Alternatively, the therapist may take the gamble that the threat will not be carried out — and lose. Even very careful precautions cannot eliminate the risk of such things. An experienced therapist may recommend that, in the patient's interest, the risk should be taken. He may be mistaken.

When patients kill themselves, everyone who was concerned with trying to help them experiences distress, guilt, anger and remorse. Suicide is always distressing. No-one should undertake psychotherapy or counselling if he feels that he would not be able to cope with such an event.

An individual who seeks to follow a career as a therapist or counsellor should pay careful attention to the advice of objective advisers. He should not have suffered a major change in his life in recent months. Someone who has been widowed recently should wait for a year or two.

The psychotherapist must be free from any serious personal problems. If he has such a problem, he will *not* find a solution by trying to solve the problems of other people. First, he must put his own house in order. There should be no problems which he cannot share with at least one other person. He should be free from any serious illness, either physical or psychological. If he has had any form of nervous illness, the doctor who was responsible for his treatment should be asked to provide a confidential report about him. If it is considered necessary, the candidate must be willing to submit himself to an independent psychiatric examination.

There will be many occasions on which the psychotherapist finds himself subjected to criticism, sometimes without foundation. He may hear harsh words from his patients, his teachers, or his peers, and he must always be willing to pay attention to them. If it seems that the criticisms are justified, he must be willing to modify his way of working. If they are not justified, he must allow the criticism to stand, without feeling it necessary to compel his critic to retract.

He will realise that in order to help one person, he may be obliged to offend others. He will try to help as many people as possible, but it is seldom possible to satisfy everyone. Some people will condemn him to his face, but others will condemn him behind his back, and he may hear about their criticisms only in a roundabout way. There may be some that he will never hear. His best intentions may be condemned from unexpected quarters. Although it may be possible to fool all the people for some of the time, it certainly is not possible to *please* them all, even for some of the time.

In a fairy story for grown-ups by Anthony Armstrong, a prince was plagued with hiccups. A magician advised that in order to overcome his handicap, he should perform a deed which would bring him the thanks of everyone. It was decided to organise a birthday feast during which wine would flow freely from every fountain in the land. He supposed that this would bring pleasure to everyone. But instead of receiving universal gratitude, he was immediately greeted with a series of complaints:

1. about the disorganisation of their service, from the Water Supply Company
2. about the small number of fountains in farming areas, from the Agricultural Labourers' Union
3. about the quality of wine supplied
4. about the quantity of wine supplied; and
5. about there being wine at all, from the representatives of fifteen temperance organisations!

The 'contract'

At this point, it is appropriate to discuss what the therapist expects of his patient and what the patient may expect of the therapist: in other words, the 'contract' which exists between them.

In the view of the author, the contract should be an unwritten one. It is also largely unspoken. It is based on mutual understanding and common sense. It assumes that the patient seeks the assistance which the therapist deems to be appropriate. The relationship between patient and therapist is a professional one, not a social one, and the contract helps to define the limits in those few cases in which they may not be clear.

The therapist expects the patient to put into words everything that he thinks and feels. He may laugh or cry and may express his emotions in words. He may not lie to the therapist, no matter how 'white' the lie may be. He may not touch the therapist, and should not drink alcohol prior to his session. He will arrive punctually and will leave when asked to do so.

For his part, the therapist will attend to all that is said, whatever it is, whether it is disagreeable, disgraceful, offensive, personal, critical or disloyal. He will not praise or criticise the patient. The information he is given will be confidential to the organisation to which he belongs. He will not accept a confidence which he may not share with that organisation. Confidentiality will not be breached, except in very unusual circumstances, such as when the therapist is ordered to do so by a Court. The therapist makes no promises to his patient. He does not guarantee that the problem will be solved, or even that the patient will benefit from his attendance.

In some centres, and under certain circumstances, it is the practice to ask patients to sign a written 'contract'. This may contain such clauses as 'I will not drink whilst in therapy'. The author sees little point in this practice. Such 'contracts' are no more 'enforceable' than unwritten ones, and may encourage barrack room lawyers to drive carthorses through their loopholes. They enable the therapist to discharge his patient if he wishes to do so, but he does not require a written contract for such a purpose. Written contracts also encourage patients to conceal breaches of them, and the therapist loses the opportunity to examine the circumstances under which the breach occurred.

Patients sometimes break rules, but there is no reason for the therapist to do so. If the patient's conduct should exceed the limitations of the contract, he should be told that his behaviour is not acceptable. If he persistently disobeys the rules, it is likely that therapy must be ended.

If limits are seriously or persistently disregarded, therapy must certainly finish. The occasions on which this ultimate sanction is imposed are rare, but when they occur, the therapist should never resume treatment with the same patient.

3

What does the therapist do?

CARDINAL PRINCIPLE: Sit down, shut up, and listen.

In fictional psychiatry, there are three characters: the psychiatrist — middle-aged, with penetrating eyes, a middle European accent and a secret sorrow; his handsome young assistant — a sort of latter-day Rudolph Valentino — a combination of detective, foil and man-about-town; and the patient — blonde, beautiful, capricious and sinful, but beginning to see the error of her ways, and anxious to reform.

The lights are dimmed. The patient burrows into the couch and pulls her skirt down to where it should have been. She tells of her childhood and her sex life, whilst the psychiatrist looks on gravely. Later, he plays a recording of the interview to his handsome young assistant, and instructs him to take her out to dinner. The sight of a child, crying in the street, reminds the patient that when she was three years old, her doll was taken away from her. In the last scene, and for reasons which are apparent only to him, the psychiatrist tells the patient that this was the cause of her troubles, whereupon her symptoms disappear and she marries the handsome young assistant.

The reader will not be surprised to learn that, in a number of respects, fiction deviates from fact. First, there is no handsome young assistant. Patients are rarely beautiful. No-one takes anyone out to dinner (patients sometimes issue invitations, but the therapist never accepts {'the transference', p. 92}). No-one marries anyone. There is not necessarily a couch, and the lights are raised, not dimmed. Above all, the therapist does not light upon a single incident from the past which explains the whole problem and leads to an instant and total cure.

The preconceptions which some readers and many patients have about psychotherapy are based on this sort of fictional model. It is necessary, therefore, to discuss in some detail just what the therapist does and does not do.

Advice

When he comes for psychotherapy, and when all extraneous material is eliminated, the patient says, basically, 'I have a problem. It must be solved. Tell me what to do.' The first point to be made is that neither the therapist nor anyone else can *tell* the patient what to do. This is usually obvious to both the patient and the therapist. But neither does the therapist offer advice to the patient, nor suggest things that he might do. Many people find this surprising. After all, the patient has come for suggestions and advice. When this is so, it indicates that the patient has a basic misunderstanding of the role of the therapist. He is not an adviser.

For *advice* to be of value, every minute detail must be known. Although the patient will give a detailed history of his problem, the only person who can know *everything* about the patient is the patient himself. It would take him a lifetime to tell it to someone else. Furthermore, experience shows that patients seldom reach the stage of consulting someone, before first considering and rejecting any suggestions which someone else could make. The therapist does *not* give advice.

This raises a new problem. The patient came for advice. The therapist has none to offer. Problems always arise between people. On this occasion, the problem arises between the patient and his therapist. If it is not resolved, psychotherapy cannot continue. The patient must come to terms with the disappointing discovery that the therapist will not advise him how to proceed. The solution can only emerge from the interaction between the patient and psychotherapist. It will arise partly from the patient's own resources. A solution which evolves in this way is quite different from being given advice. It is all very puzzling, because hitherto the patient has been unable to find a solution from his own resources. The conclusion involves the patient in difficult rethinking of their mutual roles. But problems cannot be solved without discomfort. The therapist shares the patient's disappointment that his early hopes cannot be fulfilled.

It would be pleasant for the patient and simple for the therapist if all the details of his problems could be fed into a computer which would then say, like Sherlock Holmes, 'You will find similar cases in such and such a place.' But just as no-one can learn to play the piano for someone else, or win a race for someone else, or earn a living for someone else, or fall in love for someone else, no-one can solve problems for someone else.

Reassurance

If the therapist does not give suggestions or advice, what does he do? Does he reassure? Does he say, 'You are physically sound.' or 'I can find nothing wrong with you', or 'You are eminently sane', or 'I think things will come right' or 'I don't think you need have any anxiety', or 'That sort of thing is extremely improbable'? Well, he could reassure, but what purpose would such reassurance serve? Is he totally certain of his diagnosis? Does he *know* that things will come right? Can he be *certain* that the patient need have no anxiety? Can he be *sure* that this is not one of those extremely improbable cases? Statistics are useful when planning community health services, but they do not reassure individuals. It is of no comfort to the relatives that the death of one whom they loved was caused by a million to one chance. Contrary to popular belief, *reassurance seldom reassures*.

Furthermore, the therapist may not be certain that the patient *wishes* to be physically sound or eminently sane. We shall see later that both physical and mental handicap may have advantages. Instead of reassuring, the psychotherapist sometimes goes to the opposite extreme. Far from insisting that a dreaded event will not occur, he may try to explore with the patient how he would cope if it were to happen. What would he do? It is sometimes his task to help the patient plan for remote contingencies. He will never assert that they will not happen.

Explanation
If the therapist does not advise or reassure, does he explain? Does he explain that sometimes, in states of fear, the suprarenal glands pump an increased amount of adrenalin into the bloodstream so that the heart beats faster and more forcefully, and that it may be felt as a pounding in the chest. And that this does not mean that the heart is diseased — rather the reverse. And that he can understand how frightening it must be for the patient when her husband raises his fist to her. He is a powerful man, and easily loses his temper. Some men are like that, and she knew he was like that before she married him. Marriage seldom changes people for the better. And so on and so on. At the end of a long and rambling explanation such as this, some patients are so confused that they ask, 'Do you mean that I have heart disease, doctor?' We saw in the paediatric case in Chapter 1 that explanation often confuses people. It may provide fresh possibilities for hypochondriacal preoccupation; new excuses to evade examination of the sensitive core of the problem; an opportunity to ignore the relationship between significant people, of trying to understand the relationship which has led to the problem.

Encouragement

If the therapist does not advise, or reassure, or explain, does he encourage? Does he say, 'The trouble with you is that you think too much about yourself: I used to be just the same. Then I took up golf. Why don't you do the same? You can join a golf club and meet lots of nice people and get plenty of fresh air and exercise. That's what you want, plenty of fresh air and exercise. Why don't you try it?'

This approach is particularly favoured by those who describe themselves as 'a bit of a psychiatrist m'self, y'know' — a claim made by 99 per cent of the general population and, when it suits them, 100 per cent of the medical profession. The problem is that the patient may dearly like to take up golf. One reason for seeking help is that he has not been able to do so. His cure will be signalled when he is able to follow the suggested regime. It is not the means by which cure is achieved. One might just as well encourage a patient with chronic bronchitis to stop coughing. The therapist does not encourage.

The therapist's role

The most important thing which the psychotherapist offers his patient is his undivided, uncritical attention. The reader may have very little appreciation of the difficulty and subtlety of this task. The psychotherapist *attends* to everything that the patient says and to everything he does. When it is appropriate, he shares his observations with his patient. He sees, and tries to help the patient see, he hears and tells the patient what he hears. He smells, he feels, and he observes. All the time he shares.

His attention is a questioning one. He seeks to distinguish that which comes from the heart from that which is mere conventional stereotype. The therapist attends, not like a friend, who will ignore some remarks and allow inconsistencies to pass; or like a foe, who will seize on everything that can be used to humiliate, condemn or destroy. His attention is objective and dispassionate, as far as possible free from preconceptions and prejudice. He tries to attend to what is actually there, rather than what the patient would like to be there.

If the relationship were a social one, certain conventions would be tacitly agreed. For example, therapist and patient would agree that ordinary people do not experience sexual desire for their close blood relatives, and that they do not usually hate their parents. In a social relationship, it might be 'agreed' (with a downstage leer)

that married men never look at other women. In a social relationship, one speaker may excuse himself from something which he has
said if it proves offensive to the other. He may offer an apology,
which is intended to nullify the offence. The other is expected to
accept the apology, even though it may fail in its purpose, and even
if he doubts the sincerity of the one who offers it.

Such social conventions play no part in psychotherapy. It is
assumed that the patient always intends what he says or does. There
is nothing so absurd that it can be dismissed without question.
Behaviour may not be modified retrospectively by an apology or a
withdrawal.

'Paying attention' appears to be a simple and modest requirement
but it may be much more difficult than the novice will realise. Even
when he is given advance warning of a trap, his attention may wander. He may think that something is so obvious that it is absurd to
question it. An example is given below. It will be familiar to some
readers. A phrase is enclosed within a triangle. The reader is asked
to say what the phrase is. There is a catch in it. The *wrong* answer
is given at the foot of page 46.

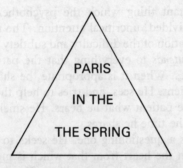

Readers who are familiar with this example may remember how
easily they were caught at first. They will still be astonished at how
easily some people, who are not familiar with it, fall into the obvious
trap.

The therapist offers not only an attentive ear, but where possible,
an understanding one. The understanding ear endeavours to be
objective. It tries to understand what is really happening rather than
what the patient would like to be happening. It 'understands' in
another sense too. It understands when 'understanding' may be difficult, painful, frightening, disconcerting, or embarrassing to the
patient. It understands that because of his feelings, the patient may
prefer a subjective lie to an objective truth.

The therapist listens to *all* that the patient says, attends to all that he does, takes notice of every aspect of his behaviour, even that which seems trivial. Sometimes this causes considerable irritation to the patient, who may complain that the therapist makes no allowance for human frailty, and treats him more like an object under a microscope than a human being. He complains that he can neither say, nor do, anything which is not subjected to careful scrutiny.

To a considerable extent, this is true. The reader will recognise that, behind these complaints, lies a plea that the therapist should be less exacting, less observant and less professional in his approach. It is really a reflection of the patient's negative transference (q.v.). The therapist would like to please his patient, but he knows that if he is to be of help, he can never be too professional. His technique may not be modified, simply because the patient finds it uncomfortable. Change cannot be achieved without discomfort.

The new therapist will wonder about paying attention: about listening, about observation, about the value of such an apparently simple exercise. He will still question the value of 'just talking' or 'just listening'. How can mere words be of help? Such questions illustrate a failure to appreciate that words are only a part of the process of communication. They help to bring precision — or sometimes confusion — to feeling and doing. When these components are added, words may raise the lover to the height of ecstatic anticipation, or to the depths of despair. Words must never be undervalued.

The act of concentrating his full attention on the patient is much more arduous than the beginner will realise. Nothing must escape his attention. Does the patient come late or early for his interview, or is he punctual? How is he dressed? How does he begin the session? How does he continue? How does the patient react to the therapist: enthusiastically, readily, slowly, reluctantly, evasively, angrily? What does he remember? What does he forget? Does he change the subject? The therapist is also searching for recurrent themes: themes which may form a pattern colouring the whole of the patient's life. Every piece of behaviour is part of the theme.

Recurrent themes

The aim is to complete a psychological jigsaw. Some pieces may be missing, but if the correct pattern has been established, none will be superfluous. When the therapist identifies a theme, he tries to share it with the patient, demonstrating how the parts fit together. When this is done, the patient sometimes finds fresh pieces, hitherto undiscovered. The patient is often unfamiliar with the total picture — indeed problems may have arisen because he was not familiar with it.

When the therapist echoes back a recurrent theme to the patient, useful elaboration may occur. Such themes, which are often unconscious, may be initiated very early in the session.

A patient was shown into the consulting room. He thanked the receptionist and said to the therapist, 'What a nice girl that is.' He then apologised for being late. It had been difficult to find a parking place, and he had been baulked by a woman driver who had cut in front of him.

The patient went on to describe a problem in the office. One of his colleagues was having an affair with a typist and the man's work was being affected. When she heard of it, the patient's wife had become very angry and had ordered him to ignore his colleague. His thoughts turned back to his courting days. Before he was married, his wife had telephoned his mother to complain that he was going to a stag party.

A recurring theme of troublesome, interfering women was identified by the therapist. The patient then remembered how his sister had always angered him by playing the role of the 'good little girl' in front of their mother, although she was often the source of the mischief for which he himself was punished. He felt that he could do nothing right in his mother's eyes and could only respond with helpless resentment when she was angry with him. He loved her dearly but seemed doomed to disappoint her. In his experience, women were always good, loved but neglectful; or wicked, dishonest and plausible. He behaved as though all women were either one or the other and never thought that there might be any who were different. These misperceptions always complicated his relations with women, his black and white assumptions creating difficulties when he tried to make satisfactory relationships with them.

Procedure

Most psychotherapists begin by taking a very full history. Several sessions may be required before it is completed. Thereafter, the therapist will be interested in the events of the days since the previous meeting. These often modify what has gone before.

History taking is sometimes skimped in medicine and consequently, significant information is missed.

At every session, the therapist makes a careful assessment of the

See page 44. The wrong answer is 'Paris in the Spring'. People who read rapidly often have difficulty in discovering the catch. If the reader persists in getting the wrong answer, he should read each line separately.

patient's mental state. This should follow the usual *medical* pattern of inspection, palpation, percussion and auscultation. In psychotherapy, the words palpation and percussion are used in a *psychological* sense. The therapist *inspects* the patient constantly, throughout the interview. In its more usual sense, 'auscultation' refers to a method by which sounds emanating from the body are amplified and brought to the ears of the physician through the stethoscope. His training and experience enables the physician to detect very delicate variations. The psychotherapist listens very carefully, not only to *what* is said but to *how* it is said. His training and experience enable him to detect very delicate variations too: subtleties of intonation, of emphasis, errors of omission and commission.

Psychological 'palpation' consists of probing for areas of 'emotional tenderness': topics which are painful, embarrassing, frightening; those which cause anger, apprehension, pleasure and so on.

In general medicine, the word 'percussion' is used to describe the technique in which echoes are caused to reverberate through a part of the body when it is tapped. In psychotherapy, the therapist attends to the 'echoes' created in the patient's mind by his questions and comments. Psychological 'percussion' is often centred upon areas which have proved tender to psychological 'palpation'.

Latent and manifest content

Everything that is said or done may be significant, even when it is 'unintentional'. Nothing that happens is dismissed as a mistake, an error, or a slip of the tongue. When the patient protests that 'I didn't really mean that', careful consideration is given to the possibility that he really *did* mean that. Everything is examined for its *underlying* meaning. The underlying meaning of a communication is called its *latent content*. The communication itself represents the *manifest content*. The translation of latent content from manifest content is called *interpretation*, and often leads to an emotional response from the patient. The response may be a flash of realisation — the 'aha!' reaction; one of indignation; of questioning; of doubt; of sadness; perhaps of pallor or blushing. The therapist should be wary of an interpretation which produces little more than good natured or compliant agreement, only mild interest or disinterest, or one which causes no emotional reaction whatsoever.

Here is an example of what may happen when the therapist pays close attention to the words used by his patient. A man was describing his difficulties with his wife. He said, 'I don't understand it. I love her. I try to be attentive to her. I am unfaith...faithful...to her.' When the last sentence was echoed back to him, he protested that it was just a slip of the tongue. It was of no significance. The doctor asked the husband to consider the proposition that it might have considerable significance. The husband became very angry. 'Of course I am not faith . . . unfaithful to her!' he protested. He became even more angry when he realised he had repeated his slip.

The *manifest* content of the communication was what the husband had twice said when he corrected his 'slip' — that he had been faithful to his wife. It was his wish that the therapist should ignore the error. The *latent* content was his unintended statement that he had been *unfaithful* to her. The therapist's interpretation, that despite his protestations he had been unfaithful, was confirmed later.

Another example is given by a patient who, some years previously, had promised to take her mother shopping for a birthday present. She had been looking forward to this outing, but when she reached the house, she found that her mother was out, and there was no message. The patient had travelled some distance, so she scribbled a note and returned home. Next day, her mother telephoned. 'You were supposed to come on Thursday', she said. 'That's right', said the patient, 'why weren't you there?' An argument developed, and the patient found herself on a totally different 'wavelength' from her mother. Then suddenly, she realised that yesterday was *Friday* and that she should have called the day before. She passed the whole thing off with a laugh. 'It must have been my unconscious, playing me tricks', she said. The therapist was very interested in this story and made an interpretation. 'It sounds as though you didn't want to buy your mother a present', he said. The patient was very angry. 'What a terrible thing to say', she replied, bursting into tears. 'I loved my mother very much. If you had any idea of how much I miss her, you wouldn't say such things'. The therapist was intrigued by the patient's angry response to his interpretation. In due course, he was to obtain evidence of its truth. The patient was very hostile indeed towards her mother, but her hostility was unconscious. She herself failed to recognise it and displaced her hostility towards the therapist.

Unconscious motivation

How can it be that attitudes can exist, of which the patient is not consciously aware? The answer lies in the concept of the *unconscious*. This is a subject of some complexity, and will be examined more fully in Chapter 5. Here we will note that thoughts, feelings, ideas and wishes which are not acceptable may become *unconscious*. They are *not* recognised consciously. The unconscious remains unconscious. The patient who said, 'It must have been my unconscious, playing me tricks,' was indicating that the true significance of her mistake was too painful to contemplate. When a 'discreditable' unconscious motive is revealed, the patient seldom receives it with enthusiasm. Instead, the therapist may be amazed at the vehemence with which it is rejected.

Sharing

Now let us consider a case in which the therapist shares his observations with his patient. It is a simple one, which does not call for any deep understanding. Nevertheless, there may be something to be learned from it.

A patient consulted the doctor for the very first time. Before a word was spoken, the doctor observed that the patient had a very disagreeable smell. It was the sort of smell about which people are not told, even by their closest friends. (To tell the truth, it is rare for such people to have close friends.) The patient complained that he had difficulty in finding friends. At least one of the reasons for this was obvious to the doctor, and it seemed surprising that it was not also obvious to the patient. But people quickly cease to notice smells. The existence of 'hospital smell', so conspicious to the patients, is often vehemently repudiated by its staff. The 'boiled cabbage' smell of a boarding house may be noticed by everyone except the proprietor. A 'gasworks smell' may be indignantly rejected by the local residents. A personal 'bad smell' usually passes unnoticed by the offender, who denies it angrily.

In the present case, the patient's olfactory sense was anaesthetised to his own offensive odour. Patients are often blind to things which are startlingly obvious to others. And unless the doctor was prepared to share his observations with his patient, there was little he could do to help the patient find friends. It might be difficult and embarrassing for the doctor, and the patient might be hurt, offended or even angry. But there is no painless way in which such information can be given. Thus, it became the doctor's difficult task to awaken the patient from his olfactory anaesthesia.

The 'insights' which occur in therapy are often painful. This cannot be avoided. The pain which is created may be the incentive which leads the patient to change his behaviour in a constructive way. The therapist cannot help his patient unless he is sometimes willing to cause pain.

In this example, the reader should note that the doctor neither told nor advised the patient what to do. He certainly did not reassure him that his impact on other people was fresh and inoffensive. He did not offer — or accept — any 'rational' explanation of the offence

('I haven't been too well lately, and when I'm not well I'm inclined to develop a slightly sweaty smell. I went to a dermatologist about it. He gave me some lotion to use.') The doctor pays attention to his patient and shares his observations with him. It is for the patient to decide whether to accept the observation, and what action to take.

Insight

The process of learning about oneself and one's idiosyncrasies, the development of self-awareness, the appreciation of how one appears to other people, is called insight. It can be extremely disconcerting.

Over the years, everyone builds up a private image of himself: what he looks like, what his strengths and weaknesses are, what he may reveal to others, and what he should conceal. However, his picture is distorted. The physical image with which an individual is familiar is strangely different from that which is known to other people, because it is his reflection in the mirror. It is difficult to find a photograph which pleases the sitter because, although the camera does not lie, the mirror does. Likewise, few people enjoy listening to a recording of their own voice. They usually look upon it as an unrecognisable catterwaul, grossly distorted and full of technical deficiencies. Yet this is the voice which others recognise, accept, and sometimes love.

Most people reject insight, preferring their own distorted picture of themselves. They dismiss indignantly anything which conflicts with their own private image. Thus, in 'Pygmalion', which was written in 1912, the irascible, impatient, intolerant, and self-centred Professor Higgins is asked by his housekeeper not to use a certain, very improper word beginning with the letter 'b'. Higgins protests loftily that 'I cannot charge myself with having ever uttered it, Mrs Pearce. Except perhaps in a moment of extreme and justifiable excitement'. His housekeeper replies, 'Only this morning, Sir, you applied it to your boots, to the butter and to the brown bread.' Higgins retorts with a rationalisation. 'Oh that! Mere alliteration, Mrs Pearce, natural to a poet'. Later, he confides to his companion, 'You know, Pickering, that woman has the most extraordinary ideas about me. Here I am, a shy, diffident, sort of man. I've never been able to feel really grown-up and tremendous, like other chaps. And yet she's firmly persuaded that I'm an arbitrary, over-bearing, bossy kind of person. I can't account for it.' And he really can't. He has no insight whatsoever. What a lonely man he must be!

4

What does the therapist say?

CARDINAL PRINCIPLE: Verbalisation precedes resolution.

Whilst he was in general practice, it was often the author's experience that he did not have to say anything. Indeed, an intervention sometimes had the effect of disturbing the patient's train of thought; and the interruption was more of a hindrance than a help.

The first rule, then, is that when there is nothing to say, the therapist should say nothing. There is nothing to be gained from talking, simply to keep the conversation going. Time and contemplation are required in psychotherapy. Solutions emerge only slowly. The instant solution, so much a feature of fictional psychiatry, should in practice be regarded with great suspicion.

Nevertheless, although much can be achieved by listening, there are many occasions on which the therapist should speak, and here we will discuss some of them.

The first reason is that the relationship between the therapist and the patient is similar to that between any two people. Consequently, effective communication between them demands an exchange of words. The relationship is however a professional one, not a social one, and it has a very specific purpose. It is to facilitate that activity which is beneficial to the patient: the communication of his thoughts and feelings to the therapist. It aims to help him to recall half-forgotten memories, sometimes proceeding to further fruitful elaboration of current thoughts and feelings. Frequently, and rather surprisingly, the act of putting a problem into words leads first to the expression of emotion, and then to the resolution of the problem. Verbalisation precedes resolution.

Facilitation is the first object of the therapist's share of the exchange. The second is *clarification*. This may be required to assist facilitation. In order to help the patient to understand, the therapist must also understand. His understanding may be only a fraction ahead of the patient's. When he asks for clarification, the content may be clarified for the patient, too.

Asking questions

It is much more important for the therapist to listen to the patient than it is for the patient to listen to the therapist, but there are times when the therapist must ask questions. He will wish to ask questions when he does not understand what is being said or when a new topic, about which he knows little or nothing, is being introduced. He may wish to ask why a patient is having difficulty in speaking about a topic, or why he appears to be evading it.

Questions should be brief, and should be phrased in simple words which can be easily understood. One question only should be asked at a time. They should be pruned of extraneous matter ('sort of thing'; 'if you follow me'; 'or what'; 'as it were'; 'and so on'). Anecdotal questions should be avoided ('I had an old grandfather who lived to be 98. He never smoked or drank. He always use to say 'if you can't think of something nice to say about someone, don't say anything'. How do you feel about saying unkind things to people?'). Technical terms should not be used.

The therapist will sometimes find that he has phrased a question badly, or that he has asked one which he did not intend. He may be tempted to rephrase the question. It is better to allow the patient to answer the 'wrong' question. This sometimes provides useful and unexpected information. The 'right' question can be put when the 'wrong' question has been answered. The patient will sometimes answer the 'right' question despite the fact that the 'wrong' one has been put.

Questions may be 'leading' or 'open-ended'. Radio and television interviewers seem to prefer leading questions. For the psychotherapist, open-ended questions are usually more informative. In them, the question is phrased in such a way that the reply demands more than a single word. 'Open-ended' questions may lead to fruitful elaboration. The leading question, 'Do you get on well with your mother?' requires only a 'yes' or 'no' answer. It may be more productive to rephrase it in the 'open-ended' form: 'How do you get on with your mother?' The answer should be attended to carefully for it may be evasive. One patient, when asked this question, replied, 'Mother was a wonderful person. She would do anything for anyone. She always had a kind word for people. They all loved her. There were more than 500 people at her funeral.' The therapist had to point out that the actual question had been evaded, and it transpired that the relationship between them had been very bad indeed.

Leading questions are more common in ordinary conversation, and many beginning psychotherapists find great difficulty in avoiding them. A simple formula for converting leading questions into the open-ended form is to preface them with the words, 'Tell me about...'

The therapist should take care not to suggest possible answers to his questions. An inexperienced therapist asked correctly, 'How did you get on with your mother?'. There was a long pause. Then he added, 'I mean, did you get on well with her, or badly, or was she possessive, or did she let you do what you liked, or what?' The patient felt that he should choose from one of these responses, when none was really appropriate. It may take time for the patient to marshal his thoughts and the therapist must be prepared to wait for the answer. He thereby acknowledges that time and contemplation are required before problems can be solved.

'Leading' questions require a specific answer, such as 'yes' or 'no', 'in 1970', and so on. They may require the patient to make a commitment or a decision. The patient may be asked when he was born, if he wishes to continue with therapy or whether he has any sexual problems. The therapist should be especially careful to avoid 'forcing' leading questions. These give the patient little opportunity of disagreeing with the therapist. An example is given by the parsimonious Aberdonian, who said to his scarcely welcome guests, 'You've had your tea, haven't you?'* Leading questions may be used as 'funnels' towards open-ended ones. Thus, 'Is your father alive? What does he do? And your mother? How old is she? How do you get on with them?' Leading questions should be used sparingly, especially in personal and intimate matters. When a patient is new to therapy and uncertain of his therapist, he may be trapped into telling a later-to-be-regretted lie. If he is asked, 'Do you have any sexual problems?', he may be reluctant or ashamed to admit that he has, and give a misleading answer. This danger can be avoided by rephrasing the question. The patient should be asked, 'Do you have any sexual problems *which you would like to discuss with me*?' If the answer is 'no', the answer is a reserved one.

The therapist should take note of *reserved* answers, because they avoid the primary question. He must remember them, because the patient may later indicate that he is prepared to give an *unreserved* answer. If a patient is asked,'Have you ever been attracted to members of your own sex?' and replies, 'Generally speaking no.', he has given a reserved answer.

Inaudible questions

If he does not hear the question, or does not understand it, and

* Such things never happen in Edinburgh.

provided that he is not frightened or over-awed, a patient will usually ask the therapist to repeat it. The therapist should repeat the question in a louder voice, using the same words. He should not rephrase it. The patient may not have heard the *words* of the question, but he has probably caught the cadence and the rhythm. If the question is rephrased, the 'tune' is changed and the patient may be confused. He was prepared for the tune of the 'old' question, and may not hear the 'new' one, either.

Interruption

As far as possible, the patient should be allowed to tell his story without interruption. However, there will be times when it is necessary for the therapist to interrupt. The patient may be in full flow, and time is running out. At a convenient moment, he should be interrupted and told how much time remains to him. Sometimes the patient will interrupt the therpist. The therapist will normally allow the patient's interruption to take precedence: he can complete what he was saying afterwards.

Participants in joint interviews (q.v.) should be discouraged from interrupting each other. If one partner wishes to interrupt, he can be assured that he will be given an opportunity of putting his point when his partner has finished.

Talking 'over' a patient — forcing views upon him whilst he is trying to express his own — is usually an expression of negative counter-transference (q.v.). The therapist should examine his own attitudes.

Comments and examples

The therapist will sometimes comment on statements made by his patient. His comments are usually intended to facilitate further elaboration. Sometimes they are an attempt to elucidate a latent meaning.

When a patient makes a generalisation, the therapist should ask for a specific example. The patient may say, 'Sometimes I find myself getting rather irritated over nothing.' The therapist should ask for an example. Some patients try to impress the therapist by speaking of exalted people with whom they are acquainted. The therapist should help the patient to speak of his need to impress.

Sometimes, when he has spoken a few sentences, the patient will pause. It is clear that he is thinking. The therapist should help him to verbalise his thoughts, perhaps by repeating his last few words. At other times, it is apparent that the patient has fallen silent because he is in the grip of an emotion. The expression of such emotions is very important, not only in understanding the problem, but also in the search for its solution. When the therapist perceives that the patient is experiencing an emotion, he should encourage him to express or *abreact* it. The lips may tremble and the face redden in grief. The blush of embarrassment, the glaring eyes and pale skin of anger should be noted. In these cases, the psychotherapist should say, 'It seems that our discussion has caused you distress' (or sadness or embarrassment or anger). When the interpretation is accurate, the emotion is usually heightened. When the therapist does not understand why a topic should have caused distress, he may, after the emotion has been expressed, ask. The abreaction of emotion is a crucial procedure in psychotherapy.

Turning propositions on their ends

Patients sometimes confuse cause and effect. A woman may say, 'I get angry when my husband leaves me alone in the evening.' Further investigation may reveal that he leaves her alone in the evening because she is angry. Another may say, 'I cannot concentrate on my work because I am unable to sleep at night.' Later, it may emerge that she cannot sleep because she worries that she is neglecting her children by going to work.

The technique used in such cases as these is given various names: turning the proposition on its end, upside down, inside out or back to front. Explanations are reversed and reconsidered. Nothing is accepted without question.

'I cannot have sex because I get a headache' might be rephrased as 'I develop a headache so that I have an excuse to avoid sexual intercourse'. If this is so, there must be something wrong with the relationship. 'I cannot bear to touch my wife because she was unfaithful with my best friend' carries several sexual implications. It suggests that the patient looks upon sexual contact with his wife as indirect sexual contact with his best friend. The therapist may wonder whether the husband has some unconscious homosexual attraction towards his best friend. The statement also suggests that his heterosexual drive is not very strong and that her infidelity provides him with an excuse for avoiding sexual contact with his wife.

Turning a proposition on its end may be useful when fears and phobias are being considered, although it may first be necessary to deal with considerable resistance. A mother who *fears* that she might injure her baby may be helped, gently, to consider the proposition that she might *wish* to injure him. Such a proposition is likely to be very alarming for the mother. Her distress will be increased still more if she superstitiously believes that speaking about such a thought might lead to its commission. The help and support of her therapist may enable her to look at her fear more objectively. If she can do so, it will often begin to abate.

When statements are turned on their ends, they should be presented as possibilities. They cannot be offered as certainties. The therapist merely asks the patient to consider them. He is not entitled to say 'it is so'. He is a psychotherapist, not a mind reader. His job is to help the patient consider all the possibilities, even when they seem absurd. Some transpositions may sound completely ridiculous, but they should not be rejected without careful consideration.

The non sequitur

The interpretation of a non sequitur may provide the therapist with some of his most spectacular successes. If he finds himself perplexed by an unexpected comment, he should refrain from asking questions too quickly. The significance may emerge much later, out of the blue, perhaps during a silence, or even after the session has been completed. Sometimes the solution is never forthcoming. We will give some examples of non sequiturs and their interpretations.

A patient was sent for an X-ray. When he returned, he commented that the machine seemed to be rather old-fashioned. The doctor correctly inferred that the patient had doubts about the reliability of the examination. He was convinced that he was suffering from lung cancer, and a normal result did not reassure him.

Early in therapy, another patient described the scene as she looked upon the dead body of her mother. 'She was beautiful' she said. 'She seemed 20 years younger. Her lips were red and her cheeks were pink. It was just as though she was asleep.' At a later session, she repeated this description, almost word for word. Then she asked the barely relevant question, 'Do undertakers use cosmetics on dead people?' The therapist was nonplussed, and was about to reply that he did not know, when the significance of her question suddenly dawned on him. If cosmetics had *not* been used, the pink-cheeked mother might simply have been asleep. By failing to draw attention to this fact, the patient would have been responsible for burying her mother alive. This proved to be her fear. She anticipated a similar fate for herself in retribution. She had left instructions in her will that one of her arteries was to be opened before she was buried. However, she did not trust her executors to carry out her wishes.

Another patient sent for the doctor when her father suddenly became very ill. The doctor did not arrive for two hours. 'Of course, he is a very busy man' she excused him. The therapist took note of the excuse and asked what would have happened if the doctor had come sooner. The patient believed that her father would have survived. She blamed the doctor for his death. She also blamed herself for his death — she should have asked another doctor to call.

A wealthy businessman, who had been charged with driving whilst under the influence of alcohol, was referred to a psychiatrist by Dr Smith, his general practitioner. After careful investigation, the psychiatrist concluded that he was insufficiently motivated for treatment. The patient was a man of considerable influence, and was very disconcerted when told that he would not be accepted for treatment. Then he said to the psychiatrist, 'By the way, I have an apology to make to you. Some months ago Jimmy Smith made an appointment for me to see you. I didn't come.' The patient assumed that he was being punished for failing to keep his appointment, although the psychiatrist had had no knowledge of what had happened. By referring familiarly to 'Jimmy Smith', the patient indicated to the psychiatrist that he was on Christian name terms with the family doctor. Later he admitted that he had hoped to revenge himself on the psychiatrist by shutting off his supply of patients, at least from Dr Smith.

Specific examples such as these are of limited general value. They illustrate how the odd, apparently irrelevant, paradoxical or superficial communication may have a significant latent meaning. They demonstrate some of the traps which await the unwary. They highlight the importance of first thinking about the inner meaning of a question, instead of immediately searching for its answer.

Forms of communication

It is customary to think of 'communication' as referring to the exchange of words. Words certainly provide a very precise medium for the exchange of ideas. By the use of words, we can agree, in the most simple and effective way, that such and such a thing is a table, or that it is hot, or that it is frightening.

However, some words are difficult to understand. They may be obscure, technical, foreign or polysyllabic. The incorrect use of a technical word may be a source of serious misunderstanding.

Some patients try to illustrate the extent of their knowledge by the use of foreign words or phrases. Sometimes they use words which are in common use and easily understandable, but sometimes they are obscure. The author requests his patients always to use simple English because, if they do not, he is eventually caught out. The use of polysyllabic words may result in floccinaucinihilipilification.

Unfortunately, words can also be used to mislead or deceive. Some patients consciously and deliberately tell lies. Others try to escape from awkward questions by using evasions. A common device is to qualify a reply. In answer to the question 'Do you ever feel angry', a patient may reply 'Generally speaking. no.' This means, 'sometimes'. If he replies, 'Never', it sounds as though he is telling a lie. One patient answered the question 'Have you ever been in prison?' with 'Not really'. He meant 'Yes'. In cases such as these, the therapist can make a reasonable guess that the patient is trying to mislead him. He should pursue any reply which he regards as ambiguous.

Non-verbal communication

The reader will appreciate that it is possible for people to 'talk' to each other without using words. Lovers squeeze each other's hands to symbolise their mutual understanding and affection. A nod of the head means the opposite of a shake. The smile that one gives on greeting a friend means the opposite of crossing to the other side of the road when an enemy approaches.

An old proverb says that one picture is worth a thousand words. Non-verbal communication is frequently pictorial.

Here are 180 words to describe a picture. The patient has consulted his therapist on 20 consecutive occasions. He has always been punctual. On the 21st occasion, he is late. He explains that there was an accident and that a long queue of traffic had formed. The therapist has sensed that things have not been going well in recent interviews, and asks the patient to consider the proposition that he was losing interest in therapy. The patient becomes angry. He asks whether the therapist is suggesting that he engineered the whole thing.

He 'quite forgets' his next appointment and subsequently telephones to apologise. At the following meeting, the therapist links the interview which had been 'quite forgotten' with the one which started late, and reminds the patient of his subsequent angry reaction to the interpretation. The patient is still more angry. He challenges the therapist to say whether he himself has ever forgotten anything — 'just by accident'; whether he has ever made a mistake. We need not continue. The picture of an angry, offended patient is clear, but it has taken many words to describe. One glance at the patient would have shown it immediately.

It is common for patients to make errors about the timing of their appointments. Sometimes they come early, occasionally several days early. Sometimes they come late. Each piece of behaviour speaks of their enthusiasm or reluctance to meet the therapist.

Patients do not always wish to keep their appointments. Things may be going badly. The patient may be growing tired — or alarmingly — rather fond of his therapist. There may be secret things to be told, embarrassing topics to be discussed, matters which the patient would prefer to leave unspoken. He may fear that, if the truth is told, his therapist will think badly of him. It is sometimes wise to discuss this apprehension. How does the patient feel when the meeting ends? Does he complain that it has been too brief or does he say that the time has passed very slowly?

Errors may take many forms. We have already referred to slips of the tongue. Why should someone make a slip? What does a man mean when he says, 'I loathe . . . er . . . love my mother.'? When two contradictory statements are made, the listener is customarily expected to pay attention to the second, and to disregard the first. Patients sometimes become angry when the therapist ignores this custom and pays attention to the first. 'It was just a slip of the tongue.' they argue, 'nothing of any importance.'

Some people make slips of the pen. In writing to thank his hosts for a 'pleasant' weekend, one said, 'I hope it will not be too soon till we meet again.' When this was drawn to his attention, he protested that he intended to write 'too long'. 'Too soon' was a slip of the pen. It was to be disregarded. However, a therapist always interested in considering the proposition that an 'error' expresses the *true* feelings of an individual. These feelings are what are sought. Words may be the means by which they are concealed.

Feelings may be expressed in ways other than verbal ones. In these circumstances, we speak of non-verbal communication. Non-verbal communication can be a potent source of expression. Smiles, scowls and tears may speak volumes. A revealing example is given by a young mother who forgot to collect her child from school at the end of his very first day. When a distasteful conclusion cannot be avoided, it must be spoken. The word 'interpretation' is used when actions are translated into words, whether they refer to conscious or unconscious behaviour.

The exposed parts of the body sometimes give important non-verbal clues. Heavy make-up will conceal such clues but may be relevant in itself. Patients may flush or go pale. Pallor usually means fear, anxiety or anger. People also flush with anger: they may blush with embarrassment. Blotchy redness may indicate some degree of erotic excitement. The redness of anger often has a slightly purplish hue. The choleric General of fiction or even real life, is sometimes said to be puce with rage. Quivering of the chin, reddening of the eyes, and the appearance of tears, are obvious signs of sadness. The patient should be allowed to weep. Silence often helps the expression of sadness. The author sometimes finds it useful to say that a memory seems to have brought a lump to the throat.

The state of the hands is worth noting. Are the finger nails clean or dirty? Are they well-manicured? Are they bitten? People who bite their nails are often chronically anxious and uncertain. If it is the therapist's practice to shake hands with his patient, he should notice whether the handshake is peremptory or prolonged. Does the patient have a tremor? The author is very familiar with a case in which the therapist does. Sherlock Holmes read much into the hands, the clothes and the perfume — his example is always worth copying. How does the patient walk? How does he sit? Where does he look?

A surprising and apparently gratifying conclusion to psychotherapy comes when the patient's symptoms disappear quite suddenly, and he reports that he is now fully well and does not need to come any more. This may be very puzzling and the therapist finds himself quite unable to account for it. It is a conclusion which is not always satisfactory. Some people call it 'a flight into health'. It may be a sign that the therapist is getting too close to a significant but possibly unconscious truth for the patient's comfort. The therapist should express his satisfaction at such a gratifying outcome but should maintain contact with the patient. He should not accept the suggestion that no further meetings are necessary. He should tell the patient that he wishes to confirm that all remains well.

We have noted that a non-verbal communication may take an apparently verbal form. For example, in Chapter 1, the anxious father asked, 'How does his heart sound?' He was using a verbal form as a device to express non-verbal anxiety about his son's health.

Some verbal non-verbal communications consist simply of noises. Obvious examples are sighing, laughing, giggling and weeping. Some patients suddenly pour out a flood of irrelevant speech. This is another form of 'verbal non-verbal' communication. The therapist should always seek the reason.

Patients often write letters to their therapist. It may be easier to put difficult matters on to paper than to speak of them openly. It is not necessarily to the patient's advantage if the therapist makes things 'easier' for him. The distress which arises from speaking is usually more productive than that which arises from writing.

Some patients write very long letters or extensive autobiographies 'to save you time'. The act of reading these epics may, in fact, take a substantial amount of the therapist's time, although some therapists encourage the exercise. It is the author's opinion that such practices deprive the patient of the opportunity of sharing his emotions with the therapist. He therefore advises against them. What is more, letters and case histories may be edited and re-written many times over. Significant factors may be distorted or may be lost altogether. Sometimes letters are used by the patient as a device to test whether or not the therapist is paying attention. Sometimes he is examined discreetly to test whether or not he has actually read them.

The telephone is used by some patients to communicate with the therapist. Once again, the therapist is deprived of much important information. He does not see the subtle interplay of emotions. He cannot know what the patient is wearing, how he is looking and who is with him. The author discourages the use of the telephone. He asks that everything should be discussed face to face. He deals briefly with telephone calls and asks the patient to raise the matter directly at the next meeting. Certain organisations, notably the Samaritans, encourage discussion over the telephone. This seems to be appropriate for their method of working. The author does not consider that it is appropriate in psychotherapy.

The therapist should never allow himself to be trapped into agreeing with something that he does not truly believe. A patient may accuse him of having said or implied something with which he does not agree. Few therapists can remember everything that is said at every meeting, and he may be unable to recall the interview in which the offending statement was made. However, if he is always true to himself, he can, if he wishes, reply, 'That is not what I believe and I do not think I would have said it.' One patient reported to her husband that the therapist had advised her to leave him. The therapist knew that he *never* gave such advice. The relationship between husband and wife was bad, and the therapist had asked whether she had ever contemplated separation. The alleged 'advice' was a carefully modified version of this question. If he should ever allow himself to say something which he does not really believe, the therapist can never make such an assertion. However, provided that his own mind is clear, he should not be in too great a hurry to dispute incorrect statements. Some represent projections on to the therapist of part of the patient's opinions, and it may first be wise to examine them from this point of view.

Patients may make complex and often erroneous deductions from questions which are put to them. One said, 'You accused me of having a guilt complex because I was unfaithful to my wife.' The author is not really sure what is meant by the term 'guilt complex' and consequently does not use it. Thus he was encouraged to look into the assertion in more detail. It transpired that the patient had mis-perceived a premature conclusion on the part of the therapist, when he put the simple leading question, 'Have you been faithful to your wife?'

When the therapist makes a promise to his patient, he must try to keep it. An adolescent boy who repeatedly played truant from school was warned that if his behaviour continued, his adoptive father would be sent to prison. He continued to play truant, and when he returned home, he was very angry to find that his stepfather was still there. It is better to avoid such promises.

Another form of a non-verbal communication occurs when a patient gives a present to his therapist. We shall say more about this later. Here we need observe only that a present represents a token of the patient's affection for the therapist. All 'non-verbal' com-munications must be put into words and interpreted. A present should be interpreted in this way.

There may be many clues to discover and much to be guessed. However, only the patient himself can tell whether or not a guess is accurate. Even when it is accurate, he may prefer to deny its accuracy. Whilst the therapist puts his observations into words, he observes the response of the patient. If the interpretation is incor-rect, the patient may respond non-verbally. A flush of anger, which is misinterpreted as a blush of embarrassment, may be heightened. Alternatively, the patient may simply reject the interpretation. A blush of embarrassment interpreted correctly, sometimes brings a verbal response of a special type to which we have already referred, such as 'not really'.

Everything has a meaning. The therapist not only hears: he sees and pays attention to everything. Every communication is carefully examined for its latent content.

Silence

From time to time, the patient will become silent. Silence is com-munication, and may have various meanings, which should always be explored. A patient may become silent whilst he considers an interpretation and its implications. This sort of silence is construc-tive and need not be interrupted. He may become silent when a new train of thought enters his mind.

At earlier sessions, the patient may be silent out of deference to the therapist. If the therapist begins an interview with a series of leading questions, silence will eventually develop whilst the patient waits for the next question.

Occasionally a patient becomes silent because his mind 'has gone completely blank'. This is a familiar experience, similar to that of being unable to recall a name which is 'on the tip of the tongue'. Here, too, 'the mind goes completely blank'. The phenomenon is usually caused by the active repression of significant unconscious emotional material. It is rarely overcome by direct questioning. The more the patient tries to remember, the more difficult does he find it to recall the forgotten thought. A better approach is an indirect one. The therapist tries to discover *why* the thought should have been repressed with such vigour. If the *reason* for the resistance can be analysed, it usually disappears. It may be clarified by reviewing the topics which were under discussion before the mind 'went blank'. Sometimes, in place of the 'lost' topic, something comes into the mind which appears to be quite unrelated. Free association (q.v.) with the 'totally different' subject matter may reveal the source of the resistance.

The patient may become silent out of shame, disloyalty, and so on. When he is reluctant to convey his thoughts to the therapist for conscious reasons, he is breaking the 'contract'. The therapist should help the patient to understand that *conscious* resistance of this sort is therapeutically harmful.

Silence sometimes springs from defiance. The patient feels hostile to the therapist and his silence says, 'It's about time you did something for a change — why should I do all the work?' When this happens, an unspoken battle sometimes develops between the therapist and the patient. Each wonders who will crack first: who will be first to find the silence intolerable. Such a 'battle' is of no value to anyone, and the therapist should not be a party to it. In this case, he need have no hesitation in breaking the silence with the appropriate interpretation, many times over if necessary. The reason for the patient's desire to struggle with his therapist should be examined — and sometimes the reverse!

Cadence and stress

We sometimes mock the Chinese for using the same word to mean 'yes' and 'no'. It seems an absurd contradiction. But we ourselves use certain phrases which can take opposite meanings, according to the way in which they are stressed. When this happens, a communication may acquire a completely new significance. For example, a family was looking forward to a picnic, but the day was dull, windy, wet and cold, and everything seemed to go wrong. 'This is a fine day for a picnic!' they grumbled. The next day was bright and warm. The sun was shining and there was a gentle breeze. The skies were blue and the birds were singing. 'This is a fine day for a picnic,' they exclaimed. The father, who did not like picnics, muttered to himself, 'This is a bloody awful day for a picnic!'

When a patient speaks of his feelings for another person, the meaning of his words may depend entirely upon the cadence and stress.

Think of the many ways that the phrase 'I love you' can be spoken, according to the way in which it is punctuated (I love you! I love you? I? — love you!). Here are some of them:

I love you.
I love you, but no-one else does.
I love you, not hate you.
I love you, not someone else.
I don't love you. Perhaps someone else does.
It's not love: I quite like you, though.
I love someone else!

A patient may make a slip, not of the tongue, but of the *tone*. It is necessary to adhere precisely to the tone when the therapist reflects the slip back to him.

Answering questions
When a patient asks a question, the therapist need not be in too great a hurry to reply. He should first consider what may lie behind the question. What relevance does it have to the present stage of therapy? Is the patient seeking an answer to a matter of fact? If so, the sources of information available to him are much the same as those available to the therapist. He himself should consult the sources. Does he seek advice or reassurance? The therapist will wonder why the patient should wish advice or reassurance at this particular moment. Sometimes the patient asks for an opinion. In medical practice, it is common to offer opinions, but the reader is reminded that opinions are based on the average 'case', and they may have little relevance to an individual patient, who is always unique.

The standard, and perhaps rather stereotyped way of replying to patient's questions is, 'Tell me your own thoughts about it' or 'What brought that question to your mind?' It is probably best to use a variation of one of these forms.

When the patient puts a question, it may be helpful for the therapist to put himself into the patient's shoes, and to ponder over the implications of the question. This often suggests a possible explanation.

For example, a patient was investigated for two or three days in a medical ward for symptoms suggestive of intestinal disease. She enquired of a nurse who was passing whether the results always took a long time to come. The nurse was tempted to 'reassure' the patient that the tests required skilled investigation and interpretation, and that they would be completed as quickly as possible. Instead, she remembered to put herself into the patient's shoes, and answered 'You must feel as though you have been waiting for an eternity.' The patient burst into tears, and cried for the rest of the day. Her father had died of cancer of the stomach, and she was sure the same fate awaited her.

The Ward Sister was not very pleased with this meddlesome interference, but the expression of her fear and the accompanying grief had a remarkable effect on the patient. By the next day, her discomfort had completely disappeared, and although several days elapsed before the tests were completed, her symptoms, her fear and here apprehension had quite gone. The fact that the test results were negative was pleasing to her, but reassurance was no longer necessary. The Ward Sister was not convinced!

The new therapist should therefore be careful about questions which are put to him. He must be on the alert for things which are not what they seem to be. He must try to free himself from preconceptions and prejudice, and should be especially careful when things seem to be unduly obvious. Even when he is asked a question to which he does not know the answer, he should still look behind it. He need not be unduly disturbed by the common, sometimes accurate, complaint that 'You never say anything'. He should never feel any need to conceal his ignorance, or to excuse his mistakes.

Intuition

The therapist should feel free to pay attention to his intuition when he is trying to help patients to put their thoughts into words. Intuition is a curious phenomenon, not easy to describe or quantify, but a very real one. It probably reflects the total impact of the patient upon the therapist. There are times when it has an almost telepathic quality, but telepathy is a 'para-normal' concept, for which there is no room in psychotherapy.

Intuition evolves from the rapid, mainly unconscious assessment which one person makes of another. It is derived from everything that he hears and sees of his companion: the empathy which exists between them, and his experience of similar people. It is as though his companion creates some sort of sympathetic 'resonance' in his own unconscious.

Intuition is a valuable asset to the psychotherapist, but it must be used with care, for it is sometimes misleading or erratic. It should not be expressed in terms of 'I think you feel' or 'perhaps you feel', but 'in similar circumstances, some people might feel.'

The therapist should avoid appearing *too* clever. A patient was giving a garbled and increasingly confused account of an episode which had occurred when she was 12. Increasingly embarrassed, she said, 'You know what I am trying to say, don't you?' The therapist was new and unwary. He had a good idea, but he could not be certain. He played his hunch. 'It sounds as though you are trying to say that you became pregnant.' The patient was completely taken aback by what she saw as his almost telepathic perception. Thereafter, whenever she had anything difficult to say, the patient insisted that it was unnecessary for her to tell the therapist, because he already knew what it was. Sometimes he was able to make a shrewd guess, but it was in vain for him to protest that he did not *always* know.

It would be very convenient for the patient and himself, if the therapist were a mind-reader. It may be tempting to 'agree' that one possesses a gift of telepathy. It is flattering but untrue. The therapist does not *know* what a patient is going to say until he says it. What is more, 'saying it' is one of the difficulties which the patient may have to learn to overcome. When he has conquered one difficulty, it may be easier to conquer others.

Conventional and stereotyped phrases

The therapist should remember that we share certain stereotyped attitudes which are seldom disputed. Such conventional points of view are tolerated with a greater or lesser degree of sincerity. It can be said of few married couples that they never had a cross word: of very few husbands that they have never looked at other women. When such assertions are made, the therapist will have considerable reservations about them. Other beliefs are so widely accepted that it may seem impertinent to question them. For example, we take it for granted that mothers love their children. This is true for most mothers, for most of the time, but it is not true for them all. If the therapist accepts such an attitude without question, he may completely miss the core of a serious problem. Other conventional points of view which are widely held but not necessarily true, include the assumption that people do not like going into hospitals, especially that they are afraid of mental hospitals, that they do not like taking drugs, or visiting doctors, and that people who commit violent, sadistic and blood-thirsty crimes *must* be psychiatrically ill. In 'Once in Royal David's City', it is affirmed that little children *must* be 'mild, obedient and good'. In fact, they may be vicious, deceitful, spiteful, inquisitive and dishonest.

Errors, lies and the truth

We have already considered some of the problems which arise from such errors as slips of the tongue. Sometimes it is difficult to distinguish between the truth, what the patient sees as the truth, and actual falsehood.

There is no way in which the 'truth' or 'falsehood' of a statement can be established with certainty. 'Truth drugs' and 'lie detectors' are fictions encouraged by liars, as a device to deceive the naive into accepting their probity.

The therapist may sometimes feel doubtful about something that he is told by his patient. He may even catch him out in a piece of flagrant dishonesty. When this happens, and especially if it happens more than once, the therapist must consider carefully whether he can continue with treatment.

In the first edition of this book, it was stated that untruthfulness is rare. The author regrets that he has been compelled to revise this opinion. Lies seem to be fairly common. Patients are sometimes more interested in securing the good opinion of the people about them than in admitting the truth about themselves. This seems to be particularly true when disagreeable matters are raised.

The patient may accuse the therapist of 'talking him into' something he did not mean, of distorting his words or even of lying. It is especially during a phase of negative transference that he may make such allegations.

Despite all this, the author believes that it is best to assume that, once a patient has accepted the need for therapy, he will tell the truth *as he sees it*. When mistakes occur, and if the therapist is experiencing a negative *counter*-transference towards his patient, he must examine the possibility that the error is his. In any case, the therapist should always discuss with the patient all possible meanings of an error. The discussion may not coincide with the patient's view of the truth, although it may later prove that he was at fault. Nothing is so absurd that it can be rejected without consideration.

Doorstep communications

Sometimes a patient will make a momentous announcement at the very end of a session, perhaps just as he is about to leave the room. Such 'doorstep communications' may be of great importance. At other times, they are employed as a means of prolonging the interview. They may then be interpreted as such. Frequently, and especially during earlier sessions, they occur because the patient has been unable to summon up sufficient courage to make his 'confession'. Time is slipping by, and if he does not say it now, it will be too late. The revelation is therefore made at the very last moment: sometimes it provides the solution to a mystery which has hitherto been completely obscure.

Doorstep communications are usually too important to be dealt with on the doorstep. It may not be possible to deal with them in the last few minutes of the interview. The therapist should try to do neither of these things. He should say, 'What you have said is of great importance. We cannot deal with it in the very short time that is left to us. We will require the whole of the next session. Will you remember to begin with it?'

The next session should be as soon as possible. The therapist should make sure that the patient raises the topic early.

The diagnosis

It would be gratifying if modern medicine were scientific and objective, but a large element of magic and mystery remains. When a patient complains of symptoms, the doctor prescribes a cure. If the patient recovers, the doctor is confirmed as being a clever man. If the symptoms continue, the patient looks for a cleverer man. If they get worse, he sometimes dies. If they stay the same, he is sometimes labelled a chronic patient.

Wedged between symptoms and the cure is interposed something called 'the diagnosis'. This seems to be an indication that the doctor knows what he is about. Provided that he recovers, it appears to reassure the patient. When a patient asks, 'What exactly is the trouble?', he is usually given a diagnosis. It may be something which sounds very precise, such as 'a right upper lobar pneumococcal pneumonia'. In other cases it may be extremely vague — a 'chill on the liver', a 'virus' or 'the blood out of order'. Nevertheless, if the patient recovers, he seldom asks any further questions.

To the clinician, however, it is different. What constitutes a really satisfactory reply to the question, 'What exactly is the matter?'? Is a precise diagnosis, such as 'a right upper lobar pneumococcal pneumonia' an adequate answer? When a doctor sees a scratch, does he really see 'The connective tissue cells growing out majestically and smoothly from the margin of the field, crossing and interlacing until a firm new structure is formed. Among these cells, others of quite different aspect, worming their way with no thought of building. Arrived at the margin where they escape from the entanglement of these more serious fibroblasts, they show their true characters. Some are polymorphonuclear leucocytes and they hop about within a limited area in a sort of ecstatic frenzy, evidently throwing out and retracing pseudopods at a great rate. Then there are lymphocytes which move, humbly like plugs crawling only a little way with head to the ground. But also there are macrophages which reach out great arms, perhaps in two or more directions and at the end of these arms, there is a flourish of clear protoplasm with out-flowing streamers that wave and search about for whatever can be seized, or else the whole advancing margin of the cell flows out and comes back like a wave, sucking in any particle that comes in its way.' (Mac-Callum quoted in Boyd). Is this the answer to the question, 'what exactly is the matter?'? If it is, does the doctor say so to the patient?

The traditional evasions employed in medicine are not appropriate in psychotherapy. Instead of receiving an elaborate but dubious reply to every question, the patient slowly realises that, however wise and experienced is his therapist, he has many areas of ignorance, and does not seek to conceal them. The therapist and the patient search together for the *solution* to his problems, which comes from within the patient himself. Some patients hope that when everything has been told, the therapist will prescribe a course of action. This is not so. The 'course of action' emerges instead from the special interaction between doctor and patient. The patient is not rejected because he becomes dependent upon his therapist, or when he is angry or unco-operative. Nothing that he says is judged. The therapist is rarely shocked or surprised. The complementary support experienced by the patient assists him in his interaction with other people. Perhaps they will not reject him, judge him or be shocked by him, either. Or if they do, perhaps he will be able to bear it.

Questions put by the patient are often very pertinent, and sometimes extremely complicated. Although the patient hopes for an answer, he cannot always be given one. There are many reasons why this should be. Sometimes, although apparently explicit, the question does not have much meaning. Some questions indicate doubt or uncertainty and then, rather than answering the question, it is the task of the therapist to help the patient express his doubt.

Patients sometimes ask, 'Have you had many cases like mine?' This is sometimes a way of enquiring whether or not the therapist's experience is sufficient to deal with the problem. Early in treatment, many patients ask, 'Do you think you will be able to help me?' This question may have a different meaning to the patient from its meaning to the therapist. At first, the therapist does not know whether the patient *wants* to be 'helped', or even what constitutes 'help'. Might the pain of *health* outweigh the pain of the *illness?*

Help sought by a patient is sometimes very selective. A man who has fallen *out* of love with his wife may want the therapist to persuade *her* to fall *out* of love with him. He is often less enthusiastic about the suggestion that he should be helped to fall in love with her *again*.

When drugs are prescribed, patients often ask 'What exactly do they do?' It is difficult to give a precise answer to questions such as this. Doctors seldom know how drugs work — there seems to be disagreement even about the mode of action of bicarbonate of soda in alleviating indigestion. The precise pharmacology of the psychotropic drugs may not be elucidated even during this century.

Many people try to deal with questions about psychotropic drugs by allocating them to categories, such as tranquillisers and antidepressants. This is helpful for journalists, but most psychiatrists regard such categorisation as misleading, and it is sometimes contradictory. A depressed patient does not necessarily feel depressed, and may object to taking an antidepressant. On the other hand, someone who feels depressed following the death of a loved relative may wonder at the reason for being refused an 'antidepressant' drug.

Patients are sometimes puzzled about the status of a psychotherapist. He usually calls himself a doctor, but he does not always behave like other doctors, and it may not be clear that he is medically qualified. Doctors in other specialities are usually prepared, when cornered, to give detailed explanations about illness. They have drugs for every disease. They realise that it is absurd, but their patients often treat them as though they are omniscient. They seldom dispute the claim.

In what way does a medically qualified psychotherapist, who works in the National Health Service, differ from the self-designated 'psychotherapist' who advertises in the agony columns of the local newspapers, along with a rather dubious collection of psychologists, hypnotherapists, faith healers, herbalists, acupuncturists and the like? Patients also wonder about the relationship between psychotherapy and the occult, telepathy, thought transference and mind reading. Most 'proper' doctors give forceful and dogmatic opinions about their unqualified rivals. The psychotherapist merely smiles enigmatically, like a medical Mona Lisa.

5

Some psychological mechanisms

CARDINAL PRINCIPLE: Everything has a meaning.

Every culture judges its members. Their behaviour may be praised for being good, or condemned as bad. In our culture, pride, lechery, envy, anger, covetousness, sloth and gluttony are bad, whilst charity and chastity, prudence, faith, modesty, felicity and honesty are good.

The comprehension of what is 'good' and what is 'bad' is learned very early in life, principally due to the guidance of the parents and other important adults. They learned it from their parents, and so on. The common understanding of what is to be praised and what condemned gives each culture its characteristic flavour. What is 'good' in one culture may be 'bad' in another.

In Western Europe, for example, it is looked upon as 'bad' for mothers and fathers to leave their children in the care of uncles and aunts, perhaps for years at a time, whilst they themselves work or study in another country. Other cultures, once called primitive, see nothing wrong in this practice. They know that their children are loved and cared for by their own people, and the children know that their parents love them.

The conscience
The conscience is that part of the personality which incorporates the cultural beliefs of the individual. It assesses his behaviour according to what is considered to be 'right' or 'wrong'. In addition, it may have idiosyncratic qualities. It cannot prevent someone from doing something which he regards as wrong, but he may be deterred by knowing that he will 'feel bad' — though he is never discovered. Even if he is the only one to know, he feels ashamed. His self-esteem is reduced.

When the conscience operates idiosyncratically, he may feel 'bad' as a result of behaviour which would be unlikely to trouble other people. For example, a young man was oppressed by the knowledge that he had contributed to the purchase of wine glasses as a gift for a colleague. He had been brought up to look upon drink as evil, and he felt he had damaged his colleague by contributing to the gift.

When someone does something which his conscience tells him is 'good', he will feel 'good' even though no-one knows of his virtuous act. People who contribute anonymously to a worthy cause may enjoy a glow of private virtue.

The 'strength' of the conscience is a useful concept, although it can be only a hypothetical one. Some people have 'strong' consciences, whilst others have 'weak' ones. Some obey the law of the land to the uttermost letter and are burdened by the slightest deviation. They would no more think of driving at 31 miles per hour in a restricted area than of taking a toffee apple from a child. Others will take toffee apples from children without a blush. The conscience of most people is 'average'. It seems to be concerned more with responsibility to individuals than to groups of individuals. To 'forget' to repay a debt to a friend is 'bad'; to evade a parking fine may be a matter for congratulation.

Problems may arise when an individual's understanding of what is 'good' and what is 'bad' is contradicted by the demands of his body. A child who grows up in a teetotal family may believe that alcohol is 'bad'. However, when he becomes a man, he may find that he likes the taste and enjoys the effect. Consequently, he develops a feeling of *guilt*. He tries to conceal his secret from the people he respects, lest they should be *ashamed* of him if they were to discover it. *Guilt* is what someone feels about his secret. *Shame* is what he experiences when it is exposed. Neither emotion is pleasant. In order to avoid shame, an individual may try to conceal his secret for as long as possible, even when the burden of guilt is almost intolerable. His greatest fear is loss of esteem. It may be a great relief when he can share the secret with his therapist.

The unconscious

The reader may wish to pause to consider the subtle concept of the unconscious, and the paradox that the *unconscious* can never be *conscious*, for then it would no longer be *un*conscious. Consequently, it will be appreciated that thoughts, feelings, wishes and ideas which are *unconscious* will not be recognised consciously. On the contrary, they are likely to be rejected out of hand, sometimes fiercely, sometimes with indifference, sometimes as plausible nonsense. They will seldom be considered seriously.

Most people have a private image of themselves which permits them to operate with a reasonable degree of self-esteem. Aspects which do not conform to the expectations of the culture are ignored or unrecognised. Their existence would present a threat to the integrity and the security of the individual, to his view of himself, to his understanding of his role in society, and to its willingness to accept him. Western cultures are expected to conform to a set of rules which were established thousands of years ago, and which are laid down as the Ten Commandments. We are expected to honour our fathers and our mothers, to be faithful to our spouses, and to love our neighbours. We may neither steal, nor lie with our sister, nor curse the dead, nor put a stumbling block before the blind, nor prostitute our daughters.

It is easy to rebel against most of these precepts, but there are some which would be hard to disobey. There is no reason why a man should not find his sister sexually attractive, except the non-logical one that 'she is my sister'. Consciously, the precept is accepted without question. If there should be any temptation, it is locked away. The unconscious remains unconscious. If the therapist reveals a 'discreditable' unconscious factor, the patient will not receive it with enthusiasm. Indeed, the vehemence with which it is rejected may be astonishing.

The unconscious is a formidable weapon in the hands of those whose aim in life is to be always right. A foolish therapist may comment, 'You hate your mother'. If his patient agrees, all is well. If he disagrees, the foolish therapist retorts, 'That is because it is in your unconscious'.

Attempts to interpret the content of the unconscious must always be made with caution. At the end of the day, only the patient himself can decide on the accuracy of an interpretation. *Speculations* about the unconscious may be made from isolated clues. Interpretation should be reserved until the therapist is reasonably sure of his conclusions.

Unconscious thoughts, feelings, wishes and ideas do not lose their strength. Indeed, confinement often seems to heighten their effect. The individual will fight off any threat to investigate them. It is as though he might be overwhelmed if they were unleashed.

Resistance is encountered when the secrets of the unconscious are about to be revealed. The doors are firmly barred, because it seems far too dangerous to open them. Resistance is itself usually unconscious. When resistance is conscious, the individual knows his thoughts, but refuses to share them with his therapist. His refusal may spring from shame, fear or loyalty. A patient who *consciously* refuses to share his thoughts with his therapist is breaking the original 'contract' (p. 38).

When resistance is *unconscious*, 'something' prevents the patient from discovering what is being resisted. The 'something' is the resistance. The therapist should try to elucidate resistance, to understand and to interpret it. Verbalisation of the resistance will usually lead to its resolution. When this happens, not only does the resistance become conscious, but often also the unconscious thoughts which were being concealed. Uncovering and interpretation of the resistance is therefore a very important and productive part of psychotherapy.

How does one elucidate the nature of resistance? Sometimes, the answer is suggested by an application of the 'principle of extremes'. What is the *worst* that might happen if the patient were to follow his thoughts along their unrestricted course? Might he murder someone? Might he start screaming and never stop? Might he be so angry that he would have a heart attack and die? Might he go mad? Might he become a homosexual?

A patient dreamed that he was shaking hands with a friend. The friend insisted on being called 'Master Bates', although this was the wrong name. The patient saw no significance in the name 'Master Bates' and none in the handshake. Later, he commented that the worst thing he could contemplate was to become a homosexual. At this point, the significance of the dream became apparent to him. He saw that it had a distinct homosexual flavouring. He recognised that the handshake was a form of physical contact between his friend and himself, and that the name, Master Bates, which was 'the wrong name' was really a pun on 'masturbates'. He added that he always became very excited when he heard of the sexual exploits of his friend.

The reader must not expect his interpretations to be greeted with enthusiasm. On the contrary, he may find himself held to ridicule. It often appears absurd to assert that things are the opposite of what they seem. Patients are sometimes so angry that they demand an apology; The *purpose* of the unconscious is to protect the individual from insight. It allows him to look upon himself as a wholesome, upright citizen.

When the therapist recognises that an unconscious mechanism is operating, he may first invite the patient to consider it as a proposition. Suppose that the patient is not as he thinks of himself, excessively gentle, but the opposite: overwhelmingly aggressive. What would that be like? What difference would it make?

Defence mechanisms

Let us consider some of the mechanisms which enable an individual to cope with the feelings about which he would otherwise be guilty. It should be noted that they usually operate without his being consciously aware of them.

In many cultures, pregnancy outside marriage is looked upon as 'bad'.* An unmarried woman who becomes pregnant invites condemnation. She may try to undo what should never have been done by asking for her pregnancy to be terminated. This too invites disapproval. Some resent the fact that the 'sinner' will escape the shame that she might have borne had she carried her child to term. Nowadays, however, she is more likely to continue with her pregnancy, boldly disputing the view that to be pregnant when unmarried is 'bad'. She rejects the idea that it is 'bad'. It is 'good'. This is an example of *rationalisation*.

Denial

Denial is a modest word for a formidable mechanism. It is much stronger in its technical sense than in its colloquial one. Denial means that, in the face of all logical evidence, something is truly *not* so.

It permits a woman with an unwanted pregnancy to *ignore* the possibility that she might be pregnant. Her periods stop. Well, she has had a heavy cold. Her periods often stop when she has a heavy cold. She starts to feel sick in the morning. Perhaps she has developed a touch of gastric 'flu'. She often gets gastric 'flu' with a heavy cold. She finds that she is passing urine more frequently. Probably the chill has gone to her bladder. Her breasts become full and slightly tender. This is because she is getting fat. She must go on a diet. Her abdomen begins to enlarge. She will certainly have to go on a diet! She feels kicking movements. Indigestion!

It does not seem credible that she can avoid the conclusion that she is pregnant. But if pregnancy is 'bad', some women *go into labour* totally oblivious of the fact. They deny something which is perfectly obvious to everyone else.

Denial is a common psychological mechanism and it is employed by everyone. It permits the individual to ignore distasteful facts completely. When something unpleasant occurs, there is no disagreeable reaction. It is as though it had not happened. The unconscious attitude seems to be that disagreeable things do not exist if no notice is taken of them. We will encounter denial again in the discussion of mourning (q.v.).

---

*The author has heard of the Permissive Society.

Another example of denial was seen in an intelligent and capable solicitor. He did well at school, gained a scholarship to his college, carried off all the prizes, and climbed rapidly to the top of his chosen profession. He knew nothing about his father. His mother told him only that he had died when the patient was a baby. He had seen no photographs of his father and his mother never spoke of him. If he asked questions, she brushed them aside, and he learned never to ask any.

He was asked by an insurance company to supply a copy of his birth certificate, but his mother refused to let him have it. Instead, she offered to send it to the company herself. The conclusion — that he was illegitimate — was obvious to everyone except the patient himself. To him, illegitimacy was totally unthinkable. It was a slur upon himself and a denigration of his mother. He could tolerate neither possibility. It was not so.

Rationalisation

'They wouldn't give me a jjjjob as a BBBBBBC announcer bbbbecause I come from Sssssssssssmmmmmmmmmmmmerssssssssssset!'

Well, perhaps he is right. But it will occur to the reader that there may be other reasons. Consider the following statements: 'I am unhappy because no-one loves me' (said by a 25 year old teacher); 'I mugged the old girl because I saw it done on the television' (said by a 19 year old youth); 'I shoplifted because I was depressed'; 'I am frightened to go into the shops because people might look at me' (said by a not-very-attractive 19-year old girl).

These statements may all be true. To the speakers, they certainly *feel* like complete explanations. How do they appear to the psychotherapist, who knows that there is nothing so obvious that it can be accepted without question. Might they be rationalisations?

Is the woman who says that she is miserable because she is unloved, really unloved because she is miserable? Does she carry an air of perpetual gloom which repels people? And if she does, what action should the therapist take? Should he say, 'Why don't you try to look more cheerful for a change!' In fact, he merely asks the patient to turn the proposition on its end. He himself does not draw any conclusions or make any suggestions.

The 'mugger' implies that violence begets violence. This is a frequent excuse and although not a very convincing one, it may be offered in the absence of any other. It does not explain why other viewers were not affected in the same way. Courts are not usually impressed by such excuses.

'I shoplifted because I was depressed' is also a common plea. When caught, shoplifters are often extremely depressed. Their depression arises directly out of the shameful consequences of their act. The individual's mental state *before* the event must be reviewed very carefully before any professional support can be given to such a plea.

The unattractive girl, who is reluctant to enter shops in case people might look at her, must consider the proposition that her real fear is that people will *not* look at her. It must be very disagreeable for a young woman to be reminded that she is not attractive. By avoiding shops, she also avoids the reminder.

Other defence mechanisms

All cultures have strict rules about sexual behaviour. Sexual activity with a blood relative is nearly always 'bad'. So too is a sexual relationship with a member of the same sex. Even the thought of such things is 'bad'. It is 'bad' for a man to contemplate sexual activity with his mother or with his sister. If such ideas come to his mind, they are instantly *repressed*. Repression means forgotten beyond any possibility of recall.

Aggression is 'bad'. It is also part of normal experience. How may one deal with thwarted aggressive behaviour? Well, it can be used to *destroy* anything that has the slightest taint of aggression. An aggressive individual may become a determined pacifist, thereby demonstrating to the world that he is not aggressive. He may *fight* for the cause of pacifism, and in doing so, gratify his aggressive drives. This mechanism which both gratifies and repudiates an unacceptable drive, is called *reaction formation*.

Reaction formation is often the mechanism of defence used by people who appear to be excessively puritanical. Such people scrutinize the most innocent book with a fine tooth comb, searching for the *double entendre*, or for any minor ambiguity which might affect public morality. In demonstrating to the world their own purity, they may be simultaneously gratifying their own unconscious prurience. The ultra-prude will read in A.A. Milne's *When We Were Very Young*

John had
Great Big
Waterproof
Boots on;
John had a
Great Big
Waterproof
Hat;
John had a

Great Big
Waterproof
Mackintosh
And that
(Said John)
  Is That

He may withhold this happy verse from his children because his prurient mind concludes that John must be a rubber fetishist.

Another way of dealing with unwelcome feelings is to *displace* them from their real object to an innocent one. Thus, anger with a mother may be displaced on to a mother-in-law. This mechanism allows mothers to be wholly good, and makes mothers-in-law wholly bad. It helps to explain the popularity of hostile jokes against mothers-in-law.

Another defence mechanism is called *projection*. The antagonism which is experienced towards someone is perceived as emanating *from* him. The 'victim' now has an excuse for reciprocal antagonism — although it is really a projection of his own.

To hate one's parents and to wish them dead is 'bad'. Nevertheless, such feelings sometimes occur. In such circumstances, the *thought* may be *isolated* from the *feeling* of hate which induces it. The individual is *consciously* aware only of the thought. The feeling is *unconscious* and he is not aware of it. The only *feeling* of which he is *consciously* aware is distress at the thought. The feeling of hate has been dealt with by *isolation*. Since it now operates at an unconscious level, it is unrecognised. Sometimes, neither the hate nor the thought is conscious. Instead, an unformulated sense of guilt or anxiety exists. The individual may try to expiate his guilt by performing some superstitious act. He often feels compelled to repeat this act many times over. The act is a symbolic one: perhaps his guilt makes him *feel* contaminated, and he washes his hands over and over again. But he never feels clean. He is not aware of the unconscious thought which made him feel unclean. This mechanism is called *undoing*.

The psychological processes which have been described are called *defence mechanisms*. Each depends upon the existence of a thought, a feeling, an idea or a wish which is regarded by the individual as 'bad'. The defence mechanism allows the 'bad' idea to remain unconscious, so that the individual is not *consciously* aware of its existence. However, the mechanism may cause considerable psychological upheaval on its own account.

Wish fulfillment

Wishes spring from biological or social needs. When someone is thirsty, he wishes something to slake his thirst. When he is covetous of his neighbour's car, he may try to buy a better one.

Some wishes may be gratified quite simply. A need for such things as a glass of water, a ticket for a football match, or even a television set, can be satisfied fairly easily. Others are more difficult. Every weekend, millions of 'investors' check their football coupons in the hope of finding the means of acquiring the house, the small business, or the ocean going yacht for which they yearn.

Wishes which cannot be fulfilled in reality may be fulfilled in fantasy. These wishes are the origins of daydreams.

Dreams

We can make certain generalisations about dreams. They are the consequence of mental activity. They usually occur during sleep, although we have mentioned a special form which occurs in the waking state. This form is called a day dream, and is nearly always pleasant.

Dreams are usually pictorial in form. Occasionally they tell a coherent story, but often they are muddled, contradictory or nonsensical. On reflection, they can often be associated with events of the previous day, events which in themselves appear to be trivial or unimportant. Sometimes they are clearly relevant to the dreamer's physiological state. A thirsty man may dream that he is drinking a cup of tea. They sometimes carry a considerable charge of emotion, perhaps of pleasure or of fear. The latter are called nightmares. The emotional charge is not always consistent with the content. Occasionally they are surprisingly lacking in emotional tone. For example, a man may dream that he is walking down a busy street, stark naked, and quite unperturbed. Sometimes they have a vivid, 'solid' quality. Some are conspicuously 'in colour'. Dreams are usually forgotten very quickly, and the dreamer may find them slipping away, even as he struggles to recall them. Psychotherapy is not concerned with magic, and dreams are, therefore, not regarded as having any prophetic significance.

Freud proposed the theory that dreams are created by casting wishes, which are usually unconscious, into concrete form. Thus, a dream about a bridge might represent a wish for sexual union. By the interplay of symbols, the dream itself allows fulfillment of the wish. The wishes are unconscious because they are not acceptable to the conscious part of the mind, and consequently the wish is disguised by some sort of allegorical transformation. If the transformation is successful, the wish is fulfilled, the dreamer experiences no anxiety, the dream is experienced as a pleasant one, and the dreamer continues to sleep. If the transformation is unsuccessful, there are two possibilities. Either the dream is experienced as disagreeable — a nightmare — since it constitutes the gratification of a forbidden wish, or the dreamer awakens before the dream is completed, and the forbidden wish remains unsatisfied. The purposed of dreams is to allow the symbolic fulfillment of unconscious wishes, and thereby to preserve sleep.

Dreams are fascinating things, and experienced therapists may make extensive use of them. The novice should be sparing of dream analysis. He may feel free to talk about them, but should be wary if his patient is constantly producing dreams for discussion. When this happens, the patient may be trying to avoid the examination of other significant material.

Symbolism

As he gives an account of his doings, it will be noticed that there is much in the patients's life that is repetitive. Even things which seem unrelated may, on detailed enquiry, prove to have an underlying similarity.

A substantial part of the psychotherapeutic process is concerned with identifying and comparing repeated themes, defining underlying patterns and ultimately deducing their sources. It is common to find that symbols are used extensively. An example has already been given in the case where a patient dreamt of shaking hands with his friend. In this, the hands symbolised the male genitalia, and the handshake symbolised physical contact, presumably mutual masturbation. The word 'masturbates' was imposed on the dream in the form of a name, 'Master Bates' which was recognised by the dreamer as being 'wrong' — in retrospect, in more senses than one.

When someone is unduly preoccupied with *recent* events, it may become clear that these are symbolic repetitions of earlier experiences. *Groups* of people may constitute a symbolic whole. Thus, people who hold positions of authority, such as members of the Royal Family, teachers, political leaders, employers, policemen, and so on, may form such a group. Ultimately, they may represent the parents. Behaviour which is rhythmic and repetitive may represent sexual activity. Such activities as losing, or forgetting names or things may symbolise hostility to the people with whom the things are associated. Starting out on a journey may be a symbol for beginning afresh. Departure may represent death.

Some events, perhaps originating early in life, are comprehended only dimly at the time. Often, their significance is completely misunderstood. They may be repeated in symbolic form in adult life.

They sometimes have rather a sinister quality and are quickly repressed. Sometimes they *repeatedly* break through in allegorical form — perhaps as a neurotic symptom. If the original event took place before logical thought was established it cannot be understood in terms of adult logic. In many cases, the therapist must learn to abandon the use of adult logic if he is to comprehend a patient's non-logical, and still infantile preoccupations.

Interlude on non-logic

Proof: That the reader will be the wealthiest person in the 20th century.

Let	$x = y$
then	$xy = y^2$
and	$x^2 - xy = x^2 - y^2$
factorise	$x(x - y) = (x + y)(x - y)$
divide both sides	
by $(x - y)$	$x = x + y$
But $x = y$	So $x = 2x$
divide both sides by x	$1 = 2$

Since the reader and the wealthiest person in the 20th century are two

And $\qquad\qquad\qquad\qquad\qquad\qquad 1 = 2$

Then the reader and the wealthiest person in the 20th century are one.

Therefore the reader will be the wealthiest person in the 20th century.

There must be a catch in it somewhere. (There is★). Otherwise it is magic. Patients frequently hope for magic from their therapist. Of course, they do not say so, even to themselves. They assure their therapist that they know he is only human, that he cannot achieve the impossible, and that they cannot hope for miracles. But it is a common complaint about psychotherapists they they cannot change dross into gold. A strong feeling seems to persist that any competent therapist should have magical powers and that if he does not, there should be someone in the world who does.

Non-logic plays a substantial part in the creation of problems, and also in the hopes which patients have for their solution. We must therefore consider the part played by non-logic and magic in our lives.

★Clue: There are no diamonds in one empty box and no emeralds in another. Does this mean that diamonds are emeralds?

Young children accept magic as a fact. Most parents encourage the belief. When Christmas comes, children are told that if they are very good, Santa Claus will come down the chimney — even when none exists — and fill their stockings with wonderful toys. And sure enough, even when they have not been very good, he does. Young children hear about fairyland from their story books. Many have funny uncles who know about magic, and can cause real money to appear from thin air. The child does not look for any trick in this because for him, there is no trick. Magic exists.

The problem about magic is that there is bad magic as well as good. There are good fairies, but there are bad fairies too. Good magic is very pleasant but bad magic is frightening. It is associated with blackness and evil; and many children, and some adults, tremble with fear when all is quiet in the darkness of the night.

The stories which entrance children are about fairies and witches, magicians and hobgoblins: about people with extraordinary but seemingly irrelevant powers; about people who give other people three wishes. The judicious interaction of these gifts leads to successful escape from predicaments which would otherwise be impossible. In fairy stories, the race is never to the swift, but always to people like the child himself, to the small and weak, the seventh son of a seventh son, or the youngest of three brothers. Maturity and experience are equated with ugliness and wickedness. The young and beautiful live happily ever after; the old are subjected to punishments which are often particularly cruel and bloody. Their limbs are chopped off, they are thrown to the wolves, or they are dropped into boiling oil.

This is not a condemnation of fairy stories. We are not suggesting that children should be told that there is no such thing as magic, or that the idea is in some way harmful. The child *believes* in magic and he is father to the man.

Adults believe in magic, too. As the first edition of this book was being written, newspapers were carrying a story about a man who could, by occult means, cause spoons to bend. Thousands believed that such a thing could happen and hundreds tried to emulate him. It was a pretty harmless piece of magic although it seemed rather pointless. Unfortunately, it did not seem possible to reverse the process.

Other things are magical; not so easily identified as such, but magic nevertheless. There is the magic of the advertiser. People really believe that they can be taught to speak a foreign language in 48 hours, to play the piano in six weeks, and to lose weight without eating less. Seven stone weaklings believe that they can, by a few simple exercises, be changed into Mr Universes. Many people, no longer very sure about an after-life, have their children baptised, to be on the safe side. There is the magic of gambling, of the football pools and of premium bonds. These are the adult equivalent of turning dross into gold. Hire purchase provides the crock of gold, with which people can buy the car for which they yearn. When later they repent, they look elsewhere for new magic. We are repeatedly assured, and appear to believe, that our economic troubles will disappear without effort if we adopt the principles of one or other of the political parties, or if we rid ourselves of trade union leaders, management or religious or ethnic groups which are different from our own.

Adults enjoy fairy stories, too. The survival of James Bond depends upon happy coincidences and ingenious gadgets which, if they occurred in real life, would surely be ascribed to supernatural intervention.

But if there were one *real* magician in the world, he could, through one single spell, lift every burden from every shoulder. All the striving, struggling, competing; all the difficulties and distress of life would be vanquished. There would be no need for psychotherapists or counsellors, no need for doctors, no need for pain or suffering, no need for work. The idea of magic is certainly a very attractive one.

People are readily persuaded that magic exists. It is often difficult to convince them that it does not. We hold on to a belief in such things as telepathy, extrasensory perception and other 'para-normal' phenomena with extraordinary tenacity. We use lucky charms, read our horoscopes and cross our fingers. Even the most *blasé* materialist finds it difficult to walk under a ladder without any apprehension whatsoever. Some people observe the superstition 'in case there is something in it'. Others cross the road, well in advance, so that their superstitious shame will be concealed. Some walk round the ladder, rationalising that 'it is the sensible thing to do: something might drop from it'. Some demonstrate that they are *not* superstitious by walking defiantly underneath it, but secretly crossing their fingers as they do so, and breathing a sigh of guilty relief when the ordeal is over. Very few really do not care.

Patients sometimes say, 'I think you must be able to read my mind', or 'It turned out exactly as you predicted'. It is rather flattering when the possession of psychic or supernatural powers is ascribed to one. It would certainly be convenient if the psychotherapist possessed such gifts. No longer would he have to ask questions, or be unsure of the truth of what he was told. He could even advise his patients what they should do.

Sometimes a patient will protest that he cannot possibly tell someone such and such a thing, because 'I know exactly what he will do'. To predict with certainty what people will do in specific circumstances is a supernatural gift. Repeated experience demonstrates that prediction is as fallible in real life as it is on the race course.

What about those who insist that they, or someone whom they respect, have had experiences which are paranormal? Such experiences are always compounded from wish fulfillment or coincidence, retrospective falsification and precision created out of ambiguity. The construction of an ordinary astrological prediction provides an example. It involves ambiguous promises ('Watch out for a letter'); generalisations ('Be careful about money matters'); things which apply to everyone ('There are occasions when you must control your temper'); faintly disagreeable allegations which can be ignored if they are too distasteful ('You are sometimes rather mean'); and a warning: if the dreaded thing happens, you have been forewarned; if it does not, your avoiding action has been successful. Those who choose, may construct very specific predictions out of vague and ambiguous generalisations. There are many who do choose.

There is statistical justification for some things which 'cannot possibly be due to coincidence'. In a group of 15 people, there is a greater than even probability that two or more will have identical or adjacent birthdays. The demonstration of this fact is always rather startling, and seems mysteriously significant to the credulous. Whatever people think of statistics, they prove that many things which seem to be 'impossible' are in fact due to coincidence.

Magic always overpowers logic. If we accept magic, we are bound to reject logic. In psychotherapy, there is no magic. The therapist tolerates his patient's belief in it, because he seeks to discover its origins and apply the necessary corrections of reality. Many people are ashamed of their belief in things which are non-logical and are reluctant to discuss them. Yet, without discussion, they can be neither examined nor corrected. In the case where $x = y$, dividing both sides of an equation by $(x-y)$ strikes at the root of mathematical logic, because you cannot divide both sides of an equation by zero. If this were not so, the reader would become the wealthiest person in the 20th century. One tiny non-logical assumption can turn a coward into a hero or a pauper into a prince.

Private logic is often internally consistent, although to the outside world it may be obviously non-logical. It is necessary for the therapist to comprehend the private logic of his patients if he is to understand their difficulties. An example is given by a patient who had been married twice. Speaking of her *first* marriage, she said, 'When my *second* husband was alive...' Quickly she realised that she had made a slip of the tongue and corrected herself. (Does the reader notice that the slip has a double implication?) The therapist asked, 'Who was your first husband?' There was a long pause, then she answered, 'There was a boy I idolised. He took me out once or twice. I was only 13 at the time. He wasn't really interested. Then I saw him with someone else...' She burst into tears and continued, 'I can still remember how much it hurt. Funny...I had forgotten all about it.' Her current problem was centred on her relationship with her present husband. If he were to die, her problems would be solved. This was the second implication of her slip. When a psychological phenomenon is caused by more that one factor, as in this case, it is said to be due to *over* or *multiple-* determination.

Emotions are frequently non-logical and are not therefore amenable to 'logical' arguments. A common example is the non-logical fear of insects and small animals. Strong men may blanch at the sight of a beetle. Michael Flanders gives a graphic description of a man struggling with a spider in his bath.

> I have faced a charging bull in Barcelona,
> I have dragged a mountain lioness from her cub,
> I've restored a mad gorilla to its owner,
> But I don't dare face that spider in the tub.
> What a frightful looking beast,
> Half an inch across at least
> It would frighten even Superman or Garth;
> There's contempt it can't disguise,
> In the little beady eyes
> Of the spider sitting glowering in the bath.

Women — and men — will scream at the sight of a mouse; mothers may squirm when their children bring them as a gift a big, fat, juicy worm from the garden. There is nothing logical in this. Obviously, it is the small animal which should be afraid.

Specific illogical fears are called *phobias*. Common examples include the fear of being alone, and the fear of heights. Later we will refer to the slight possibility that the latter is of evolutionary importance. Pathological variables include the fear of leaving the house, and fear of being in crowds.

Patients with phobias may endure a degree of fear bordering on terror. Although it is not logical, it is nevertheless fear. Phobias are mysterious things. Why should someone fear to leave the house, or to be shut in a room, or to be in a crowd of people? The patient will often say that he cannot understand it. This is because understanding requires logic, and the fear is not logical.

Why should someone be preoccupied with unwanted but horrible thoughts about the death of someone whom he loves dearly? It is not logical. Such thoughts may be very frightening in themselves, but if the therapist is prepared to share the non-logic, considering objectively its implication, he may acquire an understanding which he can subsequently share with his patient.

Some emotions are looked upon as illogical because they are associated with events which are remote in time. Time is said to be the great healer. But time is a *logical* concept, and the non-logical is not influenced by it. Emotions stemming from events which happened many years previously may persist long after the precipitating causes have been forgotten.

A striking illustration is provided when mourning has lain fallow for many years. If the circumstances of the death are 'relived', the patient may also relive the associated grief and emotion. He may weep bitterly, and talk of his anger and guilt about the bereavement. Often he will feel ashamed of being distressed about something which happened so long ago. Nevertheless, the sadness is there and he should be helped to express it. Other emotions may be relived in a similar way. The patient may recall something which once terrified him, or express anger over some long forgotten indignity. The therapist should bear in mind that things which are trivial to adults may seem very frightening to children. The process by which long forgotten emotions are relived is called *abreaction*: their expression is called *catharsis*.

An important group of non-logical emotions refers to matters of personal sensitivity. These are often of great importance to young people, and the therapist must be very careful not to dismiss them as trivial or irrelevant. A small papule of acne may feel like a flaming beacon to a sensitive adolescent, and if necessary he should be helped to say so. Older people have sensitivities too: they may be embarrassed about such bodily features as the size or shape of the nose, or the colour of the hair. Some patients experience a sense of 'intellectual' inferiority — they 'feel' ignorant about matters with which they think they should be familiar.

The therapist may often find himself tempted to 'reassure' his patients about their sensitivities, or to indicate that their concern is unnecessary. But when things are of importance to the patient, such 'reassurance' may lead him to suppose that his concern is indeed warranted.

Non-logicality may present in the form of unwanted obsessional thoughts. The patient may find himself preoccupied with a thought that someone whom he loves dearly is seriously injured, or is about to die, or is dead. He will say that although he knows that the idea is illogical, he cannot free himself of it. It is terrifying. Some patients are oppressed with thoughts about harming someone whom they love, or indulging in some form of sickening sexual perversion. They plead, 'I do not want to think about such things. I know I would not *do* them. Yet the thoughts keep coming. It is horrible.'

The management of non-logical preoccupations is the same as for other problems. The therapist attends, listens, and tries to understand. He does not judge, condemn, 'explain', or reassure. It is sometimes helpful for him to consider with the patient what would happen if a phobia were to be eradicated. What would it be like for a housewife, hitherto confined to her home with a travel phobia, if she were to be released from her fear? The usual reply is, 'Oh, it would be wonderful.' But the therapist must ask, 'Would it really be wonderful?' There would be many advantages, but could there be disadvantages, too? What are the *disadvantages* of being freed from a phobia?

People with obsessional thoughts about death, destruction or degrading perversions should be helped to visualise the scene if the dreaded event were to take place. It would be horrible, of course, but might there be something which would balance the horror? Could there even be something desirable? Phobias associated with specific objects, and those concerned with specific situations, should be examined in the light of the possibility that the phobia has a specific symbolic meaning.

Gain

The advantages of being psychopathic or neurotic*

The psychopath is allowed to talk to himself, which is very handy when he wants the railway carriage to himself.

The neurotic is not obliged to fetch the coal in, as when his wife requests him to do so, all he need do is throw down his paper and scream: 'Coal, coal, coal! Does nobody think about anything else but coal?'

The psychopath is not required to shave, thereby not having to indulge in backchat with barbers about the prospect of Manchester United.

The neurotic need not keep abreast of world affairs, since his only observation of these need be: 'Politics, politics, politics — they make me vomit!

*Selected from 'Maybe you're just inferior' by Herald Froy

The psychopath does not have to take a bath and is, therefore, less prone to catching cold, grippe, influenza or bath-rash.

The neurotic always gets prompt attention from tradesmen, who are terrified of him.

The psychopath may play yo-yo in public.

The neurotic always has right of way on the roads.

The psychopath is not expected to have a job, thereby not running the risk, which would otherwise be acute, of getting the sack.

It seems strange to assert that something as disagreeable as illness might bring advantages, but a moment's reflection will confirm that this is so. A bad cold is only mildly disagreeable, and the patient will soon recover. Until he does so, he 'will not wish to spread the infection to others' and will therefore deem it wise to stay at home. When he telephones the office, his self-denial and commonsense will be applauded by his colleagues. They, assured that their turn will come, will send their sympathy and advise him to stay at home until he is completely better. They will usually tell him to keep warm and to take things easily. The author's idea of taking things easily is to go to bed and make himself comfortable. Other people have different ideas. Some play golf ('to get out into the fresh air') or go to the theatre ('to take the mind off it'). If he is so inclined, the sufferer may, for medicinal purposes, drink whisky. If he swallows an aspirin first, he can call the combination a hot toddy, which sounds more respectable. Of course, bad colds should not last for too long. If his seems to be exceeding the statutory period, the sufferer's colleagues will start paying him visits and bringing him grapes, in order to discover the extent to which he is putting it on. Wise sufferers recover before such disagreeable enquiries are made.

Even the gravest of diseases may bring a degree of benefit. Someone who has advanced cancer will certainly be relieved of the anxieties and burdens which would otherwise have been his daily lot. The reader will understand that we are not asserting that anyone would wish to suffer from advanced cancer. The benefits of serious illness would willingly be exchanged for good health.

The advantages of an illness, whether it is physical or psychological, are called its *secondary gain*. In planning treatment, the gain must always be taken into account. A patient with a serious, although not fatal illness, such as a perforated peptic ulcer, may progress with extraordinary rapidity at first. Then, as he becomes stronger, his rate of progress unaccountably slows. He may develop new, evanescent symptoms which call for further investigations. The results are ambiguous. The clinician begins to harbour a vague suspicion that the patient does not really *want* to get well. Sometimes, when his social background is explored, the suspicion may become a near certainty. If the patient is a middle-aged housewife, with an aggressive, undemonstrative husband, a growing, rebellious family, and little time for relaxation, such reluctance is understandable. In hospital, she is visited regularly, treated with sympathy and concern, deferred to, and given every consideration. It would be almost *abnormal* for her to want to return home. The secondary gain of the illness has become paramount.

Neurotic illness provide *primary* gain in addition. Her illness entitles the housebound housewife to many of the benefits of a patient in hospital. These represent the secondary gain. The *primary* gain is that she can set aside a conflict in which opposing factors may be almost evenly balanced. Perhaps she feels unloved and unwanted, and would like to leave a neglectful husband. On the other hand, she *loves* him and wishes to stay with him. The development of a phobic illness, characterised by fear of leaving the house, solves the conflict. Her husband is compelled to pay attention to her, and she herself can no longer leave him, even if she wished to do so. The primary gain of the illness is that the conflict is set aside.

Ambivalence

Most people are aware that the feelings which they have towards people who are important to them, may fluctuate. At times they love them dearly; at others, they find them infuriating beyond endurance. Such variations in feelings are part of normal conscious experience. The word 'ambivalence' is used for the *simultaneous* experience of contradictory feelings. Ambivalence is non-logical and is only partly conscious. The individual is *consciously* aware of the predominent attitude. In the case of the housebound housewife, she loves her husband consciously, but because he does not attend to her as she would wish, it is possible that simultaneously, she *hates* him unconsciously. *Consciously*, she is not aware of her hate. It might show itself in the form of a 'mistake'. She might, for example, 'accidentally' sugar his tea with salt. She might have a dream — she would call it a nightmare — that he was dead. These are examples of psychological ambivalence.

The word 'ambivalence' is also used in a different and rather restricted sense, to describe the fluctuating *behaviour* of some patients who are suffering from schizophrenia. The therapist offers to shake hands with his patient but receives no response. He withdraws his hand, and as he does so, the patient offers his. The therapist moves to take the patient's hand, but the patient now withdraws his. Patient and therapist alternately present and withdraw their hands. The reader should be aware of the difference in meaning of the word 'ambivalence' in this context.

Free association

Free association is a fundamental technique of psychoanalysis (q.v.). The patient allows his thoughts to wander freely, without any *conscious* attempt to direct, select or modify them. One thought leads to another, then to the next and so on. The patient is asked to report everything that comes into his mind, irrespective of what it is, and whether or not it seems to have any bearing on what has gone before. The intention is to tease out and analyse the underlying unconscious threads.

A classical example of free association, and the way in which it proceeds, is given by Freud.

He was travelling with a young man who was familiar with some of his publications. During the course of their conversation, his companion wished to recall a quotation from Virgil. However, one word — aliquis — refused to come to him, although it was on the tip of his tongue. To conceal the gap, he changed the order of the words of the quotation. He knew that the quotation was wrong, and he knew that Freud knew that it was wrong! In his exasperation, he exclaimed, 'Please don't look so scornful. There's something missing in the line. How does the whole thing really go?'

Probably smiling, Freud gave the correct quotation. His companion answered, 'How stupid to forget a word like aliquis!' He thought for a moment and added, 'You claim that one never forgets a thing without some reason. I should be very curious to learn how I came to forget the word *aliquis* in this case.' Freud answered 'That should not take us long. I must only ask you to tell me *candidly*, and *uncritically*, whatever comes into your mind if you direct your attention to the forgotten word without any definite aim.'

The young man answered, 'There springs to my mind the ridiculous notion of dividing the word up like this: *a* and *liquis*.' There was a pause. Freud said, 'What occurs to you next?' Slowly his companion replied, '*Relics, liquifying, fluidity, fluid.*' Freud told him to continue. He did so. 'I am thinking of *Simon of Trent* whose relics I saw two years ago... My next thoughts are about an article that I read lately in an Italian newspaper. Its title, I think, was 'What *St Augustine* says about Woman'. What do you make of that?' Freud replied simply, 'I am waiting.' The young man continued, 'I am thinking of a fine old gentleman I met last week. His name was Benedict.'

At this point, Freud identified a common theme: 'Here is a row of Saints: St *Simon*, St *Augustine*, St *Benedict*.' His intervention had the effect of bringing another thought to his companion's mind. He continued, 'Now it is St *Januarius* and the miracle of his blood that comes into my mind.' Then he added something which is characteristic of free association: 'my thoughts seem to me to be running on mechanically.' Freud commented that St *Januarius* and St *Augustine* both have to do with the calendar. 'But won't you remind me about the miracle of his blood?', he asked. The young man answered, 'Surely you must have heard of that? They keep the blood of St Januarius in a phial inside a church at Naples, and on a particular holy day it miraculously *liquifies*. The people attach great importance to this miracle and get very excited if it's delayed, as happened once at a time when the French were occupying the town. So the General in Command took the reverend gentleman aside and gave him to understand, with an unmistakeable gesture towards the soldiers posted outside, that he hoped the miracle would take place very soon. And in fact it did take place...'

At this point, the young man paused and Freud said, 'Well go on. Why do you pause?' 'Well,' he answered, 'something *has* come into my mind... but it's too intimate to pass on... besides, I don't see any connection.' Readers who are not familiar with this incident might care to speculate what the 'something' was.

Freud replied, 'Then you mustn't insist on learning from me how you came to forget your *aliquis*.' The young man then confessed, 'Well then I've suddenly thought of a lady from whom I might easily hear a piece of news that would be very awkward for both of us.' Freud asked, 'That her periods have stopped?' Astonished, his companion replied, 'How could you guess that?' Freud answered, *'Think of the calendar saints, the blood that starts to flow on a particular day, the disturbance when the event fails to take place, the open threats* that the miracle must be vouchsafed or else ... In fact, you've made use of the miracle of St Januarius to manufacture a brilliant allusion to women's periods.' The young man asked whether it was this 'anxious expectation that made me unable to produce an unimportant word like aliquis?'

Freud answered, 'It seems to me undeniable: you need only recall the division you made into *a-liquis* and your associations: *relics, liquifying, fluid*. St Simon was *sacrificed as a child*' (as though he had been aborted). The young man later confessed that the lady involved was an *Italian* with whom he had been to *Naples*.

In a footnote, Freud mentions that whilst his companion was searching for the missing word, the word 'exoriare' thrust itself upon him with 'peculiar clarity and obstinacy'. His association with 'exoriare' was *exorcism*. Freud comments that exorcism might symbolise the getting rid of an unwanted child by abortion.

In this example, we see how the forgetting of a word with a significant unconscious connection occurred in a healthy man, not a neurotic patient. Of course, he was probably very worried. We may wonder why he challenged Freud to explain his mistake. Perhaps it was in the knowledge that Freud was a doctor, and with the unconscious hope that Freud might advise him about how to procure an abortion.

The transference

In no branch of medicine is the relationship between the patient and his doctor brought into sharper focus than in psychotherapy. This is as it should be. Careful consideration of the relationship which develops between them helps the patient to learn about the difficulties which he encounters in other relationships. It allows him an opportunity to practise such modifications as he wishes to achieve. In the course of all this, it may also be necessary for him to modify his concepts about doctors and medicine. A complementary modification is sometimes required by the beginning psychotherapist.

Patients have feelings about their doctors. Usually they like them. If they do not, they try to find another. The feelings of a patient for his doctor may be quite unrealistic. Some patients look upon doctors with a degree of awe and admiration which, to the objective observer, is absurd. The most drunken and incompetent doctor may be praised for his skill and knowledge, and the smell of whisky on his breath dismissed as a charming eccentricity.

The feelings which a patient has for his therapist are called his *transference* feelings. In psychotherapy, the patient knows very little about his therapist, and in accordance with the principle of anonymity (see Ch. 6), the therapist tries to keep that knowledge to a minimum. We must therefore discuss something of the nature of these feelings, whence they come, and what they signify.

Transference feelings may be positive or negative, and of any degree of strength. Very strong positive feelings are equivalent to being in love. The patient is constantly preoccupied with thoughts of his therapist, and yearns to be with him all the time. He tries to discover all that he can about him, and will do everything possible to please him. He may find himself unable to keep his eyes away from the therapist. Alternatively, he may be unable to look him in the face. He may wander the streets, hoping to catch a glimpse of him. The development of a strong positive transference is the origin of the common belief that patients fall in love with their psychotherapists.

When a patient experiences such strong feelings as these, the original problem is no longer of any importance, except as a means of holding on to the therapist. The patient's primary concern is how to fulfil his overwhelming affection for the therapist. A strong positive transference does not help the patient to overcome his problem —indeed it may have the opposite effect.

A strong negative transference is like hate or detestation. Once again, the patient is constantly preoccupied with thoughts of his therapist. He wishes to subdue him, to demonstrate his weakness and fallibility, to conquer, and destroy him. Subjugation is now infinitely more important than solving a problem, and a strong negative transference destroys any prospect of a solution. The patient will never permit his enemy to have the satisfaction of thinking that he has contributed towards his recovery in any way.

A moderate positive transference is helpful in therapy. The patient likes his therapist, is grateful for the efforts which are made on his behalf, wishes to co-operate, but does not mind risking the therapist's displeasure by disagreeing with him, or even defying him. A moderate negative transference hinders therapy. It shows itself by a falling-off of interest, unpunctuality, the cancellation of appointments for trivial or inadequate reasons, and ultimately the cessation of therapy.

Transference reactions may vary from time to time in the same patient. A strong positive transference may give way to a strong negative one. Elements of both positive and negative transferences may be discerned simultaneously.

Identification of the transference
The therapist should speak clearly of the transference whenever he encounters it. Examples will be given. Discussion, dissection, analysis and verbalisation will resolve it, and sometimes lead to its source. It is sometimes helpful to ask, 'What is so attractive, or so detestable about someone of whom you know so little?' The transference should always be interpreted in terms of what is happening 'here and now'. How does the patient behave towards the therapist at this *very moment*? What significance can be inferred from his behaviour?

Coping with transference

Patients use various devices to overcome the principle of anonymity. They refer to books which the therapist should have read (usually he has not), or use colloquial foreign phrases with which he should be familiar (usually he is not!). In this way, they try to gauge the direction of the therapist's interests.

It is not usually advisable to embark upon an intellectual interchange with a patient. If the therapist is acquainted with the book in question, or understands the phrase which has been used, he can be sure that his patient will refer to other books, or use other phrases with which he is not familiar. From the outset, therefore, he should always ask the patient to explain allusions, to speak in English, and so on.

The patient may express his feelings for the therapist in a roundabout way, for example, by using 'innocent' non-sequiturs. His aim is to discover the therapist's opinions, prejudices, interests and attitudes.

He may try to find out about the therapist's interests by asking, 'How do you pass the weekends?' He may ask whether the therapist is 'available' by enquiring if he is married. By asking if he has children, the patient may also be asking about the therapist's sex life. He may wonder whether his therapist is angry with him, and ask indirectly, 'Do you ever get angry with *your* children?'

He may say, 'I like your suit.' The therapist should ask, 'Are you speaking of the suit or of the person who is wearing it?'

The patient may refer to a political figure as wonderful or terrible. Here he plays his hunch and tries to appeal to what he presumes to be the political prejudices of the therapist.

He may ask, 'Don't you get tired of listening to people's problems all day long?' The therapist should point out that the patient is really asking whether he gets tired of listening to *him*.

Sometimes the patient will speak affectionately of a previous therapist. The therapist may ask, 'Do you wish you could have him again, instead of me?'

It is easy for a patient to praise his therapist, and to say how clever and symphathetic he is. It takes considerable courage to do the opposite. Trust and courage are required before a patient can criticise or condemn his therapist. It is not pleasant for the therapist to tolerate such condemnation, especially, as is sometimes the case, there is a grain of truth in what is said. However, his condemnation also demonstrates his trust. It is also a test of the sincerity of the therapist's assertion that the patient can say whatever he wishes. The author finds some comfort in these considerations when his patients are hostile towards him.

Aggression should never be met with aggression, however blandly it is expressed. ('I'm not angry, only hurt!'). There are times when the therapist must simply accept that the patient is angry with him. This is often uncomfortable, and the therapist's discomfort may be perceived by the patient. The patient will watch out for any possible 'therapeutic' counterattacks, and may be reassured when no such 'counterattack is forthcoming.

Interpretation of the transference

When an interpretation is made prematurely, there is a serious risk that it will be disregarded or lost. Conversely, the impact may be lessened if it is delayed. The timing of an interpretation must therefore be chosen carefully. On the whole, it is better to avoid interpretation whilst the patient is in the grip of a powerful emotion. The therapist should wait until it is past.

A patient became very angry with his therapist. His anger appeared to be related to the frustration which he had experienced with other men: his employer, his schoolteacher, his elder brother and his father. The therapist tried to draw attention to these parallels, but the patient became still more angry and left the room. At that moment, his anger was directed specifically towards the therapist. It is not easy to tolerate anger, even when it is misplaced. The therapist had been very uncomfortable, and had tried to redirect it to what he perceived (probably correctly) as the original source. It would have been better if he had *accepted* that, at the moment, the patient was angry with *him*. At a later meeting he did so, and the anger began to soften. The patient was then able to discuss its origins with the therapist. As he did so, he became very angry again, but his anger was now vividly associated with an incident from the past when his father favoured his brother.

Management of the transference

In order to understand this, we must revert to the patient's original expectation of his therapist: that he will be omniscient and omnipotent, powerful, worldly-wise and able to provide an infallible hand to all who come to him for assistance.

The therapist accepts this expectation. He may help the patient to put it into words. The patient may say whatever he thinks, wishes and feels. The matters which are 'confessed' often seem very trivial to the therapist, although there are times when they are indeed of substance. The therapist never judges, criticises or condemns his patient. Such complete acceptance is usually a unique experience for the patient, and as he comes to depend upon his therapist, he comes to love him, too.

When the therapist fails to tell him what to do, the patient begins to feel that he is being deprived of something important. Such deprivation may anger him, leading him to dislike, or even hate his therapist. If he expresses such feelings, he will be on the alert for the therapist's reaction. He has been told to put his feelings into words. How will the therapist react when this is done? Will he really continue to accept him?

The therapist tries to accept everything that is said, without condemnation. When the angry words have been spoken, the feelings behind them usually dissolve away.

Expression of the transference, whether negative or positive is the first step towards its resolution. Verbalisation precedes resolution. When the transference has reached manageable proportions, the constructive work of psychotherapy can continue.

It is likely that the seeds of the transference reaction were sown in the remote past. Then, the patient experienced corresponding feelings towards people with whom his relationship was similar. They were people who appeared to be all-knowing and all-powerful. They were probably parents, or other significant adults. When the storm of powerful transference feelings has passed, the patient may remember that long ago, he had similar feelings towards someone else. It may also emerge that the patient has reacted in a similar way towards corresponding figures throughout his life. Thus, he is forewarned that similar feelings may recur if the circumstances are repeated.

The counter-transference

The therapist has reciprocal feelings for his patient, and these too may be positive or negative. When they are negative from the beginning, the therapist will usually find a 'rational' reason for avoiding therapy ('He is not amenable to the type of treatment which we employ here.'). In general, therapists offer to treat patients for whom they have a moderate positive counter-transference. As time passes, the counter-transference may fluctuate, and the therapist should look into himself for the reasons.

The therapist's response to the transference of his patient may itself be an indication of his own counter-transference. If the patient becomes hostile, he may become hurt and offended, feeling that although he has worked hard, he has received little credit.

It is often embarrassing for the inexperienced therapist to interpret a positive transference ('It seems that you feel warmly towards me.'), especially when his own counter-transference is positive. However, like many difficult things, it must be done. The second time is always easier than the first.

Confrontation

When the therapist is angry with his patient, he sometimes uses a 'technique' which he calls 'confrontation'. He gives free rein to his negative counter-transference and tells the patient exactly what he thinks of him. In justification, he may remind the patient that he has often been asked to say 'exactly what you think'.

Needless to say, the use of this 'technique' is a rationalisation. Sometimes the therapist is seeking to get rid of the patient. He should take time to consider why he undertook the case. What irrational aspects of himself are revealed? It is to the benefit of future patients and for his own future comfort to learn the appropriate lessons.

Some doctors work off their irritation with patients by writing mordantly witty letters about them to their general practitioners. Unless the doctors are acquainted with each other, this can be unwise. The general practitioner, perhaps himself somewhat irritated, may show the letter to the patient. This practice is unethical, but it happens. No-one emerges with much credit, and it does not make matters easier to manage.

Management of counter-transference

The therapist is advised never to tell the patient of his feelings towards him. He himself should seek to discover their origins. If it seems to be getting out of hand – if, for example, the therapist finds himself falling in love with his patient – he must seek the assistance of an experienced colleague.

Occasions may arise when, as a result of his positive counter-transference, a therapist allows the relationship to proceed beyond the limits of what is ethically acceptable. If this should happen, the therapist *must* seek the assistance of a trusted colleague. The task of the colleague is to help the therapist to cope with his counter-transference, not to bring professional disgrace upon him. It is usually necessary for the therapist to stop treating the patient, who may complain that he has been sacrificed. Such a complaint cannot be denied. The colleague may try to find someone else to take over the case, but the patient will feel very ill-used.

6

The mechanical details

CARDINAL PRINCIPLE: The rule of anonymity.

The background of psychotherapy should be organised carefully, so that everything can proceed as expeditiously as possible. In this chapter, we will examine some of the aspects which are usually taken for granted. In doing so, we will take account of two points. The first is that the patient has a natural curiosity about his therapist, which may be used constructively. He must be given every opportunity to elaborate his own fantasies. Consequently, the therapist must remain as anonymous as possible, so that the patient's imagination is not impeded by an excess of reality. Everything which is said and done by the therapist has a meaning for the patient, just as everything said and done by the patient has a meaning for the therapist.

The second is this. Since therapy is the principal task of the therapist, he should be freed from everything that can be done effectively by others. When things run smoothly, without unnecessary distractions, the patient is given the best opportunity to avail himself of the help which is offered.

The location
Psychotherapy may be practised in the home of either the therapist or the patient, in an office or consulting room, or 'somewhere else'. Let us consider the possibilities.

The therapist's home
Patients often wonder about the sort of life the therapist leads, and sometimes 'just happen' to pass by the house in which he lives. If he practises from his own home, much of the purpose of the rule of anonymity will be circumvented. Many things which are personal to the therapist will be obvious to the patient. His curiosity will be satisfied, but he will lose the opportunity of developing his fantasies about the therapist. The therapist is therefore advised against practising from his own home.

It may happen that a patient will call at the therapist's home, asking to discuss a matter of great urgency which has just arisen. An urgent matter may indeed have occurred, but it should be made clear to the patient that he will not be seen in this way. All communications must be made through the therapist's place of work.

Incidentally, for his own sake, it is desirable that the therapist should have a place in which he can relax in his own way, free from the demands of his work and the calls of his patients. His own home is the obvious place for this relaxation.

The patient's home

If the interview is to take place in his own home, the patient will often make special preparations for the visit, especially in the early stages of therapy. At the same time, the therapist may find that he has to compete with an apparently unending sequence of telephone calls, inquisitive children, barking dogs, door-to-door salesman and visits from the neighbours. In addition, the therapist is the patient's guest and in a sense he must defer to his host. If the patient should be alone in the house, and is of opposite sex to the therapist, the therapist may sometimes find himself in a situation which, from the point of view of both the patient and curious neighbours, is at least uncomfortable and at worst compromising. What is more, the patient is deprived of an opportunity of 'acting out' certain of his transference feelings. He cannot easily 'forget' to keep his appointment, and whereas he might storm out of the therapist's room, it is not so easy to storm out of his own house, leaving the therapist in possession. Finally, the patient is deprived of the benefit of a slow, reflective journey back to his own home after the session. This may be important if the content of the interview has been distressing for him. Instead he must immediately resume his place in the household.

On the whole, it is best not to undertake intensive psychotherapy in the patient's home. However, there may be occasions when the therapist is compelled to do so. The patient may be house-bound on account of some physical handicap, or the agency for which a counsellor works may require that the client be visited at home. However, everyone should understand that this is not the best arrangement. The meetings should be transferred to the counsellor's office as soon as possible.

'Somewhere'

It sometimes happens that a patient suggests that he should meet the therapist not in his office, or in his home, but 'somewhere else'

The significance of such a proposal is usually obvious, and should be interpreted. It is an attempt to change the relationship from a professional one to a social, and probably intimate one. It should never be accepted. The therapist must not consent to any clandestine arrangement.

The office or consulting room

Without doubt, this is the best location for psychotherapy. The territory is 'neutral', usually selected and furnished by someone else. It is impersonal (although not necessarily unwelcoming) and the therapist's anonymity is thereby protected. Usually there are other people at hand if the therapist should find himself in a situation of unexpected difficulty. If he does not like what is happening, the patient can miss his appointment, 'forget' it, or walk out.

The office is the therapist's work room. It is provided for the specific purpose of psychotherapy, not for relaxation. It signals to the patient that psychotherapy is work, not just some sort of vague social interchange.

The ideal consulting room is smaller than a ballroom and larger than a telephone kiosk. Since it is provided by someone else, its size may not be ideal. If the therapist has a choice, he should choose the room in which *he* feels most comfortable. It is to be *his* work room, and if he finds it uncomfortable, he can hardly expect the patient to feel at ease.

The room itself should be well lit, and as quiet as possible. There should be provision for switching incoming telephone calls to the secretary, so that quietness may be preserved. If there is only one window, the patient should be placed so that the light falls upon him, the therapist being in the shade. Patients sometimes complain that although the therapist can see them, they cannot see him. This is an expression of the patient's wish to know as much as possible about his therapist. There may also be an unspoken irrational fear that the therapist will 'see' too much. These thoughts should be interpreted. Realistically, it is much more important for the therapist to see the patient than it is for the patient to see the therapist.

Furniture

The chairs should be comfortable but not snug. The therapist spends much time in his chair, and he should choose the one which he finds most comfortable. The *position* of the chairs is important. The patient's chair is placed so that it is well lit. The therapist's chair should be placed at right angles, reasonably close, but not so close that he and the patient kick one another if they should change the position of their legs. The therapist should not sit directly opposite the patient (for then the patient will find it difficult to look away), neither should the two sit side by side. The right angled position enables the therapist to pay close attention to the patient. The patient must turn his head slightly if he wishes to look at the therapist. When there is a desk in the room, it should not be used to separate the therapist from his patient, but placed out of the way. In physical medicine, doctors sometimes use a desk as a sort of physical barrier between themselves and their patient. This is not desirable in psychotherapy. The desk itself should be uncluttered. It is not designed to demonstrate to the world what a busy person the therapist is, how meticulous he is, or how untidy he is.

The decoration of the room and the pictures on the walls are usually the responsibility of the people who provide it. Personal photographs conflict with the principle of anonymity and should not be displayed.

An ample supply of paper handkerchiefs, and a carafe of water should be available. If he permits smoking — not all therapists do — an ashtray will be required. If he wishes to take notes during the session, the therapist may use a clipboard. Some people use tape-recorders, but there is seldom sufficient time to play back the recording and the machine soon loses its novelty. When a tape-recorder is used, the microphone should not be concealed. Patients often have elaborate fantasies about the use to which the tape is put ('Does the BBC ever use the recordings...?'). It is probably better not to have one.

The couch

The couch is the focus of fictional psychiatry, but in psychotherapy it is used regularly only in psychoanalysis (q.v.). The patient lies supine, in a good light whilst the analyst sits at the head and to one side. He can see the patient but the patient cannot see him.

This has several consequences. The patient, unable to see the therapist, sometimes has fantasies about his behaviour. He wonders whether the analyst is frowning or laughing at him or whether, when things are very quiet, he has fallen asleep. The therapist's anonymity is heightened, and the transference arises from even less reality than when the patient and therapist sit face to face. In the supine position, the patient may feel extremely passive, or like a child who has been sent to bed. The couch may be a place of romance, and the patient's erotic fantasies may be stimulated.

When they first come for psychotherapy, patients often expect to lie on a couch and are sometimes disappointed when this does not happen. Apart from psychoanalysts, psychotherapists do not normally make use of a couch. Those who wish to do so should first explore with the patient his feelings about it. Novices sometimes use the couch to impress their patients with the profundity of their calling. They would be wise to examine their own motives first, especially if the patient is blonde and pulchritudinous and they are male and hungry.

The therapist

We have repeated several times that the patient will read much into small clues; that he will try to discover all that he can about his therapist. Consequently, the therapist should give some thought to his own appearance. He is advised to dress in a way suitable to his calling. 'Way out' dress is not really appropriate, especially when one is dealing with sick people.

Most junior medical students and some doctors wear stethoscopes round their necks, in the same way that cannibals wear beads of human teeth and brothel-keepers place red lamps outside their premises; to proclaim their trade without ambiguity. Some therapists wear a white coat as a badge of office. They think that it helps patients to distinguish between the various strange people who bustle about the waiting area. Some therapists refuse to wear white coats because they consider that they form a barrier between doctor and patient. Others refuse to wear them because they do not wish to be identified with those who do. The whole subject is very complicated. The author does not wear a white coat. If he has been using one, he sometimes leaves his stethoscope on his desk. He has stopped looking for an explanation. He is proud of his job, makes sure that his patients know what it is, and is aware of no particular need either to advertise or to conceal it.

The therapist is advised to behave with courtesy towards his patients at all times. He should not indulge in the luxury of losing his temper with them. There are apocryphal stories of the beneficial outcome which has resulted when the great have told their patients exactly what they thought of them. The novice is advised to avoid such dubious precepts.

In physical medicine, it seems to be fairly common for the doctor to assure his patients that he knows exactly how it feels, 'because I have had the same thing myself'. This practice is not necessarily helpful to the patient, and the doctor is unlikely to recall the *actual* experience, because he will have taken rapid steps to deal with it. The therapist is advised to avoid the sharing of experiences. It is of little value to the patient and conflicts with the principle of anonymity.

The therapist expects his patients to exert considerable self-discipline. He himself should provide an example. Sessions should start and finish on time. If there is much to be said, and time is running out, the patient should be warned. He should be told how much time there is left, and assured that the story can be continued at the next session. If the therapist is likely to be delayed, he should try to arrange for a message to be sent to the patient. A proper apology should be given, but no explanation need be offered, however tempting it may be. ('His Royal Highness has been having another bit of trouble...') If the session is only to be brief, the patient should be warned at the beginning.

We have emphasised that the therapist offers his close, uncritical attention to the patient. The word 'uncritical' is meant literally. Not only should the therapist not *condemn* his patient, he should not *praise* him. Some therapists regard it as rather churlish not to praise a patient when he is doing well. However, if the therapist praises sometimes, 'non-praise' may become equivalent to condemnation. It is best to avoid 'criticism' completely.

Therapist and patient do not normally touch each other. Some therapists shake hands with their patients at the beginning and end of a session. Provided that both understand that this is a social convention, there is no objection to the practice, provided that it is used routinely with all patients. The handshake should never be prolonged, as a sign of encouragement, praise, or for any other reason.

Ancillary personnel

A competent receptionist is invaluable. She takes most of the administrative work off his shoulders, so that the therapist can devote the whole of his attention to the patient. She keeps the diary, makes the appointments, answers the telephone and welcomes the patients. She takes messages, looks after children and animals, and makes the tea. The patient will sometimes chat with her informally, and occasionally reveal something of importance, hoping that she will pass it on to the therapist. However, she is too wise to be caught like this. She says, 'You must tell that to the doctor yourself'. She is firm, sensible, trustworthy and reliable, and in her own way, quite as important as the therapist. One would expect such paragons to be rare: the author has perhaps been unusually fortunate, for he has known many.

The job of receptionist is often combined with that of the secretary. She is responsible for correspondence, looks after the notes and sends follow-up letters to patients who default.

There may be other people to whom the therapist can turn for advice: lawyers, accountants, social workers, and other therapists. He may seek a second opinion from them (see Ch. 7), but unless they are to take over the case, they are his assistants, not his masters.

Procedure

It is the practice of the author to adhere strictly to the ethical rule, that medical specialists may accept patients only from other doctors. He does not, therefore, accept self-referrals. He expects that the consultation will have the knowledge and approval of the family doctor. It is his experience that any attempt to bypass this rule nearly always leads to inconvenience or embarrassment, and in the long run, the patient suffers. When a patient feels that he cannot trust his family doctor, he should be advised to find one whom he can trust. Therapists who work in one of the para-medical professions usually accept patients only if they are referred by a doctor. Members of most of the voluntary counselling organisations accept self-referrals. In general, it is to be preferred that the patient should be seen by appointment, for which he should write or telephone.

The first interview sets the pattern for all that follow. It is therefore of great importance. For the patient, it may be a totally new experience, a matter for much apprehension. We have reminded the reader what it is like to see a new doctor for the first time. It can be a considerable ordeal and the patient may have had several anxious days and sleepless nights before the moment finally arrives.

The patient is usually greeted by the receptionist, and the case-notes are checked. These include details of the patient's name, age, address, telephone number, marital status, date and place of birth, occupation, and next of kin. The name and address of the patient's own doctor should also be noted. In many centres, it is still the practice to note the patient's religion, although many question its relevance. It may be important later. Most patients give a reflex reply when asked about their religion: C. of E., R.C., C. of S., Protestant, Jewish, and so on. In psychiatric practice, more patients than usual give considered replies, or argue about the relevance of the information. The receptionist need not press the patient if he does not wish to answer the question. She will mention the fact to the therapist.

Patients who arrive late often supply defiant or passive explanations. The receptionist notes these, too. It is the author's experience that all the buses in Edinburgh run late on Thursday mornings. The receptionist also makes a note if the patient arrives excessively early. From the moment of the patient's arrival, his motivation and behaviour are under scrutiny.

When the patient is punctual, the doctor should be ready to meet him. He should previously have checked that his own consulting room is free, and that the chairs are set out properly. He should also make sure that this is not the day of the decennial window clean, and that lawn mowers are not being used immediately outside his window.

The patient is welcomed into the room and relieved of his luggage and outdoor clothing. He is shown which chair to take.

When both are seated, the therapist himself should re-check the main points of identification: the patient's name, his address, his telephone number, his age and occupation, and so on. This permits the patient to settle down in the new surroundings, regain his breath, and get used to answering simple questions.

Occasionally, especially when the clinic is held in a general hospital, the patient does not appreciate that he has been referred to a psychiatrist. His own doctor speaks only of a 'colleague'. If the patient did not know that the consultation was to be a psychiatric one (he will often say, 'I didn't know, but I guessed!') he should be asked how he feels about the revelation. If he has any objection, he should be allowed to leave. He should be assured that he can return later if he wishes to do so.

The therapist should then put a fairly general opening question. For example, he may ask, 'Tell me what the trouble is' or, 'What was it that led you to consult your own doctor?' or, 'What made you seek help?'. The therapist can choose any opening question with which he feels comfortable. If he wishes, there is no objection to his asking 'What is the trouble?' or, 'What are your complaints?'. The patient who answers, 'That is what I have come to find out' or, 'I'm not complaining', demonstrates that he is a smart Aleck, more anxious to skirmish with the therapist than to co-operate with him: already allowing the therapist to know the sort of person with whom he is dealing. Perhaps it is unwise to ask, 'What can I do for you?' — the mind boggles at the possible answers to that question! Unless they are very foolish or very insincere, most patients recognise the opening question as an invitation to tell their story.

When he has put his question, the therapist must *wait* for the reply. The patient sometimes finds that his mind immediately goes completely blank. Sometimes, he needs time to marshall his thoughts. At others, he finds himself suddenly in the grip of a powerful emotion. By his relaxed attention, the therapist demonstrates that he appreciates the ordeal with which the patient is faced, that there is no hurry, and that he is not disconcerted by the patient's unforseen difficulty in presenting his problem.

During the early part of the interview, the patient may give various clues to his hopes, his apprehensions, his fears and his expectations. He should be encouraged to tell his story in as much detail as possible. If it seems that there will not be sufficient time for him to finish his story in the time allocated to the session, he should be told of this about three-quarters of the way through. He may be assured that he can continue it at the next session.

The patient will try to describe the nature of his problem and the efforts he has made to solve it. Sometimes he will claim that he has done everything that can reasonably be expected of him. At other times, he feels that he has been rather obscure. He will usually hope that the therapist will provide a solution.

Certain matters of fact are worth recording. It is useful to know when and where the patient was born, and such details of his family as the ages, marital status and occupations of his parents and siblings. If any are dead, their ages, the year and the cause of their death should be noted. Were the deaths sudden or expected? If they were expected, when did the patient *realise* the relative was going to die? What was his reaction?

He should be asked similar questions about his own family. The ages, occupations, and states of health of his spouse and children should be recorded. How long after marriage was the first baby born? If it was conceived before marriage, how did the patient feel about the pregnancy? What was the attitude of the other members of the family? If the patient is a married woman, she should be asked how many times she has been pregnant. If she is unmarried, she should be asked, gently, whether she has ever been pregnant.

The patient should be asked about his record at school and at work. Which were his best subjects at school and which were the worst? How old was he when he left school? What examinations did he pass? How many jobs has he held? What was the longest? What was the shortest? Why did he leave? Was he ever sacked? He should be asked about his hobbies and his interests. How much does he drink and smoke? What about his physical health? Does he take any medicines? Has he ever taken drugs? Has he ever been 'in trouble', i.e., involved in criminal activity?

When it is convenient, the therapist should make a detailed enquiry into the patient's sexual experiences. If he is married, how has the sexual side of his marriage been? Has he been faithful? Has his spouse been faithful? Has he ever been tempted to be unfaithful? How did he resist the temptation? Has he ever had any doubts about the fidelity of his spouse? If there have been infidelities, does the spouse know about them? If he has been married more than once, what happened in the previous marriages? Does he have children by them? He must be asked, gently, about homosexual activity and sexual deviations. In his early youth, did he ever have a close friendship with a member of his own sex? It may be helpful for the therapist to remind the patient that such youthful companionships are extremely frequent. Was any homosexual contact involved? Has he had any homosexual experiences in later life?

In helping him to express emotion, it may be useful for the therapist to enquire about the 'extremes' of the patient's experience. What is the worst thing that has ever happened to him? What is the saddest, the most humiliating, the most shameful? When has he been most angry? What is the worst thing he could imagine? What is his happiest memory? What is his earliest memory?

When he has completed the history, the psychotherapist should follow the normal medical practice of conducting a careful physical examination.

As the life history emerges, repeated patterns of behaviour may be detected. Some may suggest factors which have led to the present problem. Associations, similarities and consistent patterns of behaviour should be discussed with the patient.

Sometimes the patient will remember episodes from the past which he had 'completely forgotten'. These usually fit into a basic pattern, and when this is so, further 'forgotten' memories may be recalled. The patient sometimes talks about things that are actually happening during the course of psychotherapy. At times, he will express curiosity about his therapist and will put apparently 'innocent' questions, such as 'Are you married?', 'Do you have a family?' and 'Don't you get tired of listening to people's problems all day long?'

When this sort of question is posed, the therapist must consider with the patient its relevance to the problem which is under discussion. The patient will often give a 'rational' reply. He may say that his questions are designed to confirm his confidence in his therapist. He may ask, 'How can I trust *you* with a marital problem if you are not married yourself?' The inference is that he does *not* trust his therapist: he does not know if he is married, and an unmarried therapist would not be able to help him. This point must be explained very carefully. The patient may protest rather hurriedly that he did not mean such a thing. It then becomes the therapist's task to help the patient consider what is really true. It may be necessary, although difficult, for the patient to say unflattering things to the therapist. However, the therapist has agreed to listen to whatever the patient wishes to say. He is not concerned with flattery or disparagement. It is easy for the patient to say nice things to the therapist: the therapist should help him to say nasty things, too.

During the first interview, the therapist should tell the patient something of what is expected of him, although it may be premature to discuss the full extent of the 'contract' (see p. 38). The patient should be punctual. He should be told the duration of the sessions. He is expected to give first priority to therapy. If circumstances make it quite impossible for him to keep his appointment, he should notify his therapist as soon as possible. He may *say* anything, and should not evade anything, even if it is embarrassing, shameful, disloyal, distasteful, or apparently irrelevant. He may *say* anything he likes. He may *do* only things which would be acceptable in any professional relationship.

Letters

In medicine, all sorts of people write all sorts of letters to other sorts of people.

The first letter is often from the general practitioner to the specialist. It usually gives a short account of the patient's problems and of his current medication. It does not necessarily coincide with the patient's account of events. Sometimes it gives extensive details: occasionally it is extremely brief ('?? nerves. Please see and treat'!).

After he has interviewed the patient, the specialist replies, if possible on the same day. The author regrets that in this respect he is often at fault.

Letters from specialists to general practitioners have been the subject of much comment. They are criticised for being too long and for telling the practitioner nothing that he does not already know. Some general practitioners read the last paragraph only, because this is where the recommendations are made. Specialists should consequently reserve to the final paragraph, their advice about what should happen next.

The specialist's reply to the general practitioner may be a convenient summary of the history: for this reason it may repeat much of what the general practitioner already knows. This is a legitimate function of a letter.

Some doctors use big words and complex sentences. This may impress the cognoscenti but is not conducive to mutual understanding. Verbosity is seldom a virtue except when the omniscient Jeeves is in charge. Here, he is called to order by an American millionaire.

'Excuse me, Sir,' he (Jeeves) said, 'A seaman from your yacht has just brought this cablegram, which arrived shortly after your departure this morning. The captain of the vessel, fancying that it might be of an urgent nature, instructed him to convey it to this house. I took it from him at the back door, and hastened hither with it in order to deliver it to you personally.' Old Stoker seemed somewhat on the impatient side. 'What you mean is, there's a cable for me.' (Wodehouse, P. G.: *Thank you, Jeeves*). Little words and brief sentences are to be preferred. There is eminent authority for this practice.*

The author tries to avoid words and phrases such as 'mother figure', 'father fixation' and 'inferiority complex', but has been known to refer to an 'unresolved Oedipal conflict'.

Specialists should write occasionally thereafter to report progress to the family doctor, but there is little point in writing after every session. Progress is often slow and in the course of many months, there may be very little to report. The author tries to remember to write 'no progress' letters from time to time.

Patients sometimes write to their therapist. They may write to apologise for mistakes or misunderstandings or for their inability to attend. Sometimes they write to complain or to threaten. Some letters are very long indeed, and may be written 'to save you time'. (The author has in his possession one, illegible and unread, which runs to 150 pages.)

The author tries not to correspond with his patients. Whenever possible, his secretary replies with the comment, 'Dr Parry would like you to raise these matters when you next see him'. This is her invariable practice when the letter is heavily perfumed and marked 'Personal', Strictly Confidential' or 'For the Personal Attention of'.

Relatives or friends sometimes write about patients. They sometimes ask that the information they give should not be passed on to the patient. In these cases, the therapist should return it to the sender. Information obtained from someone else is of no value unless it can be shared with the patient. The therapist is advised to avoid *correspondence* with friends and relatives. In particular, he should avoid requests for written information. The enquirer should address himself to the patient.

Solicitors and other professional people may write for information. Unless the letter comes from a solicitor who *specifically* states that he is acting on behalf of the patient, the latter's written author-

*See Gowers Sir E 1965 Love of the long word. In Fowler's Modern English Usage. Oxford University Press.

ity should be obtained before a reply is sent. The reply should always be brief.

Doctors who 'take the case over' or who are involved in other specialist areas may request information. It is ethically correct to supply appropriate details.

Telephone messages

Although the receptionist usually deals with these, there are occasions when a session must be interrupted so that the therapist can take a telephone call. If it is about a professional matter, it should not be taken in front of a patient. If it is about a personal matter, it threatens the principle of anonymity and should not be taken in front of a patient.

The therapist therefore has two choices. He may ask the patient to return to the waiting area, or he himself may go elsewhere to take the call. If he chooses the latter course, he should remember that *patients read casenotes*. If they can, they read their own: otherwise, they read other people's — the therapist should therefore take his notes with him if he leaves the patient in possession of the consulting room. It is better to ask him to return to the waiting area.

Duration and frequency of sessions

The therapist should decide for himself the length of his sessions. The duration should be appropriate to his method of working. Certain limits are suggested.

Sessions should normally last for at least 30 minutes. A session which lasts for less than 30 minutes has scarcely had time to get started when it is time to finish. The maximum length may be about 50 minutes. Longer sessions are often too long for the attention span of either the patient or the therapist.

Patients are occasionally keen to embark upon marathon sessions which could last for several hours. Such sessions deprive the patient of valuable periods of reflection which can occur *between* sessions. Some patients seek for only one interview every year — but want it to last for 365 days.

For verbalisation to be of maximum value, the patient requires adequate time to contemplate what has been verbalised. The content of a 50 minute session is usually ample for this purpose. Many therapists allow 10 minutes between patients, five at each end of the hour. Joint interviews require more time: 90 minutes is common.

The therapist may find that the concentration required for his work makes it very fatiguing, and he himself should take several rest periods each day.

Individual sessions should be as frequent as possible. Two or three meetings every week is ideal. In psychoanalysis, the preferred frequency is five sessions every week. When the frequency is fewer than once weekly, they may be of less value. However, when the pressure of work is great, the therapist may have little choice in the matter.

Psychotherapy usually continues for at least six months. Twelve to 36 months is quite common.

Emergencies

A case is sometimes said to be urgent. Sometimes the patient is a prominent citizen. In such cases the therapist may be asked to 'fit him in' to a diary which is already full. The wisdom of this practice must be questioned.

'Fitting someone in' implies that a brief consultation will be sufficient, but brief consultations — perhaps of only five or ten minutes — are of little value, either to the patient or to the therapist. A brief interview is not sufficient for any real momentum to be developed. If something important is revealed, the therapist may be forced to call a premature halt. This is particularly true of a real emergency.

On the other hand, if the 'emergency' is to be allocated a full-length interview, the time must be taken from other patients. Even brief interviews are conducted at the expense of others. The author, therefore, finds it inadvisable to 'fit someone in'. The patient can nearly always be given 'first aid' treatment by his general practitioner, until a proper consultation can be arranged.

True emergencies are uncommon is psychotherapy. There may be occasions when the patient feels an urgent need to contact his therapist, but he should be discouraged from doing so. Contact should be limited to the appointed times. Patients who are seen several times each week are unlikely to encounter a matter of such great urgency that it really cannot wait until the next session.

Emergencies are more common in very dependent people, and represent their imperious demand for instant relief. Tolerance, patience and self-discipline are integral parts of therapy, and the patient must learn to tolerate a certain amount of discomfort and distress. It may sometimes be necessary for the therapist to take a calculated risk. The therapist may make it plain that he does not regard it as being necessarily in the best interests of his patient, to be stampeded by an angry demand for immediate succour. It may be unpleasant to wait until next time, and is not always easy. Some patients react with anger, recrimination or blackmail. But when the first emergency has been faced successfully, it becomes easier to overcome the subsequent ones.

Smoking

It is not surprising that many psychiatric patients smoke. It is a matter of observation that many people who work with psychiatric patients also smoke.

Smoking is supposed to promote relaxation, and many patients expect to smoke during psychotherapy. Some of them ask permission first.

Whilst psychotherapy is concerned *ultimately* with relaxation, it does not follow that the therapist wishes his patient to be relaxed *during* sessions: sometimes he wishes the opposite.

If a psychotherapist is really concerned with the health of his patient, he will discourage him from smoking. He will certainly discourage smoking in the consulting room. If the patient asks for permission to smoke, he may be told, quite politely, 'no'. If he takes out a cigarette without asking permission and the therapist prefers him not to smoke, he should say so.

When the therapist permits smoking and smokes himself, should he smoke in front of his patient? If he does so, custom demands that when he takes a cigarette, he should offer one to the patient. When the patient takes a cigarette, custom demands that he offer one to the therapist. So a complex exchange of cigarettes builds up, patient and therapist each trying to keep up with, yet neither wishing to overtake the other.

Smoking in company, with such traditions as passing round the packet, is a social practice. Like other forms of social intercourse, such as eating and drinking, smoking does not mix with psychotherapy. The therapist would be wise not to start.

Presents and favours

It is not uncommon for a patient to offer a gift to his therapist. There may be times when it is tempting to seek the assistance of a patient. When one is facing the purchase of an expensive item, it may seem foolish to reject a patient's offer 'to let you have it cheap'. There may seem little harm, when one is having car trouble, to accept the offer of a motor-mechanic patient to 'put it right for you'. The therapist is advised to avoid these temptations. If he does not, he will sooner or later have cause to repent.

When a present is refused, it is understandable that the patient should feel hurt and rejected. He may plead that the therapist quite misunderstands the purpose of the gift. It is not meant to be a bribe;

it is an expression of gratitude and perhaps of his affection. Often it seems churlish to refuse. Nevertheless, the therapist should refuse.

If the patient particularly wishes to do so, and when counselling or therapy is completed, he may make a contribution to the parent organisation or to an associated charity. The therapist should not accept a personal gift.

7

Problems for the therapist

CARDINAL PRINCIPLE: There is no Santa Claus

We have reiterated that problems always arise between people. Most commonly, they occur when a change takes place in the relationship between them. Whilst Jack loves Jill and Jill loves Jack, there are no problems. Each is idyllically happy, totally preoccupied with the other. Each yearns to spend every waking — and sleeping — hour with the other. Each wishes to live happily ever after.

But life is not a fairy story. Jack wants to go to a football match. Jill is bored by such things. Jill changes her hairstyle. Jack does not notice. Jack wants to visit his parents, but Jill does not like them. Jill wants to visit her parents, but Jack does not like them. Jack wants to watch 'Monty Python' but Jill thinks it's dull. Suddenly, terrible gulfs appear. Jack argues that it is unreasonable to prevent him from watching football. Jill retorts that if he really loved her, he would stay at home with her: and that if he cared about her, he would notice when she tries to make herself look nice. Each thinks that the other should try to 'like my parents for my sake'. There is no chance that Jill will ever find anything amusing in 'Monty Python' or that Jack will understand why she does not fall about in convulsive laughter at every episode. Each is discovering that the other has personal needs in addition to shared ones — sources of pleasure which are outside the pleasures of companionship — that each has likes and dislikes which, to the other, are dislikes and likes. At the same time, neither wishes to hurt the other. Both would like to return to the previous idyllic relationship. But now it seems that this can never be.

New problems arise. Can Jack and Jill satisfy their mutual needs well enough to permit a successful modified relationship? Are they willing to *accept* a modified relationship? Can either tolerate a role which on certain occasions is second best? Or must Jack turn to Joan and Jill to John?

Incompatibilities in a relationship are usually discovered by one of its members before the other. The anguished, sometimes terrified reaction may heighten the difficulties, although it does not follow that the foundation of the relationship must be affected. One or both partners may seek help. If one turns away, the other will plead for guidance as to how to put things right again. Sometimes, the solution is simple, and the couple can revel in the sweetness of reconciliation.

As it develops, nearly every relationship encounters difficulties, and these are sometimes profound. The resolution of some difficulties will help to strengthen it, but some problems are insoluble, and may be the harbingers of its destruction. If the partnership appears to be doomed, one of its members may turn for help. In this way, it frequently happens that the psychotherapist is asked to help when relationships become damaged.

Joint interviews

These are very important, since they permit the therapist to examine the problem in pure culture. In this way, he can gauge the relative strengths and weaknesses of the partners, their resources and their motivation. Some therapists never see a patient individually. The patient is always seen with his partner, even at the very beginning of therapy. More commonly, joint interviews are undertaken only after one of the partners, labelled, often rather arbitrarily, 'the patient', has presented with the problem. The other partner may be seen by someone else. A joint interview is a technique by which the problem is examined. It may also be the means by which it is resolved.

It is the author's practice to conduct joint interviews only after each partner has been seen individually. He may himself have seen both partners; at other times, he has seen one and a co-therapist has seen the other. In the latter instance, he and the co-therapist first exchange the information they have obtained about the partners.

Co-therapists should agree upon certain technical matters before the joint meeting is held. These include such things as where everyone is to sit, who is to open the session, who is to finish it, how long it is to continue, what subjects are to be covered, and whether there should be tentative plans for further meetings.

The first joint interview may be started by asking the couple to express their feelings about the procedure. They usually reply that they are well satisfied, but if either therapist detects any reservations, he should say so. It is a basic rule of psychotherapy that resistance must be dealt with as soon as it is perceived. Speaking about it helps to resolve it.

The 'patient' is then asked to re-state the problem. He should be helped to cover all aspects, including the disagreeable ones. His partner may wish to interrupt, to correct, to 'put the record straight', or to explain 'misunderstandings'. He should be asked to reserve his comments for later. Initially he should listen to what is being said. Often, this is the first time he has done so.

When the 'patient' has completed his account, it is the turn of the partner. He is asked to give his account of the situation. The therapist ensures that he too covers every aspect, omitting nothing. This time, 'the patient' may wish to interrupt. In turn, he is asked to wait and to listen. Often, this is the first time he has done so.

When each partner has given his account, when each has heard the account of the other, the therapists should try to iron out the discrepancies, to clarify the inconsistencies, and to correct the misunderstandings. The partners should be helped to agree on as much as possible. One partner may accept that he has over-stated one aspect of the case, or admit that he has little or no memory of a particular episode. The other may have to concede that however vivid is his own memory, his partner has no recollection of an incident. Some differences cannot be reconciled. Then the partners must be helped to accept that they have seen the same event through different eyes.

During joint interviews, certain basic points should be clarified. Do the partners really want the problem to be solved? Although they give a hasty affirmative, further questioning may reveal areas of doubt. How will they feel if the problem cannot be solved?

Couples will often continue their discussions after the joint interview, sometimes encouraged by a new-found understanding of each other. This is especially so when each has listened to the other's point of view for the very first time. Previously, perhaps, they had stormed out of the house, or found some other way of not listening. In some situations, a threat of violence is used. In the consulting room, the couple often have an unspoken and quite unrealistic fantasy that the therapists have the resources to prevent unseemly behaviour.

The co-therapists should work together closely. They should devote time both before and after each session to discuss the contribution of the other. This is expensive of therapist time, but provides each therapist with a unique opportunity of learning about his own performance and behaviour. Each co-therapist is able to observe and later to comment upon his colleague's technique, without appearing to intrude.

On occasions, two therapists will discover that they have been individually involved with two partners. They may find it valuable to combine to conduct joint interviews,

Problems sometimes exist between more than two people. They may exist between two or more *groups* of people. The method of joint or multiple interviews is also applicable and the outcome may be very gratifying.

Admission to hospital

At the beginning of psychotherapy, or occasionally during its course, it is necessary to consider admitting a patient to a psychiatric unit. Such a decision should be made only after the implications of the step have been examined carefully.

We have already noted that illness may bring advantages. Admission to hospital may bring substantial advantages. If the patient is a busy housewife, she will be relieved of many dreary, everyday chores. Someone else will be responsible for keeping the house clean, cooking the meals and making the beds. The patient will expect the flowers, grapes and compassion which are due to the invalid from a hitherto neglectful family.

One day, however, it will be necessary for her to return to her former dreary existence. Thus, the very act of admission to hospital can create a problem.

It is certainly easier to deal with a severely distressed patient in hospital. There, although he may disturb other patients, he will not disturb the neighbours. The relatives of a suicidal patient may feel more secure if he is in hospital, Where there is serious domestic friction, there may be something to be gained from separating the antagonists. Such separation can be achieved with dignity and without loss of face when one of them is admitted to hospital. It may be difficult to choose which is to be labelled as 'the patient' and some units solve problem by admitting all the antagonists.

When a doctor advises a patient to enter hospital, his message is essentially this: 'You are ill. The situation is too complicated to be managed by your own people under your own roof. We will provide more experienced people and a better roof.'

However, this is not necessarily true. There are very few illnesses which cannot be managed perfectly well in the patient's own home, provided that certain basic facilities are provided. However, Britain is a hospital-oriented country. If beds are available, they may not be left empty. It may be less desirable for the patients, but it may be easier for the therapist to treat several together at one centre.

If admission is accepted, certain consequences must be faced. The most important of these is that sooner or later, the people between whom the problem existed must be reunited. Although 'the patient' may be visited regularly, and his partner interviewed, the separation is an artificial one. One day, they must go back to the beginning.

Many patients who seemed to be overwhelmed with hopeless despair when they were in their own home, improve very rapidly after admission. Perhaps they feel 'safe'. Others, although they would repudiate the idea with some vehemence, prefer the role of the 'sick' person. The demands and limitations of treatment are found to be preferable to the freedom, independence but conflicts of their own home. Patients such as these often protest, 'You don't think I *like* it here, do you? The answer should be a gentle question. 'Could it be possible that you prefer hospital to your own home?'

Although he may have reservations, the therapist may decide that it is wise to provide a temporary haven. However, this procedure, which may solve *all* of the patient's difficulties for *some* of the time, is only a temporary one. One of the principal aims of therapy will be to help him to return home as soon as possible.

Information from friends and relatives

Friends, relatives, employers, neighbours, workmates or others who know the patient, will sometimes offer important information about him. Two conditions must be satisfied before this information can be accepted. The first is that the therapist should be free to discuss the information with the patient. When information is given under a pledge of secrecy, it is of no value, and should not be accepted. If information is accepted under an inadvertent pledge of secrecy, the therapist may find himself in a very unsatisfactory position, because he is unable to use it, even though it may truly be of importance. Someone who wishes to impose a condition may be asked for the reason for secrecy. Sometimes it transpires that the informant expects to receive an antagonistic response from the patient. Such fears are not usually justified. The difficulties should be discussed with the informant, and his apprehensions examined. The need for the pledge (like other problems) then usually disappears, and the information can then be accepted without any preconditions. If a pledge is still demanded, it should not be given. The informant should be told that he can contact the therapist at a later date if he is willing to supply the information freely. Very often he does so.

The second condition is that no-one who wishes to give information should be seen unless the patient has prior knowledge and has given consent. A therapist who agrees to see an informant without first obtaining the consent of his patient, is risking a breach of confidence, which he may later regret. If the patient refuses permission, his reasons should be discussed. He objections often disappear when this is done, but his final decision must always be respected.

Confidentiality

Patients frequently, and sometimes with anxiety, ask, 'This is confidential, isn't it?' When this question is put, the therapist should help the patient to share his fears of what it would be like if other people were to know. Patients often have elaborate fantasies and imagine that the most innocent piece of behaviour will be of consuming interest not only their nearest and dearest, but also to their townsmen, their countrymen, and occasionally even to the whole world. Some believe that they would become the subject of universal derision. Such grandiose fantasies as these must be discussed carefully.

Having dealt with the fantasies, the facts must be acknowledged. In Britain, neither doctors, nor counsellors of any sort can claim the privilege of confidentiality in respect of matters discussed with them by their patients. If ordered to do so by a court, they must reveal the information they have. Privilege may be claimed by ministers of religion only in respect of information which has been received during the course of confession. It is seldom possible, therefore, for a therapist to give an *absolute* guarantee of confidentiality. The patient will usually understand that this is so. However, the therapist will endeavour to respect the confidentiality of what he is told. He will not disclose it unless the circumstances are exceptional.

There are occasions when a breach of confidentiality must be considered. For example, the therapist may hear of a criminal act, either contemplated or completed. Careful thought must then be given as to whether or not such information can remain confidential. It is generally considered that the public good outweighs the rights of the individual. Where such ethical problems arise, the therapist should consult with senior colleagues or professional advisers before reaching his decision. The doctor should consult his defence union, the voluntary counsellor should consult the agency's legal adviser, and so on. Nevertheless, the final decision is his own.

There is a second problem about confidentiality. To *whom* is the information confidential? If the therapist works in a hospital, does the information belong to him or to the hospital? Should a junior doctor be free to discuss confidential information with a senior colleague? When a counsellor belongs to a voluntary counselling organisation, does the information belong to him or to the agency? If the therapist moves away from the district, may information obtained by him be passed on to his successor? If the patient leaves the district and is treated by a new therapist, may the new therapist have access to information obtained by the previous one?

It is generally best to regard information as being confidential to the organisation for which the therapist works, although there are a few exceptions. Thus it may be undesirable that information confided by an employee to his welfare officer *who is also an employee* should be the property of the organisation for which they both work. There will be occasions when the therapist can do little more than assure his patient that he will do his best to respect his privacy. Absolute confidentiality can not and should not be guaranteed.

Scapegoating

Nowadays, very few people seem prepared to accept responsibility for their own mistakes. Errors of commission or omission are blamed on to others, or ascribed to the vagaries of inanimate and defenceless objects such as computers. Popular repositories for blame are government departments and the nationalised industries. Pride of place on the list of popular scapegoats must surely be given to the postal services, which, more than any other, are unjustly blamed for the shortcomings of the people who forget to use them.

Scapegoating is common and in psychotherapy it is usually easily identified. It is a form of self-deception which borders on dishonesty. The patient may be reluctant to acknowledge this, but when necessary he should be helped to do so.

Acting out

Reference has already been made to the fact that the patient is expected to express his thoughts, feelings, ideas and wishes in words (see 'The contract', p. 38). A patient who expresses them by other, more direct means, is said to be 'acting out'.

He may demonstrate his hostile feelings towards his therapist indirectly, by going to another doctor and asking for a tranquilliser. He may show them directly, by being constantly late for appointments. Sometimes, an attempt at suicide is used as a device to express feelings of being neglected. Someone else may then be compelled to take care of the patient. Conversely, he may express his affection for his therapist by prolonging the end-of-session handshake. These devices are means by which the patient 'acts out' his feelings towards the therapist, against him or towards other people.

By expressing his feelings in behaviour, instead of in words, the patient evades the spirit of the contract.

'Acting out' must always be interpreted. The therapist should translate the acting-out behavior into words, such as 'You seem to be angry with me', or 'You seem to feel that I do not care enough', or 'You seem to be very fond of me'. Patients who repeatedly act out their feelings are not suitable for intensive psychotherapy. They should be warned that therapy will cease if acting-out continues.

Joking

There are several jokes in this book. Jokes are appropriate in education, when they may be used to emphasise a point. They are not appropriate in psychotherapy. The therapist is advised not to joke with his patient, or to respond to jokes made to him — rarely a difficult matter. The patient may accuse the therapist of being cold and humourless, perhaps expressing his negative transference by this statement. He wishes that the relationship between them could be warmer. An appropriate interpretation should be made.

Occasionally, a patient will present a serious personal problem in the form of joke. He may, for example, tell an anecdote about homosexuals. The therapist should always examine such matters according to the principle, 'true words are often spoken in jest'. It would be fatal to the relationship if the therepist were to fall into the trap, and treat as a joke something which was felt deeply by the patient.

In the social context, a joke is a useful device for softening hostile comments, or for introducing provocative ones. They give the listener the choice of taking a topic seriously or of ignoring it altogether. Patients' problems are not matters for jokes.

Second opinions

The therapist may sometimes find that he himself is in need of guidance or advice. He may be out of his depth or feel that he is getting nowhere. Sometimes he would like an acceptable excuse to get rid of a difficult patient. Occasionally, a client tells his counsellor of physical symptoms, and both will wonder whether these indicate the presence of organic disease.

When a second opinion is thought to be desirable, the therapist should first clarify his own need. Sometimes the request for a 'second opinion' is really an attempt to unload a difficult or unrewarding client on to someone else. If this is the therapist's wish, he should not shrink from admitting it, either to himself, or to the person whose opinion he seeks. It may then be possible for them to consider together how the situation has arisen: whether it might have been foreseen, whether it can be changed, and whether it might indeed be better for the patient to be treated by someone else.

There are certain situations in which a second, medical opinion *must* be sought — at least by a non-medical therapist. These are when there is a clear-cut *change* in someone who has passed his mid-30s. The change may be in his physical health or in his psychological outlook. It is emphasised that a *change* should have occurred. A person who has been chronically anxious for the whole of his life need not be sent for a second opinion, merely because he has passed his 36th birthday. On the other hand, a patient who, up to the age of 40, has seemed reasonably well adjusted, and who then develops persistant symptoms of anxiety for which there is no obvious cause, should be given the benefit of a second opinion.

In the case of a counsellor working in a voluntary agency, the referral should be made to the client's family doctor. The counsellor should never permit the family doctor to be bypassed. The client may plead that, for one reason or another, he does not wish his general practitioner to know what is happening. The counsellor may have a medical friend. Nevertheless, the general practitioner often has important knowledge about the client and his family, and it is he who is ultimately responsible for the patient's health. If the client lacks confidence in his own doctor, he should find another. Sometimes it is easy and convenient to bypass the general practitioner, but the counsellor is advised against doing so.

When the therapist is himself a medical practitioner, or is a member of a medical team, it is easy to obtain another medical opinion when one is required. The therapist will always keep the general practitioner informed.

When a second opinion is sought, it is best to *write* to the person from whom it is requested. The letter should be brief, should indicate the interest of the writer, and should describe the difficulties which have arisen. The letter is not a device to demonstrate to the recipient how clever, hard-working or well-informed the writer is. If a counsellor wonders whether a psychiatric opinion might be desirable, he may mention this in his letter to the general practitioner He may not, of course, 'order' it. The writer should express his willingness to provide further information if required. This may be given in another letter, by telephone, or by direct discussion.

If the person who is to give the second opinion wishes to see the patient, the therapist should not try to predict what will happen. In particular, he should not make any promises on behalf of the other person. He should not, for example, tell the patient that a particular investigation will be undertaken, or give him premature warning that he will be expected to attend the clinic twice every week for at least 12 months.

When a second opinion has been given, the therapist has the right to decide whether or not he will accept it. He is not bound to do so, but he usually will. If he does not, he should tell the patient of his decision. It is *not* permissible to seek a third opinion, if one disagrees with the second opinion. To shop around for an opinion which agrees with one's own is not seeking a second opinion at all. Such a practice is unfair to the patient and dishonest to the person who gave the other opinion.

Use of technical words

A technical vocabulary is important for the exchange of ideas between specialists. However, it must be acknowledged that specialists do not always use technical words in precisely the same way.

Certain technical words have been adopted, not always accurately, into the ordinary vocabulary. At one time, poliomyelitis was commonly known as infantile paralysis. Now the technical term is universally used. Certain psychological terms like 'paranoid' and 'ambivalent' seem to have been adopted into everyday use: regrettably, in a careless and imprecise way. A word which causes much confusion is 'schizophrenic'. In everyday speech, it is often used when an individual has conflicting attitudes towards a single object. People will say, 'I am schizophrenic about Royalty', when the they wish to convey their opinion that there are both advantages and disadvantages to the system.

A special problem arises because schizophrenia is one of the most serious of psychiatric illnesses. It is not easy to describe. The commonly used translation, 'split personality' is incorrect. The personality is not split. But when someone finds that he has a conflicting attitude towards Royalty, or, more ominously, towards someone whom he loves, and when he reads such phenomena described as 'schizophrenic', he may wonder whether he has the dread disease. Of course, if he has, his problem *may* be solved. Even schizophrenia has its advantages. He may be relieved of responsibility for his actions. Instead, he may be confined in a mental hospital (see 'Gain', p. 87).

Another word which sometimes causes confusion is 'depression'. Its technical meaning is similar to its colloquial one. However, since the advent of effective drugs for the treatment of depressive illnesses, the word is sometimes applied to other emotions as well.

When a patient complains of depression, it may be necessary to ask him to elaborate. Some doctors, for no very obvious reason, apply the diagnosis of depression to people who have a bad temper, and it has even been used to describe people who are happy and cheerful. (A few drug companies have revelled in the dubious concept of 'the smiling depression'. This means that people who cry require antidepressants, and so do those who laugh! In fact, it is seldom difficult to detect a tear behind the rather watery 'conventional' smile of the depressed patient).

The habit of using the same word for different things and sometimes to use different words for the same thing, can be the cause of much perplexity. The therapist must acknowledge such difficulties and make allowances for them.

Thus, when doctors make pronouncements, there may be apparent differences in their opinions, which cause consequent confusion to their patients, who infer an alarming conflict of medical opinion when there is none. In these circumstances, the therapist may hear terrifying stories of how doctors have differed, when he knows that there was no disagreement. The patient usually allies himself with the view he prefers, imagining that he is in opposition to the other.

It may be difficult for the therapist to listen to criticism of other doctors, especially when he is a doctor himself . Some think that in order to keep in the good books of the General Medical Council, or because 'there but for the grace of God go I', they must rush to the defence of their colleagues. Some therapists fear that if they do not defend their colleagues, it will be assumed that they are joining the attack.

Patients often reflect crucial aspects of their personalities in their attitudes towards doctors, and may express wholehearted admiration of one, or very serious criticism of another. The criticism may be unspoken but if the therapist is willing to attend, it may be there. ('Dr A was a bit lost. He sent me to Dr B. It was *he* who made the diagnosis.').

When a patient criticises a doctor, the therapist need not immediately seek to defend him. It is his task to help the patient say whatever he wishes to say. If the patient feels that a doctor has behaved badly, he should be helped to say so. The therapist does not necessarily support the criticism by this practice. Sometimes it appears that the patient is justified in his criticism. Occasionally, by reason of personal acquaintanceship with the circumstances, the therapist will know that it is justified. However, these are relatively minor issues. The patient should be helped to say what he wishes to say.

It is unfortunate if the medical profession is unduly sensitive about such matters, but it is not relevant to the patient's welfare.

Short cuts

Intensive psychotherapy may be long and hard work, and therapists often wish that there were some means by which the work could be accelerated or simplified. The patient, too, would prefer a speedier and less exacting means of obtaining relief. Occasionally he will wonder whether he might be helped by hypnotism, relaxation, drugs or acupuncture, or by more mystical means such as yoga, prayer or transcendental meditation.

If these techniques would bring quick and effective results, there would be every inducement to employ them. Unfortunately, the high hopes which they offer seldom materialise. It would be very pleasant if everything could be resolved by the induction of a cosy hypnotic trance. The patient would simply go to sleep, obey the commands of his hypnotist, and waken with his problems solved. Unfortunately, the matter is more complicated than this. First, since problems exist *between* people, they would all have to be hypnotised. A sonorous hypnotic assurance that 'You will no longer be frightened when your husband raises his fist to you' is not likely to be very effective.

It should be obvious that drugs cannot solve the difficulties which arise between people. They may, it is true, dull perception to a limited extent, so that less immediate distress is suffered. Some counsellors advise their clients to 'get something from the doctor if you cannot sleep', thereby making a promise on behalf of someone else. Others believe that it is more important to look for the reasons for the patient's inability to sleep, than to prescribe a chemical which will induce not only unconsciousness, but also a state of dependence.

The use of tranquillising drugs and antidepressants is very specific, and they rarely make good partners in intensive psychotherapy. If a drug can do the job speedily and effectively, there is no need for psychotherapy. Drugs are sometimes proposed as an 'adjunct to psychotherapy'. This may be profitable for the people who manufacture them, but it is questionable policy for the psychotherapist. When a change occurs, is it due to the drug or to psychotherapy? Can the therapist be sure that the patient's symptoms have not simply been suppressed by the drug? Is a patient psychologically 'well' if he is able to sleep only with sedatives? When drugs are employed, is the patient 'well' or 'ill'? Is there a pathological state to which the problem can be ascribed? How much of the patient's difficulty is to be ascribed to 'disease' and how much to other factors? When things go well, is it because of the drug or due to the efforts of the patient?

Some therapists use a procedure known as 'drug abreaction'. The patient is given a drug which alters his state of consciousness. A slow intravenous injection of a weak solution of Pentothal or Methedrine may be used, or the patient may be given ether, nitrous oxide or CO_2 to inhale. As a result, some diminution of the patient's inhibitions may occur and he may then produce new material. Sometimes, he undergoes a profound change in his affective state. However, when the procedure is concluded, the patient may have little memory of it. Alternatively, he may say, 'It was not I who said that' (or who felt like that), 'it was the drug!' The author's experience is that, with patience, equal and generally better results can be obtained in clear consciousness, without the use of abreactive drugs. Consequently, he does not favour this method, although others find it useful.

The role of prayer and meditation depends upon the circumstances in which they are used. True believers will usually find help from their devotions, and such practices are entirely appropriate when the counsellor is working with a religious organisation. True unbelievers will find rational explanations for the benefits which are claimed. The author acknowledges that many people have found great help from such courses. They are not, however, short cuts.

More mystical means of help range from the sublime to the outrageous. The author is unable to believe that problems can be solved by sticking needles into selected parts of the body, or by encouraging patients to twist themselves into transcendental postures. He has no wish to argue with those who do.

Alcohol

It is not possible to conduct psychotherapy with a patient who is under the influence of alcohol. To make the matter absolutely plain, the author expects his patients to abstain from alcohol completely on the days on which they come for therapy. They may not drink until the session is completed. Patients who disobey this rule are reminded of it and the current session is terminated. Such an attitude may appear harsh and dogmatic, but even a minor degree of intoxication reduces the value of psychotherapy, whilst states of moderate or severe intoxication make it a total waste of time. The patient who repeatedly disobeys the rule may, of course, be addicted to alcohol. When this is so, he will need assistance to stop drinking before psychotherapy can proceed. When abstinence has been achieved, he must *remain* totally abstinent. Part of the psychother-apeutic aim will be to help him observe this requirement.

The patient who is not an alcoholic but who repeatedly disobeys the 'no drinking' rule, is challenging his therapist. For him, con-frontation seems to be more important than therapy. If this is really so, the therapist will have little hesitation in terminating treatment. At other times, patients drink to give themselves courage to visit the therapist. The reason for their difficulty must be explored in clear consciousness. Exploration will involve the patient in some discom-fort as well as considerable self-discipline, but such things cannot be avoided.

Sleep and sleeping pills

It is extremely disagreeable to lie awake all night. The experience is one which is familiar to most people. Even more unpleasant is insomnia which persists for several nights. Then one may be tempted to ask for, or to prescribe sleeping tablets.

Psychophysiologists who are interested in the problems of sleep find great difficulty in keeping people awake! Even those who claim not to have slept for months on end, fall into a peaceful doze shortly after being connected to the leads of the electro-encephalogram (by which the onset and depth of sleep can be gauged). On wakening next morning, they exclaim triumphantly, 'There you are! I didn't sleep a wink.' In fact, they have usually had several brief spells of wakefulness between long periods of sleep. They remember the for-mer, but not the latter. This is probably the explanation of the dis-putes which sometimes occur between night nurses and patients in hospitals. The nurses report that the patient was soundly asleep at all visits: the patient accuses them of being asleep themselves. The *subjective* experience is that the patient was awake for the whole night. This experience is no less unpleasant for being subjective. The sense of tossing and turning, changing from one side to the other, listening to the hours chiming away, leads some people almost to the brink of despair. 'I won't be good for anything tomorrow', they cry.

But again, on psychological and physiological testing, people who have been deprived of sleep seldom demonstrate any serious dete-rioration in performance until the loss of sleep has been substantial. So even this fear is without foundation.

The reasons for the *subjective* distress of insomnia are complex. Some originate in childhood. Most parents consider that it is important for their children to have plenty of sleep. Children are sent to bed early 'because you are growing'. Sometimes, going to bed early is a punishment. Children often stay awake to hear what is going on between their parents. Sometimes they are frightened of bedtime and darkness because they fear they will see ghosts. Even fairly grown-up children, and many adults, are frightened of the dark. Some people are frightened to stay awake because of their thoughts. Others are frightened to sleep because of what they may dream.

Many of these difficulties can be solved simply and quickly by the prescription of sleeping tablets. These are cheap, effective and (in the prescribed dosage) safe. Since it is 'healthy' to sleep, it may appear legitimate to ask for them to promote health. The patient nearly always assures his doctor that he 'wants them only for a night or two' and that he 'doesn't want to get used to them'. But, in the United Kingdom alone, the number of people who have 'got used to them' runs into millions. The sleeping tablet habit presents a serious problem of drug misuse, and it has been created largely by the medical profession.

Like alcohol, sleeping tablets are bad partners in psychotherapy. They emphasise the patient's dependence and gratify his hope that difficulties will be solved quite passively, the only effort required of him being the ability to swallow. Sleeping tablets inhibit dreaming, so that dreams, described by Freud as the 'Royal road to the unconscious', are impeded. A marked increase in dreaming is regularly reported when hypnotics are withdrawn. Finally, the subjective ability to sleep *soundly* is a good index of psychological health. How can the therapist assess the wellbeing of a patient who is taking hypnotics?

Two questions regarding the use of sleeping tablets will be dealt with here. The first is, are there ever circumstances in which the prescription of hypnotics is justified; the second, how may they be withdrawn from people who are dependent on them?

Obviously, it is a kindness to prescribe hypnotics for patients who are suffering from serious *physical* illnesses. However, it should be borne in mind that some hypnotics *accentuate* sensitivity to pain. In painful conditions, the prescription of an analgesic may be more effective. In psychiatric illnesses, the use of hypnotics is justified only in *acute* conditions accompanied by marked emotional perturbation, such as that seen in agitated depression and in severe acute reactions to stress. Hypnotics should never be prescribed solely in order to assure the doctor of an undisturbed sleep! A doctor who prescribes sleeping tablets, should make it his personal responsibility to withdraw them as quickly as possible. He should not leave the task to another.

Treatment of established hypnotic dependence is usually easy provided that the patient is willing to follow one or two simple instructions. Although at first he is likely to experience one or two uncomfortable nights, he may be assured that he will, within a week or ten days of withdrawal, be sleeping as well *without* a hypnotic as he was when he was taking one. He may notice that the *frequency* of dreaming is increased, although the dreams will not necessarily be unpleasant. Within three or four weeks, he will be sleeping *better* without hypnotics than he was whilst he was taking them. If the patient has been taking sleeping tablets for many years, the first night or two following withdrawal may *feel* extremely sleepless, and will be experienced as correspondingly disagreeable. It is, therefore, wise to undertake withdrawal at the beginning of a stress-free period. A long weekend is very suitable for the purpose.

The patient should limit his 'sleeping time' to any selected eight hours of the day (for example, from midnight to 8.00 a.m.). If his habitual bedtime dose has been up to three sleeping tablets, it may be stopped immediately. If the dose has been higher, it should first be halved. In this case, the process will take longer.

Before going to bed, the patient should provide himself with an alarm clock set to ring at the end of the 'sleeping time'; a bedside lamp; suitable reading material — *Basic Psychotherapy* is ideal; a transistor radio with an earpiece; a thermos flask containing a hot drink; a hot water bottle or an electric blanket; and a convenient means of emptying the bladder.

Many people find it helpful to take a milky drink before settling down — hot or cold, according to taste, but not tea or coffee! When the 'sleeping time' comes, the patient should turn out the light and wait to see what happens. He should not try to *make* himself go to sleep. If (as is usual)he finds himself wide awake, he should, after a few minutes, switch on the light and read or listen to the radio. When he is ready to settle down again, he should take another drink and empty his bladder. He should always ensure that he feels warm. Patients sometimes ask if they may keep a sleeping tablet at the bedside, to be taken if they have not fallen asleep by a certain hour. Since the object of the exercise is to stop sleeping tablets, the answer is 'No'.

The patient usually finds that he is dozing off, just as the alarm clock rings for the end of 'sleeping time', and he is tempted to turn over for another half hour. But sleeping time should be limited to the selected hours and he should not have another half hour in bed! Quite frequently, he feels sleepy after lunch, and contemplates the possibility of having forty winks. He should not have forty winks. He is creating a 'physiological' sleeping tablet, which must be preserved for the selected sleeping hours.

This simple routine usually works very well. In the early stages of psychotherapy, a patient's willingness to follow it may be a useful measure of his motivation.

Change

During psychotherapy, there are occasions when the patient suddenly realises that all his problems will be solved if he divorces his wife, marries his mistress, sells his house, becomes a vegetarian and emigrates to Bolivia.

It is rare for problems to be solved by impulsive decisions of this sort. Patients should be advised to make no major changes in their way of life during therapy. Those who ignore this advice usually regret it, and may find themselves without a wife, a home, a job, or even an English speaking tax inspector.

Case discussions

Many organisations hold regular case discussions. These should be regarded as an *essential* part of therapy. It is the therapist's *duty* to his patients to attend them regularly, and to take an active part. He should not regard such meetings as an idle distraction from the real work of therapy, to be attended only if time allows.

The ideal discussion group has about eight members, all of roughly the same level of sophistication. Sometimes it has a more experienced leader. The meetings are held regularly, preferably every week, for about 90 minutes. Its members should give the meetings priority. Each takes it in turn, not necessarily in strict rotation, to talk about a case with which he is dealing. The case need not be one which has posed any particular difficulty. It is often most valuable when presented extemporaneously, without notes or previous preparation. The members of the group discuss the case, the roles of the participants and particularly the involvement of the therapist. They will often help him to examine his counter-transference.

Such a group, meeting regularly, can be of great benefit to its members who may become very adept at picking up their various blind spots. Consequently, the effectiveness of their work is greatly increased.

Is it worth it?

In every therapist's life, there are times when everything seems to go wrong. His patients get worse instead of better, and lose no opportunity of telling him so. His colleagues complain about his incompetence, simultaneously sending him more patients. His car develops an expensive rattle, and his wife threatens to leave if he wants her to stand by him; or to stand by him if he wants her to leave. Finally, to crown everything, an eminent authority publishes yet another paper demonstrating that psychotherapy is a waste of time.

The eminent authority usually compares two groups of patients. He demonstrates that, after a year or two, those who have had psychotherapy are no better than those who have not, and that in the end, it makes no difference. He infers that psychotherapy is a waste of time, of money and of energy and that those who practise it are at best well-meaning simpletons, and at worst charlatans.

We have already emphasised that psychotherapy is an arduous and time-consuming procedure, and criticisms such as these must be considered very carefully. If it is really a waste of time and effort, the practice of psychotherapy should certainly be abandoned. However, the reader will appreciate that the question is far from being settled.

The first point to be made is this. In medicine, the physician is concerned as much with the means to an end, as he is with the end itself. Most people would make a complete recovery from pneumonia, without treatment. Antibiotics are not withheld because of this. Fractures could be reduced without anaesthesia. Most patients suffering from agitated depression will recover spontaneously, without the use of E.C.T. or antidepressant drugs. But it would be unnecessarily cruel to withhold such things. The aim of medical treatment is to speed the process of recovery, to minimise discomfort whilst spontaneous recovery takes place, and to make life endurable when no cure is possible. If psychotherapy can serve any of these purposes, its value is assured.

Unfortunately, it is not easy to make valid comparisons. How *can* one compare the discomfort endured by patients who are suffering from similar *physical* illnesses? Attempts at comparison have very little meaning. The distress of many physical illnesses is certainly alleviated by such *psychological* measures as compassion, concern and tenderness. Many forms of psychiatric illness can also be helped by these methods.

The crucial problem is that of measurement. A few psychological variables (for example, the I.Q.) can be expressed numerically, but even then, comparison does not mean very much. Apart from the fact that one man is brighter than the other, little useful information can be inferred from the statement that two men have I.Q.s of 75 and 150 respectively. When personality is measured, numerous factors must be taken into account. Ingenious attempts are constantly being devised to differentiate, isolate and measure them, but there are many technical problems and it appears that many years must pass before they are perfected.

However the 'Is psychotherapy of any value?' controversy still excites attention from time to time. Insofar as it encourages research into the measurement and comparison of personality, it is of considerable importance. One day, there may be a satisfactory answer.

Until that day arrives, most practising physicians will consider that the only worthwhile guide is what the patient says and what he does. He seeks help and usually he perseveres with it. No-one can say how he would have been if he had not done so. For whatever reason, he usually feels better off with help than without it. Objectively, and at the end of the day he might have been equally well off without help. No-one behaves as though they seriously think that this is true.

8

Patients with difficult problems

CARDINAL PRINCIPLE: 'Tell me about it'.

Problems of delicacy and intimacy

The management of sexual difficulties

There are certain problems which seem to cause almost as much anxiety to the therapist as they do to the patient. This may be the case when a patient complains of a sexual difficulty.

The reaction of the doctor sometimes borders on panic. He scribbles a hurried referral letter and pushes the patient out of the room as quickly as possible, burbling, 'I am not trained to deal with such things. You must see a psychiatrist.' Let us consider the consequences of such behaviour.

What must it be like for someone who is worried about his sexual function? His problem is a very personal one: something of great delicacy, involving things about which he may be deeply ashamed. Some people would try to reassure him by saying that he has no reason to be ashamed, because there are lots of people in the world with similar difficulties. Nevertheless, he *is* ashamed. He is often frightened, anxious and embarrassed. He will wonder where he can turn for help and advice. Naturally, he will choose his confidante with great care. It is likely to be someone whom he knows slightly, someone whom he respects, someone in whom he feels able to repose some trust. In the whole world, there may be only one person in whom he feels able to confide. So he seeks out that one person. Often, it is his own doctor.

Unfortunately, doctors do not know everything. Their training does not cover all aspects of living. What is more, there are some things which interest them and some which do not. There are some matters with which they can deal competently and confidently, and others about which they feel ignorant and inadequate.

Many doctors feel that they are 'not trained' to advise their patients about sexual problems. Often they too are embarrassed by them. Consequently, when a patient confesses that he has such a problem, the doctor's first thought may be to refer the patient to someone else, as quickly as possible.

The 'someone else' is often a psychiatrist. There is no particular reason why this should be so. Psychiatrists are rarely better 'trained' to deal with sexual difficulties than their colleagues. However, they may have learned to be a little less shy when asking questions about sexual matters.

Meanwhile, what of the patient? Often he is in a turmoil of anxiety. After weeks, months or sometimes years of worrying, he finally decides to seek help. What should he say? What words should he use? What will he be asked? Will the doctor laugh at him, or scold him, or be angry with him? Will he be able to do what he is told to do? For several days before the dreaded interview, he may be so anxious that he is unable to sleep. Eventually, the moment arrives and, frightened and embarrassed, he tells his tale.

Until it happens to them, doctors seldom give thought to what it is like to be a patient. They forget the doubt, the anxiety, the apprehension and the private rehearsals which precede a consultation. It is rare for them to appreciate the extent of their impact on their patients. So how will the patient feel when the doctor, whom he has chosen with such care, tells him, 'You must see a psychiatrist'?

The patient is unlikely to know much about psychiatrists. He will have some vague ideas about them derived from television and the newspapers. They seem to be rather strange people, perhaps themselves a little mad. Sometimes they appear to be little better than the people they claim to treat. Unless the courts are vigilant, they may help criminals to escape punishment for terrible crimes, by saying that they are ill. They have extraordinary theories about little boys being in love with their mothers. They are not quite respectable.

So, when the doctor tells the patient 'You must see a psychiatrist', often he *does not go*. To make things worse, he then fears to speak to anyone else about the problem, lest he should be given similar advice. As a result, the difficulty may remain a private and permanent anxiety which affects the whole of his life, sometimes changing him into a chronic neurotic semi-invalid.

We therefore consider that the guiding principle in the management of sexual difficulties is this: in the first instance, *the person to whom a sexual problem is confided should be the person who tries to deal with it*. He should *not* refer the patient to someone else. He should sit very tight and say, 'Tell me about it.' Then he should listen to the reply as carefully as he can. However alarmed, unsure or confused he may feel, he should listen and try to understand. He need not worry about making suggestions or giving advice. At the end of the session, he should say that he and the patient require time to consider what has been said. Then he should ask the patient to return.

As happens so often, the rather surprising consequence is often that verbalising the problem leads a considerable way along the road towards its resolution. When the patient returns, he will often say that things seem to be a little easier. Almost certainly he will have had further thoughts, memories and observations to add to what he has already said. Three or four sessions of this sort may be sufficient to resolve the problem. When this is so, the doctor may feel that he deserves very little of the credit. It is certainly true that much of the credit for successful psychotherapy belongs to the patient. But the doctor may be assured that by offering his sympathetic attention, he has made a significant contribution to the satisfactory outcome.

Of course, sexual problems are not resolved so easily every time. After a few sessions, the doctor may form the view that a specialist opinion is required. The specialist to whom he turns may be a psychiatrist. But by this time, the patient is accustomed to talking about his problem. It is no longer a shameful solitary burden. He has shared it with his doctor, and he knows that his doctor has tried hard. Now, he is often much more willing to accept the proposal that a psychiatric opinion be sought, although his attitude towards psychiatrists may not have changed.

It is always helpful for the psychiatrist to know that the doctor has proceeded in this way. To tell the truth, if the 'simple' procedure has not been successful in bringing about the required change, it is unlikely that a psychiatrist will have greater success. He often represents a final Court of Appeal, whose task is to say that the situation cannot be changed. The doctor who made the referral may then wish to help the patient come to terms with this unwelcome fact.

Sexual difficulties arise principally from disorders of either the *direction* or the *strength* of the sexual drive. Normally, the sexual drive is directed towards an adult of the opposite sex. Instead, it may be directed towards the self (masturbation); to an adult of the same sex (homosexuality); towards something associated with the opposite sex such as clothing (fetishism); towards a non-genital part of the body such as the hair; or, rarely, towards children, animals or things. Well adjusted heterosexual adults may show traces of these deviations.

Masturbation is so common, especially in young people, that it should be regarded as normal. It is also fairly common in older people who have no sexual partner. There are some doctors who would regard someone who has never masturbated as abnormal. Masturbation has no damaging consequences, but many people are ashamed of having practised it, and the consequent anxiety may lead to problems. These difficulties usually disappear quickly when the patient realises that his therapist is not alarmed.

Homosexuality is much more frequent than is commonly supposed. Four per cent of the males interviewed in Kinsey's classic survey were exclusively homosexual, whilst 37 per cent had had some sort of homosexual experience in their life, usually in youth. Homosexuality must therefore be regarded as a variant of normal sexuality. Most normal heterosexuals will show slight traces of homosexual interest and most homosexuals show traces of heterosexuality. The relative proportions of the homosexual and heterosexual components of an individual varies. Most people are predominantly heterosexual: a few are predominantly homosexual. Some people have homo- and hetero-sexual drives in approximately equal proportions. They may marry, have children, and continue a homosexual relationship.

Awareness that his drive is homosexual usually dawns only slowly, and the individual has ample time to adjust to it. It need cause few problems in itself, and in most Western countries, there are no legal sanctions. Most homosexuals are content to accept their orientation and to gratify it discreetly.

People who are heterosexual must understand that homosexuals may fall in love just as deeply as they, and feel just as deeply the anguish of rejection. The person who is exclusively homosexual feels just as much revulsion for heterosexual activities, as does the heterosexual for homosexual ones. Homosexuals have no more wish to be changed into heterosexuals than heterosexuals have to be changed into homosexuals. In the few cases where such change has occurred, it would be presumptuous of the therapist to claim the 'credit'. It was probably to happen anyway.

The limits of psychotherapy in homosexuality were described with characteristic kindness by Freud, in his reply (written in English) to a letter from the despairing mother of a homosexual son. He wrote:

9th April, 1935

Dear Mrs...

I gather from your letter that your son is a homosexual. I am most impressed by the fact that you do not mention this term yourself in your information about him. May I question you, why you avoid it? Homosexuality is assuredly no advantage, but it is nothing to be ashamed of, no vice, no degradation, it cannot be classified as an illness; we consider it to be a variation of the sexual function produced by a certain arrest of sexual development. Many highly respectable individuals of ancient and modern times have been homosexuals, several of the greatest among them (Plato, Michelangelo, Leornardo da Vinci, etc.). It is a great injustice to persecute homosexuality as a crime, and cruelty too. If you do not believe me, read the books of Havelock Ellis.

By asking me if I can help, you mean, I suppose, if I can abolish homosexuality and make normal heterosexuality take its place. The answer is, in a general way, we cannot promise to achieve it. In a certain number of cases, we succeed in developing the blighted germs of heterosexual tendencies which are present in every homosexual; in the majority of cases it is no more possible. It is a question of the quality and the age of the individual. The result of treatment cannot be predicted.

What analysis can do for your son runs in a different line. If he is unhappy, neurotic, torn by conflicts, inhibited in his social life, analysis can bring him harmony, peace of mind, full efficiency, whether he remains a homosexual or gets changed. If you make up your mind, he should have analysis with me!! I don't expect you will!! He has to come over to Vienna. I have no intention of leaving here. However, don't neglect to give me your answer.

Sincerely yours with kind wishes,

Freud.

P.S. I did not find it difficult to read your handwriting. Hope you will not find my writing and my English a harder task.

Homosexuality may be a source of distress to parents when they learn of it in their children, and of great sadness to spouses when they learn about it in their partner. When the discovery is made, a total reorientation of attitude may be required. Relatives sometimes ask for 'treatment' of the homosexuality of their loved one, seeing his 'perversion' as evidence of 'disease'.

But it is they who need help. Their reaction often follows a pattern similar to that which is regularly seen in mourning (q.v.). First, there is denial. It cannot possibly be true — hence the conclusion that homosexuality is some sort of disease. Second, distress at the realisation that it *is* true. Finally comes the stage of restitution ('... after all, many of the world's greatest men were homosexuals ...').

One of the principal problems of homosexual relationships is that although they may appear to be firmly founded, they do not always have the inherent stability of heterosexual ones. They lack the (sometimes questionable) security of marriage vows, and the stabilising influence brought about by the birth of children. Further, they lack support and encouragement from the community, which, on the contrary, exerts pressure towards the break-up of such relationships. If an association should end, the homosexual may find it more difficult to establish a new relationship than a heterosexual.

Consequently, homosexual relationships are innately less secure than heterosexual ones, although one does not need to doubt that the desire for stability is sincere. Homosexuals have as much need for support and reassurance as their heterosexual brethren. They love as deeply as their fellows. In those sad cases when the relationship becomes precarious, or shows signs of disintegration, one or other partner may be driven to despair.

Disorders of the *strength* of sexual drive are frequent in neurotic disorders, the most common being a reduction in the strength of sexual drive. This is called impotence in men and frigidity in women. Naturally, both partners are affected — an obvious example of the maxim that problems always arise between people. There may be little to be gained in treating one partner without the other, and the joint interview becomes of great importance. Even after many years of marriage, a couple may have difficulty in talking to each other about intimate matters. The therapist's first task is to help them overcome this difficulty. The new-found ability to communicate will often continue outside the consulting room.

A certain mystique, associated with the names of Masters and Johnson, has emerged in the management of sexual disorders. Basically, Masters and Johnson try to facilitate *communication* between people who are experiencing sexual difficulties. In the course of this, the gently erotic practice of mutual exploration is encouraged. Much attention has been given to their ingenious suggestion that full intercourse should be proscribed in the early stages of therapy. This advice minimises anxiety and avoids the risks of failure. If intercourse is feasible and the need urgent, no 'therapeutic' proscription is likely to be heeded.

Powerful emotions such as anxiety, depression, fear and anger may impair sexual relationships which were previously satisfactory.

When such emotions exist, they must be examined, expressed and dissipated before progress can be made.

The *attitude* towards sexual intercourse often differs between the sexes. For the male, it is often an end in itself, whereas for the female it may be a means to the end of pregnancy. If *conception* should be the woman's sole object, it will not be surprising that she should become frigid when contraceptive measures are used. Most women can obtain full sexual satisfaction only from men whom they truly love: the opposite is not always true, and many men can have a good *sexual* relationship with women whom they dislike, despise or even hate.

The need of both partners to please the other is important for each. A woman will often feel that the pleasure which she is able to give to her partner compensates for her own frigidity: the man may feel that his own pleasure is diminished if he is unable to bring his partner to a climax.

The therapist should help the couple to discuss all of these matters, and everything else which is important to them. The object of therapy is to encourage freedom of mutual expression without prompting or interruption. The therapist should be on the alert for attempts to evade or minimise subjects which are difficult, embarrassing or painful. Everything must be discussed openly.

It must be conceded that sexual problems cannot always be overcome. When this is so, the therapist must discuss the choices which are open to the couple. Amongst these is the possibility of separation. The therapist need not feel obliged to try to restore a marriage which is damaged beyond repair. In such cases, the couple may need help in order to separate. But there is more to marriage than sexual intercourse, and the existence of an insoluble sexual problem does not mean that the marriage cannot continue. On the contrary, when such a fact is faced frankly, many couples decide to remain together.

Problems of control and indulgence

Alcoholism

There are three certain ways of insulting a man: by doubting his sense of humour; by criticising his driving; or by implying that he has a problem with drink. Of these, the latter is usually the worst. The label 'alcoholism' suggests a drunken, bleary-eyed sot; maudlin, dishevelled, irresponsible, selfish, neglecting his obligations: a picture of pathetic contempt. Although such a picture is seen sometimes, it is by no means typical. Many alcoholics are hard working, responsible people, who are very concerned about their dependence.

It is in alcoholism that the mechanism known as *denial* operates at its most insistent. The reader is reminded that denial operates at an unconscious level, and is able, in the face of all the evidence, to say that something really and truly is not so. It is not mere refusal to face facts. The facts are rejected, scattered and defeated. All conclusions drawn from them are completely routed.

Thus, for many reasons — shame, fear, dread of the consequences, pre-existing low self-esteem — the alcoholic often continues to insist that there is no problem, however obvious it is to other people. Doctors often fail to appreciate the significance of denial, continuing a fruitless frontal assault, readily sidetracked into perpetual and interminable arguments about definition, quantity, type and frequency. Repeatedly defeated, they ultimately lose their temper, curse the incompetence of psychiatry and decide to wash their hands of the whole thing.

As for patients, some go to their death denying their alcoholism. The real constructive work of treatment and recovery can proceed only when denial is overcome.

Alcoholics who are concerned about their state often have a poor opinion of themselves, and feel that the drunken stereotype is too good. Their low self-esteem usually precedes their drinking, and the development of alcoholism reinforces it. They feel that they are unworthy of the concern of anyone: and that they can turn only to those whose plight is similar to their own. This may be the origin of the frequent but inaccurate assertion that only alcoholics can help alcoholics.

However, not every alcoholic who acknowledges the diagnosis is concerned about it. Those who are unconcerned are unlikely to change their ways. They cannot be persuaded to stop drinking. 'After all', they argue, 'it's a free country and I enjoy it.' Such people as these see no reason why they should not beg, borrow or steal in order to maintain their supplies. They assert that they are 'entitled' to live on Social Security because they have 'paid in for it'. They are not prepared to take any responsibility for themselves or their families. Some are content to play the role of the jovial drunk, and fail to appreciate that the joke can become extremely tedious. They are self-centred and irresponsible and are usually impossible therapeutic prospects. Their conscience is feeble and they have no motivation to change their way of life. It is they who represent the popular stereotype of the alcoholics: in fact, they are the minority.

Many alcoholics care very much indeed. They are hard working and responsible — sometimes too hard working and too responsible. They set targets for themselves which they cannot possibly maintain.

They use alcohol to dull their nagging consciences and thus find themselves even less effective. The burden of guilt increases, and a vicious spiral is created. Such people may be able to find nothing of merit in themselves whatsoever. They become more and more aware of their dependence upon alcohol, and depend more and more upon alcohol to free themselves of the awareness. As they contemplate their progressive deterioration, they feel helpless, hopeless, feckless. They are worthless drunks. If they had venereal disease, it would at least be the consequence of an excess of daring-do. But they are merely alcoholics.

Excessive drinking is common in neurotic patients, and the therapist sometimes finds that a problem has existed long before he became aware of it. Sometimes it is acknowledged only after many months of therapy. The patient now has an additional problem: how to confess his 'indulgence' to his therapist — how to admit that he has added the misuse of alcohol to his other difficulties. The problem may be increased because by now, the therapist has become a very important figure in his life. He wonders what his reaction will be. Tentatively, he may test his therapist's response, perhaps by making a little joke about drunks, but always watching carefully. Such a trap constitutes a reminder that there are no jokes in psychotherapy. Everything must be examined for its latent meaning. For if the therapist laughs heartily, how will his patient be able to tell him...?

When a patient confesses that 'I think I may have been drinking a little too much', the therapist should, as always, endeavour to conceal his surprise, responding instead with an unstartled, 'Tell me about it'. He must not condemn, reassure, advise or refer to someone else. In particular, he should not be ready with an instant, 'Of course you are *not* an alcoholic'. Such a reply combines reassurance with condemnation, and indicates certainty in the face of ignorance.

We have already stated that drinking and psychotherapy do not go together. Neither do drinking and problem solving. If the patient is using alcohol as a tranquilliser to give him courage to overcome his difficulties, he should stop drinking. If he has become addicted, he *must* stop.

The details of the diagnosis of alcoholism will be found elsewhere: here we will remind the reader that there are four groups of symptoms, each of which is pathognomonic. If one or more is present, the patient is an alcoholic, and most physicians consider that he should stop drinking completely.

The first group of symptoms is characterised by the development of episodes of amnesia for the period in which he is drinking. The patient is not necessarily drunk, and his behaviour may seem normal to those around him. However, when he comes to review the events of the previous evening, he will find that he has little or no memory of them.

Episodes of tremor, often accompanied by a feeling of apprehension, beginning several hours after the last drink was taken, and relieved by another, are also diagnostic. It is common for such tremors to occur upon wakening in the morning. If they continue, they may proceed to the development of delirium tremens (D.T.s). Delirium tremens is the third condition which indicates alcoholism.

The fourth symptom is a diminution of tolerance to alcohol. The patient finds that he can no longer 'hold' his drink as well as he could. He often blames this on to 'getting older'. In fact, it is a common symptom of advanced alcoholism.

There are two major difficulties in psychotherapy with alcoholics. We have mentioned the first. It is the problem of overcoming denial, and helping the patient to accept the diagnosis. The second is to help him maintain total abstinence. Time and patience may be required before denial is overcome. The patient may be invited to undertake a simple diagnostic test: for example, to remain *totally* abstinent for a limited period, such as four weeks. He will often accept this challenge, but he is seldom successful. The test is not an easy one — the reader who thinks otherwise might wish to try it for himself. The patient sometimes claims to have cut down, or to have succeeded, except on one very special occasion. Regrettably, this means that he has failed the test. It is important for the therapist to make this clear, although never in a whirl of triumphant vindication. He should neither adopt a 'holier than thou' attitude, nor say even, 'I feared it might be so'. For the patient, the implications of failure are profound. Is it true that he is an alcoholic? How will he face his friends? Worst of all, if he is using alcohol as a prop, what will happen if he tries to manage without it?

Patients who are worried about their drinking often have underlying neurotic problems. Hitherto, they have 'dissolved them away' in alcohol. Additional problems are created by the misuse of alcohol, so that there is then a double burden to shoulder. The psychotherapist can offer great help in the treatment of alcoholism provided that he will follow the ordinary rules of therapy — remembering especially that the patient is constantly looking for anything which may confirm him in his low self-esteem.

Many patients who are addicted to alcohol find themselves unable to stop drinking unless external controls are imposed. Alcoholism, therefore, is one of the conditions for which in-patient treatment may be necessary. Admission also gives the therapist an opportunity to attend to his patient's physical health, which may be seriously impaired.

Alcoholism is a chronic, insidious disease. Alcoholics are subjected to the same stresses as non-alcoholics. Sometimes they are more susceptible to them. Consequently, when pressure is great, they may turn to that source of relief which is taken for granted by their more fortunate fellows, and they relapse. If this should happen, the therapist need not feel too disappointed or surprised. Relapses should be accepted in the spirit of 'a man who never makes a mistake never makes anything'. They may be useful for both the patient and the therapist. They provide a dramatic illustration of the need for constant vigilance.

It is the opinion of the author that if an alcoholic is to remain well, he must remain completely and permanently abstinent. There can be no deviation from this rule. There are times when it appears to be painfully and unjustly rigid, for example, when a patient pleads, not unreasonably, 'Surely I may have half a glass of champagne to toast my daughter on her wedding day?' However poignant the circumstances, the answer must be an uncompromising 'No. Not even a sip.'

Many patients try to modify this rule. They ask 'Is it all right to take just one glass and no more? I am sure I can control it. If I am wrong, I will not take any more.' The paradox here is immediately obvious. If they are 'wrong', they cannot 'control it'. *Control* is the major problem in alcoholism. Instead of facilitating control, alcohol impairs it. The good intention is thus twice destroyed.

Some readers will have encountered 'controlled drinking programmes' and their patients may ask for permission to experiment. There is no objection to an experiment, provided that it is understood that no conclusions can be drawn until it is completed. From his own observations, the author has concluded that permanent 'controlled drinking' is unattainable, however desirable and attractive it may appear.

Alcoholics with neurotic conflicts are often very suitable candidates for psychotherapy. Neurotic patients go to their doctor as soon as they encounter a difficulty, but the alcoholic tries to do something himself — to 'treat' himself with alcohol. The treatment is inappropriate and ineffective, and ultimately creates more difficulties than it solves, but at least the patient has made an effort to achieve independence. When they have stopped drinking, this valuable streak of independence may be used for more constructive purposes. With sympathetic help, the same determination can be employed to free them both of their problems and their dependence.

Some therapists, out of conscious virtue and unconscious distaste, choose to reject alcoholics as potential patients, either because they *are* alcoholics or sometimes because they have relapsed. This is unfortunate. When reasonable selection criteria are employed, the treatment of alcoholism may be very rewarding.

Problems of disease, death and bereavement

The physically ill

The urgent preoccupation of those who treat people who are physically seems to be to reassure them that there is nothing seriously wrong, and that a cure will be achieved speedily and without undue discomfort. Consequently, many patients are deprived of the opportunity of talking about their real anxieties. These may be quite irrational, and completely unrelated to the condition for which they are being treated. The doctor should always listen carefully to what his patient wishes to say. As so often happens, the mere act of 'saying' it to someone who is willing to listen, and who does not show undue concern or agitation, may go a long way towards alleviating the anxiety. It is of course legitimate to reassure a patient who has a serious physical illness, but the therapist should clarify for himself the nature of the reassurance for which the patient is asking. Whilst it is not necessary to force disagreeable facts down his throat, it is proper to listen to what he asks, and to reply as carefully (and probably as truthfully) as possible.

The dying

Once, the author was asked by a patient who was dying of cancer, whether he was dying of cancer. The author, frightened and uncertain, gave a dishonest reply. The patient died a few days later, knowing that his doctor had lied to him. The author has neither forgotten the experience nor forgiven himself for it.

Patients rarely ask such questions unless they already know the answer. Of all patients, those who are dying are certainly the most in need of sympathetic and unhurried attention from the doctor. He can seldom have 'more important' things to do. When he is asked such a question, the doctor should, if he is not already doing so, sit by the bedside and give a gentle and honest reply. He should then wait for the patient's response. It may be sad and very slow. The patient may cry, shrug his shoulders, or sigh. At an appropriate moment, the doctor should ask whether the patient has any other questions. He should try to answer these honestly. He may make any reasonable promises, but should not offer unsolicited reassurance. He should tell the patient that he will return soon, and that he will be happy to discuss any other matters. He should visit the patient again as soon as he can.

The bereaved

The bereaved are people who mourn for the death of those whom they love. 'Mourning' is the name given to the process by which they become reconciled to their loss. Grief is the emotion which they experience. The process of mourning follows an orderly pattern, in which there are three overlapping stages: denial, acceptance and restitution. It will be convenient to begin by discussing the response to the sudden and unexpected death of someone who is much loved.

When such a death occurs, the immediate reaction of the mourners is one of denial. The word 'denial' is used here in its technical, psychological sense (see p. 75). Sometimes the mourner says, 'There must be a mistake. It cannot be so. I was speaking to him only this morning. It must be someone else.' At other times, he thinks, 'I am asleep, and this is a bad dream. I will waken in the morning and find that it was just a nightmare.' Responses such as these are common. They protect the mourner from the fact of death.

Some bereaved people have no *intellectual* difficulty in accepting the death, but they demonstrate *emotional* denial. The mourner says that he feels stunned, in a daze, unreal, or numb. Sometimes he says that he feels nothing. It does not *feel* as though it has happened. In these cases, the mourner often takes charge of the funeral arrangements in a curiously dispassionate way. He conforts others, registers the death, and so on. The people around him comment with surprise on 'how well he has taken it'. Sometimes he surprises even himself. In fact, he has not 'taken it'. The appropriate emotional response has been denied.

'Denial' was manifested dramatically by Queen Victoria through most of her widowhood. Her consort's room was always kept as he had left it. His clothes were laid out for him each day, as though ready for his return.

Denial gives protection from the painful second stage of mourning, the stage of 'acceptance'. Basically the 'pain' is emotional, but it may take a physical form. When death has been preceded by physical symptoms, the mourner's 'emotional' pain may show itself as a similar physical pain. During acceptance, the mourner may weep. He may cry silently, sob bitterly or sigh heavily. Often he has no wish to live. He does not think of taking his own life, but indicates that in death, he would find a welcome reunion with his loved one.

Acceptance and denial alternate, especially in the early stages of mourning. For a brief moment, the mourner will forget that his loved one is dead, and turn towards his chair to speak to him. Then, abruptly, he remembers his loss. Sometimes, he 'feels' a presence in the room, or he may 'hear' the voice or 'see' the form of the dead person. These experiences, which are presumably the origin of the belief in ghosts, are comforting, not frightening.

The dead person usually continues to 'live' in the dreams of the mourner. These may be happy, vivid 'discoveries' that it was 'all a mistake'. On other occasions, to his distress and dismay, the dreams are not of happy reunions, but are horrible nightmares. The mourner may dream that he is pleased to hear of the death, perhaps that he himself has murdered the loved one, or that he is singing and dancing over the grave. Such dreams often cause great distress. 'Why' pleads the mourner, 'should I dream such a thing? I never felt anything like that in my life.' (The reader should consider the answer to this question, remembering that there is nothing so absurd that it can be dismissed without consideration).

In most cultures, a formal funeral ceremony is held after death, in which relatives and friends gather together. Many know little of the deceased, and the more distant relatives may have few feelings about his death. Old enmities are usually forgotten, and the presence of the mourners gives support — and comfort — to the bereaved, although the platitudes with which they indicate sympathy are often rather trite and meaningless. The *fact* of death is sometimes reinforced by a ritual viewing of the body. At the funeral itself, the coffin is lowered into the ground (symbolically, when cremation has been chosen) and the person conducting the ceremony offers words of inevitability ('Dust to dust, ashes to ashes') of sympathy, and of hope.

The grief of mourning often continues for many months. In the first year, every week brings its anniversary. The friends of the mourner are sometimes baffled and unsure about how best to bring consolation. Such phrases as 'It could have been worse', or 'At least he did not suffer', or 'Now he is at peace' are shown for the empty clichés which they are. Friends are sometimes disturbed to find themselves becoming angry with the mourner. 'Life really must go on, you know', they protest, or 'You must pull yourself together — for the sake of the children, as well as for yourself.' The mourner nods his head, smiles briefly, but continues to be preoccupied. Why did it happen? Might it have been foreseen? Could it have been avoided? He ruminates upon his own behaviour and often finds fault with himself. If only he had paid attention to what seemed to be a trivial incident. If only he had insisted. If only help had been sought sooner . . . Often, the only counter to these arguments is that of improbability, and this is seldom adequate. The mourner blames himself, over and over again. 'If only I had acted differently...' is the recurrent theme of this phase.

Eventually, usually after the first anniversary has passed, the tenor begins to change. Life really must go on. 'He would have wished me to continue in the way he had started...' This final stage is called restitution. The loved one is idealised. One does not speak ill of the dead. His faults are ignored or forgotten, his virtues acclaimed. Slowly, the mourner takes up the reins again — often in a way which he believes would have been wished by the deceased. Sometimes he adopts the mannerisms, the gestures, even the mode of speech of his beloved.

The sequence which has been described applies to sudden death, for which the mourner is unprepared. When death is lingering and painful, the mourner may have had months of preparation. In these circumstances, the process of mourning begins when the mourner *realises that the loved one is going to die*. It is as though death had occurred at that point. A mourning process which has not been completed can sometimes be reinstated by putting the question 'When did you realise that he was going to die?'

The horrified realisation leads first to denial. 'Something can surely be done. Someone must give a second opinion. They have developed a new drug in America. What about a faith healer? Someone, somewhere *must* be able to do something.' Acceptance develops as hope fades, and denial is overwhelmed by the obvious physical deterioration of the dying patient. The relatives become sad and preoccupied. When mourning starts some time before death, acceptance may have been completed when death actually comes. When this is so, restitution can begin immediately. The mourner may truly say, 'It was a blessing. He suffered so much and complained so little.'

Dying patients sometimes need help to mourn their own death. First, there is a long period of denial. The patient is quite unable to understand why he is not getting better. If he should be a doctor or a nurse, this is very puzzling to the onlookers. Then, briefly, and usually quite late in his illness, he passes through a sad stage of acceptance. Finally comes restitution, in which he seems calmly reconciled to the approach of death.

So far, we have been speaking only of death. But other losses must be mourned, and the three stages may be seen in many circumstances. When the loss is a significant one, it follow a similar pattern of denial, acceptance and restitution. A sick person may mourn the loss of an organ such as a limb, a breast, or part of the stomach. Even the loss of a tooth may be mourned. Doctors assume rather too easily that because an organ is internal and invisible, its loss is not of significance. They should understand that the loss of an invisible organ such as the womb, may be of great importance to the patient.

There are other losses to be mourned too: the loss of youth, of vigour, of sexual attractiveness, and of reproductive capacity at the time of menopause. The fact that 'everyone has to face up to such things' is obvious, but it does not make them easier to accept. Loss of employment, of status, of promotion prospects, or the frustration of ambition, may be mourned. There is the loss, through marriage, of one's children. People will mourn the loss of a valued possession: perhaps one which symbolises a relationship. In all of these examples, the one who loses says first, 'It cannot be so'. Then he acknowledges that it is so. Finally he often discovers new comfort from what remains.

A potent source of distress is the death of a household pet, especially a dog. The therapist should be careful not to identify himself with those who say, 'You mustn't upset yourself. After all, he was only a dog.'; or 'Just go out and buy yourself a puppy. You'll soon forget all about him.'

The relationship between man and his dog is one of considerable psychological interest. Man often insists that his dog 'understands everything that I say', or that ' he knows exactly how I feel'. Since the dog cannot speak or complete a questionnaire, it is difficult to dispute this assertion. Dogs often do behave as though they love their masters, however badly they may be treated. This combination of apparent understanding and unwavering constancy makes them very significant objects, especially to those whose life is one of loneliness and lack of love. In such circumstances, grief may be considerable. The patient must be helped through the mourning process in the same way.

The three phases of mourning are seen in psychotherapy as the patient develops insight. For much of his life, he has enjoyed a distorted view of certain aspects of his personality. As treatment progresses, he discovers that he must abandon a favourite view of himself. First, he will deny an interpretation heatedly, and may try to persuade the therapist to alter it. Sometimes he threatens to withdraw from therapy. Acceptance follows slowly. The patient becomes preoccupied; sometimes he is morose and withdrawn. His friends sometimes say 'therapy is not doing you any good...you should give it up'. Finally comes restitution and reorientation: 'Well, if that is how things are, I shall have to do something about it.' As he abandons a cherished but neurotic image of himself, the patient finds a new freedom to adopt a fresh, more constructive attitude to his problems.

Overwhelming problems

Suicide

When someone encounters a very serious problem, and when other solutions seem remote, it is possible that he will think of killing himself. If the relationship with his therapist is satisfactory, a patient will be prepared to discuss such a possibility, and the therapist will not wish to ignore such preoccupations.

One important generalisation about suicide can be made immediately. It is this. At some time or another, nearly everyone has wondered — perhaps only momentarily — whether it is worth while to go on living. Would it not be easier to die? Therapists, and especially counsellors are sometimes reluctant to ask their patients about suicidal thoughts, 'lest it should put the idea into their head'. Indeed some patients will say that they had not considered such a thing 'until you mentioned it'. In fact, it is very difficult to put an idea into someone's mind if it is not already there — or at least, very nearly there. The therapist should never evade such a question, just for this reason. Suicide is one of the many difficult things which therapist and patient must be willing to discuss with complete honesty.

Some therapists prefer to lead gently towards the crucial question. They ask, 'Have you ever felt that you didn't want to go on? Have you ever felt that life isn't worth living? Have you ever thought that you might as well be dead? Have you ever thought of taking your own life, of committing suicide?' The reader will note that leading questions are used. This is because committed answers are required. The therapist should eventually use the word 'suicide'. If he receives an affirmative answer, he should try to discover what the patient's thoughts have been, whether he has formulated any plans, and whether he has taken any steps to implement them.

Sometimes the patient replies to a question about suicide before it has been put. He says, 'I hadn't thought of suicide, if that's what you mean.' If the therapist has not used the word 'suicide', the answer seems to indicate that the patient has thought of it.

When, eventually, the question is put, the patient may respond in several ways. Sometimes he weeps and confesses that he has thought of it. He may pause and say, thoughtfully, 'Well, no...but...' He may become heated, and vehemently reject such an idea. At times, his response is quite unemotional and carries with it a feeling of assurance that indeed the idea had not occurred to him. As always, the therapist must attend carefully to the reply. 'Just talking' minimises the possibility of suicide.

A 'successful' attempt at suicide has a very profound effect on those who are close to the victim — his relatives, his friends, and, of course, his therapist. The latter may be shocked, sad and self-reproachful. Sometimes he is angry. He will wonder how the tragedy could have been avoided, will question his own behaviour and search for where he went wrong. Sometimes he may find himself trying to pass the burden of guilt on to the shoulders of someone else.

People who consider suicide often think carefully about the effect that it will have on other people.* Some are prepared to subject themselves to situations of considerable danger if, by doing so, they think that they can manipulate a desirable outcome. An angry lover may take a considerable overdose of a drug, not really to kill herself, but to bring her partner to heel. Such an attempt at suicide, which is also known as 'para-suicide', has been described as a 'cry for help'. Sometimes it would seem more appropriate to call it a 'scream of rage'. Although death is not necessarily intended, the attempt may go wrong, so that the victim dies 'unintentionally'. An apparently minor attempt at suicide should never be dismissed as being of no importance.

Some people make very serious attempts at suicide. Their argument seems to be, 'If I die, it won't matter. In any case, everyone will be so distressed that they will be forced to *do* something'. This outlook has been compared to the game of Russian Roulette, in which life or death is staked on the spin of the barrel of a revolver.

When the therapist is treating someone who has strong preoccupations with suicide, he may find himself in a dilemma of considerable ethical and emotional proportions. Should he take the gamble that the event will not occur? Should he reassure himself that 'people who talk about it rarely do it'? Sometimes they do, and the maxim — which is still commonly believed — is a reassurance, not a guarantee. Should a counsellor immediately say, 'Then you must see a psychiatrist'? A panicky response such as this is no more appropriate to the confession of suicidal thoughts than it is to the admission of a sexual difficulty (see p. 133).

* 'I'll just die, then you'll be sorry...' (one of Ronald Searle's schoolgirls, crossed in love).

The best response is, 'Tell me about it.' As always, the person to whom suicidal thoughts are admitted should, in the first instance, be the one to handle the case. Of course, this is a matter in which there will be great pressure on him, greater than in any other situation. If he is inexperienced, he will certainly wish to consult with a more experienced colleague. But no-one can predict with certainty what will happen. Sometimes, it will be considered advisable to deprive the patient of his freedom, and to admit him to a psychiatric unit so that he can be observed more carefully. This gives no guarantee that he will not succeed in taking his life. Alternatively, the risk may be taken, and sometimes the gamble is lost.

The final decision is based on an assessment of the probabilities. What is the best thing for the patient? If he is admitted to hospital, his therapist may be compelled to pass the case on to someone else and much of his own work will be wasted. The patient may look upon such a decision as a serious breach of faith on the part of his therapist. Alternatively, the therapist may decide to ride out the storm, and lose his patient.

Suicide is not common when patients have a close and continuing relationship with their therapist. It is much more common in the absence of such a relationship. It is always a source of anxiety and uncertainty for the therapist, which can never be completely eradicated.

9

Problems with difficult patients

CARDINAL PRINCIPLE: Don't judge a chapter by its cardinal principle.

The phrase 'difficult patient' is often an evasive euphemism for a 'troublesome patient'. Although he may be suffering from a 'real' illness (whatever the other sort may be) he does not behave in a manner which might be expected of an Englishman and a gentleman. He may in fact be neither, but this is not the point. He does not *behave* like one. He muddles his appointments, insults the nursing staff, threatens the receptionist and insists on seeing the head doctor. He is continually telephoning about something or another, writes long and indecipherable letters, fusses about innocent investigations and makes a general nuisance of himself. He does not seem to appreciate that investigations take time; that emergencies must be dealt with first; that he is not the only person who is sick; and that doctors cannot perform miracles. As a punishment, he is sometimes referred to a psychiatrist, but psychiatrists are often worse at handling troublesome patients than other specialists, and the referral merely adds to everyone's sense of grievance.

It is not easy to understand the behaviour of such people, but little can be done unless an attempt is made to do so. Let us therefore begin by considering the chronology of their illness. It begins with a symptom. The patient does not know what it signifies and hopes that it will go away. Sometimes it does, and all is well. Otherwise, he may experiment, perhaps with a patent remedy, recommended by friends or relatives. However, if the symptoms persist for more than a week or two, he visits his doctor. The doctor listens to the story, sometimes makes a cursory examination, and writes a prescription. He is told to return if he is not better in a week. The medicine sometimes cures him, and the doctor receives credit due to a very clever man. But sometimes, the symptoms continue. The patient returns and is often given a change of treatment. If this does not work either, the doctor may decide to refer the patient for a specialist opinion.

Several weeks have now passed, there has been no change in the symptoms, and it is becoming increasingly clear that the doctor does not know what is causing them. The prospect of a specialist consultation is always alarming, and a week or more may elapse before an appointment can be obtained. When the time comes, the patient tells his story yet again; the specialist listens and says, 'We will have to make some investigations. Come back again next week. We should have some results then.'

Thus a few more weeks pass by, and the symptoms continue. The patient can scarcely be blamed for becoming increasingly alarmed. Eventually a time comes when he can stand the uncertainty no longer. '*I want something done, now*', he explodes. From that moment, he may be labelled as a difficult patient.

Yet it must be very difficult to tolerate disagreeable, unexplained and possibly sinister symptoms for several weeks, without becoming frightened. Even the most sanguine would find his patience strained. When, as is often the case, the patient is not psychologically robust, the tension sometimes becomes unendurable. *The difficult patient is a frightened patient.* He will not be made less so by 'punishment', whether it is the obvious one of making him wait a little longer, or the more subtle one of referring him to a psychiatrist. Such reponses are likely to make him worse, not better.

How then should he be handled? Surely he should not be allowed to 'jump the queue'? Wouldn't that make him worse? Paradoxically, instead of making him worse, such a step sometimes makes him better. There is something to be said for seeing troublesome patients sooner, rather than later. In doing so, the staff demonstrates its concern for the patient's symptoms and its wish to help him. The patient's anxiety is eased more rapidly, to the benefit of the hospital staff as well as to himself. And when, as is often the case, there was nothing to be anxious about anyway, the patient may be less frightened at a future occasion.

Doctors should never refuse a patient's request simply *because of the way in which he makes it*. His reasons may be wrong, but there may be an ultimate logic in what he asks. A very immature woman completely failed to mother her first two children by retreating into neurotic illness for months on end. She then *demanded* of her gynaecologist that he should sterilise her. She described her gynaecological history in terms of florid exaggeration ('...the flying squad had to pump gallons of blood into me — literally! There were seven doctors there, and they *all* said they had never seen such a *terrible* miscarriage. I cannot *possibly* go through it all again...'). The insistent, importunate quality of the patient's presentation so antagonised the gynaecologist that at first he decided *not* to sterilise her. Then he realised that her attitude towards further pregnancies was the precise reason for performing the operation. Perhaps she knew instinctively something that was not immediately apparent to others – that she was unable to cope with motherhood. Unfortunately, she made her request in the form of a self-centred, neurotic, *demand* of a difficult patient. Careful consideration was given, and it was decided to perform the operation. Subsequently, she became much more calm and contented — never the most stable of women, but much less troublesome than before.

Patients with imaginary symptoms

Can there be any such thing as an imaginary symptom? Someone who says 'I think she is just imagining it' is usually voicing anger and frustration with the patient. Needless to say, such comments often make her worse.

Pain is a subject of great psychological and philosophical interest, and it is one of the main *raisons d'êtres* for the medical profession. *What* is it? Where is it *really* experienced? How can it be measured? How can it be described? How can someone compare his experience with being stabbed with red hot needles when he has never been stabbed with red hot needles? Does the dentist, who had toothache yesterday, share the immediate experience of his patient, who has toothache today? Why is gall-bladder pain felt in the shoulder? Why does the amputee suffer severe pain in a toe which is no longer there? How does 'real' pain differ from 'neurotic' pain? When is a pain not a pain?

There is a kind of answer to some of these questions. However, there may never be a way of measuring the *subjective* experience of pain, or of comparing it with other types of pain. The headache due to a cerebral tumour may be very severe and persistent: so also may be that due to migraine. A surgeon who develops a tension headache after he has completed a long and difficult operation will have no doubt of the reality of his experience. It will not be alleviated if someone ascribes it to 'anxiety following partial gratification of unconscious aggressive drives'. He is in pain, and there is no more to be said.

The fact that a doctor is unable to find an organic cause for a symptom does not cause it to disappear. After making an exhaustive physical examination, doctors will sometimes say, 'I reassured the patient'. It is not clear what this phrase means. If the symptom should continue, the only matter on which the patient can be assured is that the doctor does not know what is causing it.

The matter is sometimes complicated because, when a potentially sinister group of symptoms is presented, and routine investigations are negative, the patient may be subjected to an exploratory operation. Laymen assume that operations are concerned with getting rid of diseased organs, and their surgeons rarely disillusion them. When an exploratory operation is negative, some meaningless evasion is often presented as the 'diagnosis'. If the symptoms continue, the doctors who are asked to treat them, are expected to support the meaningless diagnosis. In this way, they are entangled in the patient's logically sound but factually incorrect assertion that 'they wouldn't have done an operation if it wasn't necessary, would they?'

A common but unwise aphorism in medicine is that organic disease must be excluded first. It is unwise because it assumes that all physical illnesses are more serious than all psychological ones. Nearly every day, patients die by their own hand whilst time is wasted in the investigation of the physical symptoms of their obvious depressive illness. Many early schizophrenics are allowed to deteriorate whilst months are spent in undertaking elaborate but irrelevant biochemical investigations. It is unwise because it assumes that the exclusion of organic disease is always possible. Many therapists are familiar with 'organic' cases in which organic disease 'has been excluded'. The organic signs usually develop after the case has been referred to them. Regrettably, this may happen after the therapist has already embarked upon 'treatment'.

Three important consequences follow when one is dealing with 'imaginary' symptoms. The first is that a diagnosis of neurotic disorder should be made only for positive reasons. The 'exclusion of organic disease' is *not* a positive reason. The second is that the therapist should always make himself personally responsible for confirming the absence of organic disease. He should perform a careful physical examination before he embarks upon treatment. Symptoms often precede physical signs by many months, and the therapist sometimes discovers an organic disease which has been 'missed' by his medical colleagues. (He need not expect them to receive his discovery with enthusiasm. It is more likely that he will be rewarded with a gloomy assertion that 'she was all right when I examined her', and a veiled hint that the signs are due to psychiatric meddling.) He may, in these circumstances, encounter the disagreeable but not uncommon experience of being 'blamed' for 'missing' the patient's illness and for her being labelled a 'psychiatric' patient. This is due to displacement of the guilt and anger of the relatives. Finally, it is never wise to make a diagnosis of a *primary neurotic* disorder in an individual who has passed the age of 35, and who has *never* before shown any evidence of instability.

The bad tempered

People are occasionally referred for psychotherapy because they have a bad temper. The referral sometimes angers them but they usually keep the appointment.

Individual traits of personality, such as warmth or coldness, placidity or volatility, even temperedness or bad temperedness, are usually fixed. Like hair colour, height and bodily configuration, they cannot be changed. The therapist is therefore compelled to tell the bad tempered patient that the only advice he can offer is to try to control his temper. This advice is rarely accepted with good humour.

It should be understood that 'bad temper' *per se* is not an illness, is not modified by drugs, and is rarely a matter of psychiatric interest.

The unwanted

Some people are simply unwanted. They have no friends and although they may try hard, they seem to have an easy capacity for alienating people. They are obviously lonely and sometimes turn to alcohol for consolation. As a result, they are even less wanted. They form a poignant group. Sometimes they commit suicide, and everyone is very sorry about it. Doctors do not want them, and often refer them for psychotherapy, sometimes with a letter requesting 'help with this distressing case'. (This well-worn phrase is very familiar to psychiatrists, and is often used by those who combine the minimum of compassion with the maximum of rejection). Unfortunately, they are not wanted by psychotherapists either, but they may be directed towards self-help groups. Church organisations carry a substantial number of people such as these, but may find it difficult to conceal their distaste.

Some unwanted people are middle-aged or older women, unmarried, widowed or divorced. Men seem to be able to find one of the women to take care of them. The rest have to manage as well as they can. They often do so with great fortitude.

The impossible

Impossible patients are impossible. There is no psychological technique which will make them otherwise. Much time may have been wasted before they are distinguished from the merely difficult. The therapist may eventually be faced with the fact that the patient on whom he has spent so much time and trouble is impossible, and that all his therapeutic good intentions have been wasted.

When someone finds that their patient is impossible, nearly everyone else will find him impossible too. There is no group of specialists, such as psychiatrists, who relish the prospect of coping with impossible patients or who find them of particular professional interest. The counsellor who accepts an impossible client will consequently find it very difficult to persuade someone else to take him over, if he can no longer cope.

Such people may be rejected for *intensive* counselling without difficulty, but it may be less easy to deny them supportive counselling. Some organisations give their clients a prescriptive 'right' to attention. These include some Government departments – the Department of Health and Social Security is an example – and outright rejection is not possible. A few, very charitable organisations (for example, certain evangelical Christian ones) believe that no-one is impossible. They will always be willing to offer some sort of supportive counselling to those who ask for their help.

Naturally, impossible people frequently plead for help, and their pleas may have great poignancy. They may be depressed, suicidal, hopeless, homeless and helpless. Their lives are in a mess. It is rare for them to have a job. They have often been deserted by their families. They move in and out of prison and may show a marked tendency to alcoholism. Women may indulge in prostitution. They often express the wish to reform, and their plea carries more than a semblance of sincerity. They repeatedly ask for 'just one chance'; for help to start afresh. Often it seems churlish and unkind to speak of them as impossible. Occasionally they become unexpectedly tractable, and eagerly agree to any new way of life which is proposed. However, it is rare for early promise to be maintained. A lapse occurs, and is confessed with shame and remorse. Forgiveness is begged and readily granted. Then comes a second lapse, then a third and a fourth in rapid succession. How can such incorrigible people be helped?

They cannot; and paradoxically, *if this is accepted*, one or two of them seem to change. It is as though some of them can change only when they are *truly* accepted for what they are, and not regarded as lumps of human clay, to be forced into a mould chosen by someone else.

Most psychotherapists carry a few patients such as these. They can be very wearing, and the beginner is advised not to expend too much energy upon them. He should not agree to counsel more than one or two, for he must stand by those whom he accepts. If he regrets his selection, there may be no-one to extricate him from his difficulty. For him to pass them on to someone else would be unfair to the patient and untrue to himself. He must accept the burden, however much he may subsequently regret his decision.

The double discovery, first that he is accepted for what he is; and second, that no-one is trying to get rid of him, even for such solicitous reasons as 'he knows more about your sort of problem than I', is often a new and quite unbelievable experience for the patient. He may try to test out his therapist. He gets even worse, still more incorrigible. He may try to persuade the therapist to abandon the case. But if the therapist persists in accepting the patient as he is, ignores discouragements, and tries to share his world, he will, very occasionally, provide an impossible patient with an experience which is so unique that it sometimes offers the possibility of a true change. However, the therapist must not *expect* a change. If he does, he will certainly be disappointed. If he is disappointed then he can be sure that his original expectations were too high.

The reader may be very dissatisfied with advice which is as vague as this, totally lacking in any straightforward and practical way of dealing with impossible patients, offering no suggestions which would be at least worth trying. He may feel that what has been written is all very well, but that it does not help him in the management of such patients. Surely, there must be *some* way of making them see what a mess they are making of their lives, of helping them to face up to their responsibilities, of forcing them to behave like adults, of demonstrating the selfishness of their behaviour to them.

Such pleas as these are particularly poignant when, as is so often the case, the patient is young, attractive and intelligent. It is then particularly that the therapist feels that someone should be able to do *something*. Naturally, as the patient grows older, becomes more dissipated, more obviously incorrigible, the pleas tend to be muted. Even then, however, some patients retain the ability to make others feel that they have never had a proper chance: that they have been maligned and misunderstood from the very beginning.

Part of the difficulty arises from the fact that such people, although physically mature and of normal or even of above-normal intelligence, have some *emotional* retardation. Their *behaviour* is like that of young children rather than that of adults. Like children, they are impulsive and self-centred. They give little or no thought to the needs of others. They seem completely unable to plan for the future. They do not seem to learn from their mistakes, and completely fail to appreciate such virtues as responsibility, industry and perseverence. Often, they seem to be seriously lacking in conscience.

Their pleasures are often quite simple, and centred on such mouth activities as smoking and drinking. They can often talk very persuasively. Their emotions may be turbulent — they may be overwhelmed by anxiety or possessed by an indescribable fury, which can lead to unrestrained aggression. They are unable to comprehend what it means to love or to cherish other people, although they usually expect undivided attention for themselves. If they embark upon a sexual relationship, it is often out of pure animal longing. Consequently, they are usually promiscuous, and may be hetero- or homosexual according to the whim of the moment. Needless to say, they take no responsibility for their sexual partner or for any children whom they may father.

It is not easy for a 'mature' adult to feel his way into a personality such as this, for he has left such attitudes far behind. Mature people plan for the future, learn from their mistakes and take into account the needs of others. It is difficult to conceive of people, apparently adults, who are so immature that they cannot comprehend such things. Even the most experienced therapist finds difficulty in communicating with such people in any meaningful way. Young children mature spontaneously: it is not something which is learnt. There is occasionally a remote hope that the 'impossible' patient will mature at a relatively late age. Although it is unusual, it sometimes happens.

Many readers will question the value of simply accepting these people for what they are. It is much more difficult than it sounds. The therapist will frequently find himself angry, frustrated and exasperated. At times, he will feel disconsolate. He will frequently feel that he could use his time more profitably and wonder whether he should leave incorrigible patients to the experts. But the 'experts' are no better at managing them that anyone else. In addition, most 'experts' already have a small band of their own, and are not keen to accept more. When the therapist accepts the buck, he must usually keep it.

Money

Most organisations have an unalterable rule about money. They will help the client to manage what he has, but they will not, under any circumstances, give or lend him any. When this is the rule, it *must* be obeyed. Sometimes, the counsellor is tempted to bypass it, but he does so at his peril. Money and counselling do not mix.

Some organisations are willing to give a limited amount of money, food, shelter and clothing. When this is so, the client's motivation often seems to be based more on the prospect of financial gain than on any desire to change his way of life. He is often remarkably well acquainted with the parable of the Good Samaritan if the organisation is a voluntary one, and with his 'rights' if it is governmental. In the latter case, he is swift to point out that he has 'paid in for it for years'. Needless to say, this is usually quite untrue. If there is anything in the purse, he expects to have it. If the counsellor should point out that there are limits and that he is not empowered to extend them, he will be rewarded with surprise, reproof and offended virtue. The problem of conforming to limits is often one of the client's main difficulties, and it would be against his interests for the counsellor to extend them. The most important demonstration for the client is also the least palatable. It is, that limits are limits. If he can teach this lesson, the counsellor will have achieved a notable success.

The prospect of obtaining money, especially state money, usually brings out the worst in any potential beneficiary. He looks upon the counsellor as the keeper of a bottomless purse, and behaves as though he has an absolute right to all that is available — to all that he requires. If he is given less than he demands, he seems to think that he is being treated unjustly. He may even threaten physical violence. If this seems to be a genuine risk, the counsellor should have no hesitation in seeking the help of the police, although this may add to his difficulties with the client.

In dealing with such people, a frontal assault is rarely of value. The counsellor should remain sympathetic, but he must be firm, objective and quite implacable. A verbal battle is usually a waste of time. Occasionally it may be possible to divert the client's hostility to other, more constructive directions. An example of such a transposition, stripped of embellishments, is as follows:

The client comes to the desk, scowls horribly, and says to the counsellor, 'I want some money.' The counsellor, knowing that he has already had his entitlement, replies 'You have had all that you are allowed.' The client becomes threatening. He says, 'If you don't give me some, I'll bash you.' The counsellor is alarmed and his hand moves towards the alarm bell. Several replies are available to him. He might say, 'You can't have any.' But he has already said this. It would be best not to repeat himself. He could say 'The law says that you have reached your limit. It is not within my power to give you more. If it were, I would.' (Would he?) From the point of view of the client, the counsellor and the 'law' are identical, and this reply amounts to an arbitrary decision to refuse him what he wants. In either case, an argument between counsellor and client may develop, each operating at different levels, and neither really understanding the other.

The alternative approach is for the counsellor to try to 'feel' himself into his client's shoes, to 'feel' what he feels, and to translate the feelings into words. The counsellor counters the threat of being 'bashed' with the words, 'It sounds as though you feel angry.' The client may reply 'So I am! Bloody angry! You would be angry too, if you were in my position.' The counsellor must avoid moralising or reverting to a bureaucratic role. He should try to stay in the client's shoes. Perhaps he says, 'Your position must be a very difficult one. Tell me what it is like.'

It begins to dawn on the client that the interview is not following the familiar pattern, and indignantly he tries to bring it back to more familiar lines. He says 'Look here, Jock,* I didn't come here to be psychoanalysed. Are you going to give me that money or are you not?' The counsellor reminds him that he has already answered this question. The client, baffled, decides to change his tactics and threatens the counsellor with an appeal to 'higher authorities'. He says 'I can't get any bloody sense out of you. I'm going to write to my Member of Parliament.' (or to the Queen, or the Prime Minister). The counsellor is enthusiastic about this idea. He says 'That's a very good idea indeed. You will get the address from the library. Next time, tell me how you got on.'

Thus, the counsellor acknowledges the fact that the client is in difficulties and that he is angry. He encourages his own suggestion that there is something that he himself might do.

Many readers will say of this dialogue, 'It sounds all very simple, but you don't know my clients. They are the most difficult people in the world.' It is true that the writer does not know the reader's clients, but he knows many people like them, and does not underestimate the difficulties. However, unless something of the sort is tried, nothing will ever be achieved. Of course, the chances of success are very small, but if one client carries out his threat, he will have made a start, and that will make it all worth while.

Violence

A patient may not touch his therapist. This is part of the 'contract'. It includes the assurance that the patient will never offer physical violence towards his therapist. His violence must be limited to words. If he wishes, the patient may *say* 'I am so angry that I am going to strike you.' But he may not *do* so! Obviously the threat of

*A different word is used south of the border.

violence cannot be tolerated. If the therapist should believe that he is truly in danger, he cannot continue with therapy. If therapy should be stopped for a reason such as this, it can never be resumed — at least with the same therapist. Neither can physical violence towards others be tolerated, nor any form of criminal or illegal activity. If he should consider it to be necessary, the therapist should have no hesitation about making these facts explicit.

If the patient wishes to do so, there is no objection to his reverting to the language of his Anglo-Saxon forebears in order to express his violence. Such words as **?*!!***, **@@@**!!????!! and **!!!????!! can be spoken with considerable vehemence, and carry a considerable aggressive charge when addressed to the right person, such as the therapist when he is being obstructive.

Another effective way of expressing violence is by becoming tight-lipped and silent, or replying only in grunts. This is variously called sulking and dumb insolence. Psychiatrists prefer the elegant variation, 'passive aggression' which means the same thing.

Slamming doors, stamping, and throwing plates, count as physical violence, and are not permitted.

There may be circumstances in which the therapist's public duty overrides any consideration of professional confidence. Problems which are properly the concern of psychotherapy are never amenable to violence. When difficulties arise, the therapist should always consult senior colleagues and, where appropriate, legal advisers.

A special problem arises when a patient is threatened with violence. In such circumstances, the one who is making the threats is usually beyond the influence of the therapist. (There may be exceptions, for example, in marital counselling, when one partner threatens the other). If a patient truly believes himself to be in danger, the therapist may help him decide to whom he should turn for protection. The therapist himself cannot offer protection, and it is probably better that he should not ask others to provide it. If necessary, the patient can ask the police for help, and if it seems advisable, he should be encouraged to do so.

Therapy under compulsion
In this section, we will consider two groups of people. All have been found guilty of a criminal offence. The patients in one group have accepted that they are in need of treatment, and this has been offered to them, usually as a condition of probation. The patients in the other group are detained in prison or a similar institution as a punishment for their offence.

A patient who is receiving psychotherapy as a condition of probation sometimes protests that he himself does not wish to be treated, and says that 'treatment' has been 'ordered' by the court. Technically, this is not correct. The patient has been offered treatment and, of his own free will, he has accepted it. As a result of his agreement, the court has excused him from punishment. Although this is the *technical* situation, it is understandable that the patient should feel that he has been 'sent' for treatment, because a choice between punishment and therapy is not really a choice. In these circumstances, it is natural that the patient should feel that treatment has been imposed upon him. The consequence is that his motivation may be seriously deficient, and treatment is often unsatisfactory.

The situation raises the problem of insight, and the wisdom of offering treatment as a condition of probation. Why, if he appreciated the need for it, did the patient not seek treatment before he committed the offence? In most cases, it is difficult to avoid the conclusion that treatment is looked upon as a soft option, clearly preferable to punishment.

There are occasions when a criminal offence is the direct consequence of a pathological state of mind, but these are uncommon. They may occur in, for example, a patient with a severe depressive illness who commits 'social' suicide, by shoplifting. A well-known broadcaster recently followed her 'social' suicide with actual suicide. When the diagnosis is certain, it is appropriate to offer treatment for the primary psychiatric illness in place of punishment. When there is doubt, it is usually better for the court to impose punishment. The patient can be treated afterwards, if he wishes.

The problem of someone who is already detained in prison is slightly different. Psychotherapy, particularly group psychotherapy, is sometimes offered to selected prisoners. Even then, there must be a suspicion that such occasions provide welcome relief from some of the drearier routines of prison life. Furthermore, the prisoner will have few opportunities to practice his new found insights. Therapy is most likely to be of value when the prisoner undertakes to continue with it after leaving prison. He is usually enthusiastic in giving this 'promise' but regrettably, although perhaps inevitably, the failure rate is high. A few prisoners hope that, by continuing with therapy after leaving prison, they will have a convenient excuse for subsequent criminal acts. They may be warned well in advance that this will not be so. Patients who are receiving psychotherapy are expected to conform to the law. Psychiatric illness is not an excuse for breaking it. The courts are sometimes indulgent to patients who are suffering from severe psychiatric disorders, but the therapist always expects his patients to behave lawfully.

Pastoral counselling

Counsellors who are members of religious organisations are often looked upon by their clients as men of God — as His direct representatives — sometimes even as God himself. Their clients often expect them to behave in accordance with their own, sometimes idiosyncratic concept of perfection, and condemn any deviation. The counsellor may protest that he is just a man, like other men, but his pleas are not likely to be heeded. He is firmly cast into a role and there may be little point in engaging in fruitless argument about it. Parishioners often expect ministers of religion to behave like saints, greeting anything which verges on the self-indulgent, such as smoking, or which appears to be mildly sinful, such as buying raffle tickets, with the shocked reproof 'I wouldn't have expected a clergyman to do something like that!'

Many of them find the expectation that ministers should be perfect, difficult to tolerate. However, it cannot be denied. The evidence is based partly on the avidity and enthusiasm with which laymen read stories of fallen clergymen. Stories such as these sell nearly as many newspapers as stories of fallen doctors. Perhaps it is best for the minister, of all men, to adhere to Polonius's adage, 'To thine own self be true'. The clergyman knows what he may expect of himself, and of the difficulty of obeying many of the precepts of the Bible. He must forgive his own failures because others will be less willing. To his sorrow, he will discover that compassion and understanding does not cure everything, perhaps not even his own problems.

In counselling, clergymen may wish to employ some of the general principles discussed in this book. They are, however, in the unusual position of being able to give advice, based on biblical authority. Naturally, they will not wish to depart from this authority or to modify it. They may find it helpful to concentrate on the frailty of man and the problems of adhering to biblical precepts. When it is appropriate, they will naturally emphasise the Christian message of forgiveness.

Members of some church organisations feel obliged to counsel everyone who asks for their advice. They feel that no-one should be rejected, however unpromising he may appear to be, and that they should be prepared to listen to everyone who calls upon them. This point of view is a noble one, but it will be seized upon by a small but troublesome group of people, who will provide the counsellor with every opportunity of fulfilling his Christian duties. In such cases, the counsellor might be wiser to accept his own limitations and frailties.

God alone has all the resources of the universe at his disposal. The supplicant has precisely the same access to God as does the counsellor. Counsellors need not be too disconcerted by their pained response. Neither need they be unduly troubled by the client's close familiarity with the parable of the Good Samaritan. Such clients conveniently misunderstand the parable, choosing for themselves the role of the man who falls among thieves. They expect others to play the part of the Samaritan and ignores the fact the virtue is ascribed to the Samaritan's behaviour, not to the victim's.

Patients from different cultures

To be successful in psychotherapy, it is necessary for the therapist and patient to be able to communicate easily with each other. The attitudes, philosophies and behavioural patterns of one culture may be very different from those of others. If they come from different backgrounds, it may be difficult for patient and therapist to get on to the same 'wave length', despite the fact that both speak the same language. If they do not even speak the same language, the difficulties are formidable. The therapist whose culture is different from that of his patient will do his best, but he should not underestimate the difficulties. It is better to seek the help of a therapist from the same culture. If this cannot be arranged, the problem of communication must be accepted as an important factor militating against success. The criteria for selection should be modified accordingly.

Parents, children and other relatives

When children require psychiatric treatment, their parents will expect to be involved, although they are often anxious about the implications, and frequently apprehensive of blame. Parents may believe that psychological illness in children stems from 'faulty upbringing', and may fear that this should be so in their own case. They will feel, usually with justification, that they have tried to do their best, but will recall incidents from the past which they will wish had never happened. They will hope to be told 'precisely what the trouble is' and will expect the therapist to tell them, in a few simple words, how to put it right.

It may be helpful to the parents of a child with a nervous illness if they are first encouraged to express their feelings about it. The subsequent discussion will include their own sense of guilt and possible attempts to evade responsibility. ('Could it be hereditary? My husband's uncle had a nervous breakdown.')

Parents are likely to become very defensive when they anticipate blame, and the therapist should try to avoid anything that may be taken as criticism. When they discover that they are not to be scapegoated, important information and assistance may be forthcoming.

Relatives who offer information about patients may hope for information in return. The therapist should be careful to avoid any breach of confidence. The reader is reminded that information given under a pledge of secrecy is of no value (see p. 118).

Sometimes relatives come, not to offer information or help, but to make it clear that they have none to offer. They often present the well worn excuse 'I am not well myself. I am under the doctor.' If this familiar evasion is encountered, the therapist may feel that there is little point in prolonging the interview.

Relatives sometimes ask how they themselves should behave towards the patient during his treatment. Should they make special allowances, and go out of their way to humour him? If they feel angry, should they clench their fists and count to ten? Patients usually detect insincere behaviour very quickly, and their reaction may be magnified in proportion. It is best for relatives to behave in the way which reflects how they truly feel — anything else would be dishonest and unhelpful. The patient is not helped by learning to cope with shadows. He must deal with people as they are. It may be distressing to the patient when his wife acknowledges that his behaviour makes her angry. It is better that she should say so during treatment, than confess later that there are certain things which she dislikes about him.

You cannot win
There are certain patients with whom people find themselves constantly at loggerheads. The most innocuous remark is turned into a battleground. Some patients seem to spend the whole of their lives in this way. They relate to people by fighting with them. The therapist himself may fall into the trap. Everything he says seems to provoke the patient, and ultimately he finds that he is provoked by everything that the patient says. Eventually he despairs. 'You just cannot win!', he cries.

When this happens, the therapist should ask himself, 'Do you *want* to win?' After all, psychotherapy is supposed to be a constructive exercise, not a destructive one; a collaboration not a battle.

When the therapist discovers that he is becoming insidiously and imperceptibly at loggerheads with his patient, he should first consider his own share of the exchange. It is not sufficient simply to deduce that this is how the patient handles *his* relationships. How has it come about on this occasion? When the therapist has thought about his own contribution, it is appropriate to discuss with the patient the question, 'How is it that you and I always seem to be at odds with each other?' The therapist is better able to help the patient to examine his contribution after he has examined his.

The eccentric

There are some people who choose not to conform to the ordinary modes of life. This does not seem to follow from failure of maturation, or from psychological abnormality. It happens because they seem to prefer a way of life which others regard as eccentric. Such people are not likely to seek help on their own account, but their baffled friends and relatives may urge them to do so. They may good-humouredly agree to participate, but therapy undertaken solely at the behest of someone else is rarely of value, and the therapist will feel that if modification is to be achieved, something more than good-humoured acquiescence is required. There does not seem to be much point in persevering with such cases.

The flirtatious

Early in his career, and sometimes much later, the therapist will encounter patients who seem to be more interested in achieving a social or even a sexual relationship with the therapist than a professional one. We have emphasised that social relationships are of no help in psychotherapy: sexual ones are even less so! If a therapist should discover that he has embarked upon psychotherapy with a flirtatious patient, he should interpret the patient's every attempt to change the relationship. He need not hesitate to speak about sexual undertones.

Such cases are sometimes difficult and can be extremely trying. If he feels that he is getting out of his depth, the therapist should consult a more experienced colleague. He may be advised to terminate the case and if this should be so, he should follow the advice. He may be greeted with the scandalised reproof of offended virtue: 'You told me that I could say anything. Surely you didn't really think...?' But this comes only when the patient has failed to add a valuable scalp to his collection. The therapist need not feel too distressed.

Le Bovarysme

This is 'a condition occurring in dissatisfied young women; in whom a mixture of vanity, imagination, and ambition, has induced ideas above their station in life, especially in matters sentimental'.*

This condition is so beautifully described that the author could not resist the temptation to include it. Cases are particularly frequent when royal princes become engaged. They are aggravated when royal tongues are heard to slip over their marriage vows.

* Forfar and Benhaman, French-English Medical Glossary: I, The Lancet, Page 789, 6th October, 1973.

10

Some schools of medical psychology

A classical Freudian approach?

Some readers of the first edition of this book commented, slightly reprovingly, on its 'classical Freudian approach'. They complained of its 'failure to take account of the tremendous advances which have taken place since Freud's time', seeming to imply that much of Freud's work is out-dated, out-moded and unworthy of consideration.

It is true that Freud's name occurs here several times. He was the first to describe many of the phenomena which we now regard as commonplace. He was one of the first to present in a coherent and consistent way the idea that there is an active part of the mind which operates without the intervention of consciousness. This was then a unique concept, but is now rather stale from familiarity.

Over one hundred and twenty years have passed since Freud was born and it is more than forty years since he died. Many have condemned his work, some without apparently having read it. A cheap edition of his books is readily available and many psychiatrists keep them on their shelves, next to the Bible and the collected work of Shakespeare. They remain there. Not everyone appears to have understood, for example, the subtleties of the Oedipal phase of development. It is, therefore, appropriate to remind the reader of his place in medical history.

Freud was not a long haired eccentric, with patched jeans and bare feet. He was a gentle man, an astute physician and a very acute observer. His wisdom, experience and knowledge, the originality of his thinking and the intensity of his application entitle him to be numbered among the intellectual giants of his generation. He was trained as a physiologist, but marriage led him to seek a more substantial living, and he decided to specialise in neurology. His most important mentor was Breuer, whose name was mentioned in Chapter 1.

Freud conducted his investigations with objectivity and precision. Many of his critics are prejudiced and obscure. A common complaint is that his theories have not been subjected to statistical analysis. Constant attempts are being made to construct suitable programmes, but the matter is of great complexity. The same complaint might be made against even the comparatively simple things of medicine, such as the efficacy of antibiotics.

Freud was one of the great theorists of medicine, and it is a great honour for modern psychiatry that he should have been one of its founding fathers. However, this book is *not* based on his, or any other single theoretical viewpoint. The concepts used are acceptable to most schools of medical psychology. We are not concerned with presenting any individual one. When psychotherapy is broadly based, as it is here, it is usually described as 'eclectic'.

The different 'schools' of psychotherapy have many features in common, and their differences lie predominantly in thier philosophical background. In their actual approach to the patient, their similarities are probably much greater than their differences. Nearly all claim to respect the patient as an individual, to adopt a non-directive approach and, as far as possible, to avoid unconscious bias. All try to be objective and nonjudgemental. Some claim to offer more 'encouragement' than do others, but such things are likely to vary more with the individual practitioner than with the school to which he adheres. This book might consequently claim to be an elementary textbook of the *practice* of all of them. The author does not expect to receive a round of applause at this point.

Sigmund Freud

Even at the end of the 20th century, some of Freud's observations are shocking and disquieting to many enlightened people. His most disturbing observation is that, during the third and fourth years of their lives, young children develop a considerable interest in genitals, both their own and those of other people. They begin to ask questions about where babies come from. Little boys speak of marrying their mothers when they grow up, and little girls, their fathers.

These activities may cause a certain amount of perplexity, distress and embarrassment to their parents. Little boys get erections. Little boys and girls are usually gently discouraged from manipulating their sexual organs.

Parents often make brave promises that when the time arrives, they will answer all delicate questions with complete honesty. But when the moment comes, they lose their nerve. At the last moment, they give evasive answers, babble about eggs and pollination, and tell the child that he will learn about such matters when he grows older.

Freud postulated that all children, male and female, know about the male penis, usually from personal observation, but possibly from some sort of innate knowledge. They believe that *all* children started life *with* a penis. The difference between the sexes is that some have retained the penis (the males) and some have lost it (the females). The penis is a source of pleasure and little boys are concerned to ensure that they do not become one of those who lose it (castration anxiety). Little girls wonder how they can obtain another (penis envy).

For all children, their mother has been present from the dawn of memory. She provides love, comfort and succour. It is she who wakens them in the morning and who soothes them to sleep at bedtime. It is she who feeds them, plays with them and loves them. For a long time, father remains a shadowy figure, who materialises only at the extremes of the day.

However, his importance gradually increases. He is big and tall; clever, rich, brave, strong and powerful. His word is law. He is the source of retribution and the heavens tremble when his anger is aroused. It is father who says what is good and what is bad. He rewards good behaviour and punishes bad. He is the law-maker, the judge and the executioner. (The whole constitutional theory of the United States is based on ensuring that never again should the powers of the executive, the law-maker and the judge, be incorporated in the body of one single individual!) Father's pockets are crammed with wealth. His wisdom is immense. He is also great fun, and his child loves him, and admires him deeply.

Father and mother have a secret. It appears to be centred on the bed which they share. For most of his life, the child is excluded from this bed. His friends' parents have similar arrangements, and it seems that the world is divided into mothers and fathers who share beds, and everyone else.

For as long as he can remember, the child has shared his pleasures with his mother. He has shared the pleasure of suckling, of eating and drinking, of playing. Freud claimed that a stage comes in which children find pleasure in excretion. Initially they try to share this pleasure with their mother, too. Eventually, during the phase known as toilet training, they reject the pleasure, because it is her wish. The child then discovers that manipulation of his genitals gives him pleasure. It is understandable that he should naively, expect to share this pleasure with his mother.

Thus begins the genital stage of development. The child seeks actual genital contact with his mother. There is no reason — other than that which is most potent of all, because it is subjective and emotional — to call his desire anything other than sexual. However, great offence is caused to many people by saying so. They argue passionately and sometimes angrily that childhood is a stage of innocence. There is no reason to spoil it by introducing adult concepts such as genital sexuality. Such ideas are horrifying to many enlightened minds. *It can be predicted from Freudian theory that it should be so.* During this stage*, the little boy tells his mother that when he grows up, he intends to marry her. She tries to explain that it cannot be. His attempts to share his genital pleasure with her are gently but completely rebuffed. He is discouraged from 'playing' with himself, and his mother refuses to take any part in the 'game'.

The child is thereby faced with two mysteries: his mother's rejection, and the secret of the parental bedroom. These mysteries are developed before logical thought has been established. The solution perceived by the child is therefore not a logical one. He concludes that his father is his *rival* for his mother's affection. If this is so, he must be his father's rival! But father is a giant: big, tall, strong, rich and brave. Compared with him, the child is a dwarf: weak and defenceless. If his father should inflict upon him the ultimate punishment for his lascivious desires... This terrifying fantasy is the source of his 'castration anxiety'.

The reader should appreciate that the *facts* which we have been describing are matters of observation. The theories are an endeavour to formulate the child's *fantasies* about the facts. It is true that parents *are* often uncomfortable about the behaviour of their children when it is overtly sexual. If there should be a childlike fantasy about castration, it has no foundation in reality —although some little boys are warned that 'it' will drop off if they do not stop 'playing' with themselves, and some are even threatened with having 'it' cut off.

Freud called this situation the Oedipal conflict. The term is derived from Greek mythology, where Oedipus, a Theban prince, unknowingly killed his father and married his mother. This is the conflict into which the child seems to be drifting.

Several elements contribute to the fully developed Oedipal conflict, and they will be listed in personal terms.

1. I love mother and she loves me.
2. I want her to love me in a special way, but she refuses to do so.
3. Mother reserves part of her life for father. I am excluded. It

---

* This account is given from the point of view of the male child. The process in the female is similar, although slightly more complicated. The interested reader should consult the literature.

seems that she reserves for him the pleasure which she denies to me.
4. If this is so, father is my rival.
5. If father is my rival, I am his .
6. Compared with me, he is a giant. Unless the fairy stories are true, and little people can kill giants, I will lose the battle.
7. But I love my giant father. I don't want to fight him.
8. My giant father seems to love me, although at times he has a funny way of showing it! He does not seem to want to fight me.

The reader will recognise that many aspects of this conflict are reflected in the fairy stories which enthrall young children. Freud suggested that the child may be biologically prepared for these postulates, just as he is biologically prepared for the acquisition of language. He proposed that the manner in which the conflict is resolved may also be determined biologically.

The Oedipal conflict is *resolved* when part of the child's personality, called the *super-ego*, differentiates to become, almost literally, the *father*. The consequences of the formation of the super-ego are as follows:

1. I love mother and she loves me.
2. I do not wish mother to love me in any other way. Any special way is gratified vicariously, through that part of me which is father.
3. Because part of me is now father, I do not have a rival, and neither does he. There is no need for a battle. If there were to be one, we would both be destroyed.
4. Within me, I now have someone whom I love and admire. One day, I will grow up to become a man, just like him.
5. Within me, there is now a part which says what I should do and what I should not. It makes me feel good when I behave well and bad when I behave badly. It is called my conscience.
6. My conscience says that it is wicked for boys to have incestuous thoughts towards their mothers. Therefore I must *forget completely* everything that has happened. I must vigorously deny, even to myself, that such a thing could have occurred.

The super-ego comprises two parts, the ego-ideal and the conscience. Stage four represents the formation of the ego-ideal and stage five the formation of the conscience. Stage six is the source of the massive repression which occurs when the Oedipal conflict is resolved. It explains why people are unable to recall many of the happenings of infancy, and particularly such a monstrous series of events. It also explains their anxiety, anger and rejection when anyone suggests that such a thing might be so.

Thus the resolution of the Oedipal conflict is achieved by a process of *identification* with, and *introjection* of, the parent of the same sex. It leads to the creation of the super-ego, which consists of the ego-ideal and the conscience.

The super-ego is the part of the personality to be developed last. At birth, the personality consists of a primitive, undifferentiated structure called the id. The id is totally self-centred and the locus of all primary desires. It demands instant and total satisfaction of all bodily needs, and takes no account of reality . The relief of its needs is pleasurable, and it is said to operate according to the *pleasure principle*. The ego develops from the id, and orients the id to the reciprocal demands of reality. It operates according to the *reality principle*. The demands of society are acknowledged only when the conscience is formed.

The development of the Oedipal conflict is the culmination of the third stage of 'libidinal development'. When it is resolved, a period of latency ensues. This occupies most of the schooldays , and concludes with adolescence. The first two stages of libidinal development are the oral stages and the anal stages.

These stages are focussed sequentially on maturing centres of bodily sensitivity and excitement, called erotogenous zones. They are respectively the mouth; the anus and urethra; and the genitals.

The oral (oral dependent) stage of development begins at birth. It continues until the child begins to acquire voluntary control over its excretory musculature. For most of the oral stage, the child is totally dependent on the adults around him. His pleasures are located in the region of the mouth. Mouth pleasures continue into adult life. They include eating, drinking, sucking, chewing, and talking. Mouth activities may be comfortable and enjoyable. In states of displeasure, they may be involved in biting, cursing, screaming, shouting and swearing. In anger, the lips may be pursed, or closed altogether in silence. It is very rude to open the lips and protrude the tongue!

The reader should note that we reserve certain oral pleasures for adult life. These include smoking, drinking alcohol, and kissing erotically. As children grow up, they begin to copy these activities. Certain major psychiatric illnesses (e.g. severe depression) are characterised by a loss of oral activity.

The infant has no understanding of the demands which may be

made upon him by the outside world. Through his mouth, he can effectively demonstrate his pleasure and displeasure. If he is angry, he can shout and scream. He takes no account of father's need to sleep, mother's headache, or the desirability of pleasing wealthy relatives. The conscience has not yet developed.

The anal stage of development is one with which many people find it difficult to identify. During this stage, it is claimed that children derive pleasure from excretory activities. That this is undoubtedly true of certain adults convinces no-one, for they are dismissed as perverts.

The young child certainly *uses* his new-found ability to control his bowel and bladder to control others—a fact which is very familiar to most mothers. During the course of development, and in obedience to the wishes of his mother, the child must *continue* to control his excretory activities, but *abandon* the pleasure which he derives from them. As he 'becomes clean', the child learns that his excretions are foul, dirty things, and that people who say otherwise are foul and dirty creatures.

During the anal stage of development, valued traits of personality, such as orderliness, obedience, tidiness, punctuality and cleanliness are acquired. The child learns to do the right thing, at the right time, in the right place; in particular, to empty his excretions into the pot when his bowel and bladder are moderately full, and when his mother tells him to do so. Thus the child learns to distinguish dirt from cleanliness, and to obey others. He learns that obedience brings approval. Approval itself is pleasurable. Children sometimes learn that they can control others by obstinacy—by not doing the right thing at the right time, in the right place.

The aspects of Freudian psychology which we have been describing are called respectively structural, topographic and genetic. We must refer to two more, the dynamic and economic.

Everything that happens is related to what has gone before. There is nothing new in the world: no such thing as an accident. Everything is driven by the complex interaction of many factors. The whole is in a state of equilibrium. If energy is required for one activity, it must be taken away from another.

Two further concepts must be introduced in order to understand the formation of character and the development of psychological illness. These are 'fixation' and 'regression'. Some individuals fail to progress through all the stages of libidinal development. If progress is halted, they become 'fixated' at that particular stage. Thus, people who are completely amoral and hedonistic, who show no regard for the rules of society, who have apparently no conscience to deter them from eating, drinking and smoking all that they can beg, borrow or steal—the situation found in people whose personality is said to be psychopathic — may be 'fixated' at the oral stage.

People who are excessively preoccupied with such things as orderliness, punctuality and the extreme rule of law — obsessional personalities — may be fixated at the anal stage. Fixation may be due to innate biological factors, to external pressures or anxieties, or to undiscovered factors.

Under certain circumstances, for example when disease supervenes, the individual may 'regress' to a previous fixation point. If severe Oedipal anxieties are re-awakened, the individual may 'regress' to the anal stage of development, and develop an obsessional psychoneurosis.

A Freudian headache*

Let us consider the formation of a disagreeable physical symptom, such as a severe headache, for which no organic cause can be found.

A neurotic symptom partly punishes, partly gratifies, and partly distracts attention from the source of an unresolved unconscious conflict. Suppose that a female patient has an unresolved Oedipal conflict — an unconscious desire for sexual contact with her own father. If she were simply told this, she would certainly be angry, incredulous and dismissive, and her headache would certainly not get better. This is because the sexual tension is *unconscious*.

The tension is *displaced* to an area far away from the genitals, perhaps to the head. Thus tension is experienced in the head, and the patient suffers from a tension headache. Some patients simultaneously lose genital sensation and become frigid. Attention is now concentrated on the painful area. The patient may screw up her eyes and retreat into a darkened room. Some readers will wonder what it is that she is reluctant to 'see'.

The patient may take the painful 'area' to someone who is clever, knowledgeable, wise, strong and powerful (her doctor). When she has told him about it, she often feels better. She may be relieved if someone will gently soothe the painful area (a husband or a lover). Thus the desire is partially gratified and the area of tension relaxed.

Finally, let us agree that a tension headache is extremely disagreeable. The original, unconscious, unacceptable desire has been painfully punished.

---

* If the reader is suffering from a headache as he reads this, it is suggested that he should retire to a darkened room until he feels better!

Homosexuality

The Freudian view is that a man who is homosexual has an over-whelming but unconscious fear of castration. It is therefore impos-sible for him to share his sexual activities with a female, because, lacking a penis, she is a reminder both of his incestuous wishes and their possible outcome. In consequence, he can share his sexual needs only with someone who *already has a penis*, that is to say, homosexually. A woman who is homosexual experiences overpower-ing penis envy. She cannot tolerate any reminder of that of which she has been deprived. Consequently, she can share her sexual needs only with someone who lacks a penis, that is to say, homosexually.

Adler and Individual Psychology

Adler and Jung were amongst Freud's earliest supporters and col-laborators. Both broke away and founded schools of their own.

Alfred Adler was the first to separate. He rejected most of Freud's teaching, and established his own school of 'Individual Psychology'. Each individual is regarded as unique. There is no preconceived progression through developmental stages, no Oedipal conflict: very little unconscious.

The individual's behaviour is directed solely by the way in which he perceives, and copes with, his areas of *inferiority and weakness*. From his earliest days, the individual strives for superiority. There are many adult examples. Demosthenes overcame his stammer by declaiming to the waves, and in due course became a great orator. Helen Keller overcame blindness and deafness, and became a great writer and teacher. Sir Douglas Bader, having lost both legs in a plane crash, became an ace fighter pilot in the Second World War.

The mode adopted by the individual to cope with his feelings of inferiority is called his Life Style. This varies from one person to another, so that there is an infinite variety of patterns. Adler described some frequent responses to common situations.

Position in the family is important. The eldest child is the leader of his younger siblings. After a year or two, during which he has the exclusive attention of his parents, he is deposed by the next child. It is the eldest child who is most subject to parental authority, the most knowledgeable, but also the most vulnerable, for the second child is always at his heels.

The second child is forever trying to catch up with the eldest, but feels that he can never succeed in doing so — whatever the reality of his situation.

The youngest child remains the baby of the family, with older and more powerful siblings always ahead of him, never experiencing the jealousy which is associated with the birth of a younger child.

Sexual role may be a determinant of strength or weakness. In our culture, woman is often looked upon as the weaker vessel. In consequence, she may develop a 'masculine protest'. She may become aggressively masculine, or alternatively, retreat into ultrafemininity. She masters her environment by exploiting her feminine wiles. (She is characterised very effectively by Ann Whitefield in Bernard Shaw's 'Man and Superman'. 'Superman' is, of course, woman!)

The male too, may show a 'masculine protest'. If a male feels insecure in his role, he may acquire the attitude of a 'He-man'. Alternatively, he may surrender completely to passivity and effeminacy.

Some individuals choose a neurotic road to superiority, and use neurosis as a cloak for their weakness. There is no task which the individual could not achieve if it were not for his 'illness'. The illness forever precludes his putting his 'strength' to the test, and in fantasy it remains unsurpassed.

Adler's teaching, though rather simplistic, had, at one time, considerable influence. Now it has greatly decreased. His concept of the Life Style is sometimes called 'repetition compulsion' by Freud. The diagnosis of the Life Style requires careful scrutiny of the patient's total life history, in order to identify recurrent patterns of behaviour. Careful scrutiny such as this has importance for all schools of psychotherapy.

Jung and Analytical Psychology

Whilst Adler focussed increasingly on conscious mental activities, C. G. Jung's interest shifted to those which were unconscious.

He was the author of an early word association test and proposed an early theory of psychological types, which was later to be recreated and elaborated by the distinguished behaviourist, H. J. Eysenck. Mankind was divided into two basic types: introverts and extraverts. These words have passed into common use and will not be defined further.

Jung broke with Freud shortly after Adler. He considered that Freud ascribed excessive importance to infantile sexuality. He founded his own school of Analytical Psychology. In doing so, he moved away from his original, highly objective approach and became more mystical and less scientific. He developed a 'theory of opposites'.

Man's psyche is a balance of opposing factors, the total operating in a state of equilibrium. There is the conscious and the unconscious, the persona and the shadow, the rational processes and the irrational ones; and the four functions: thinking, feeling, sensation and intuition. These combine with extraversion and introversion to form eight psychological types. Jung believed that the unconscious comprised two parts: the personal and the collective. The 'personal unconscious' is self-explanatory. He regarded the fact that themes, myths and symbols are repeated throughout all cultures and religions of the world, is an indication that there is a more primitive part of the personality which is inherited from one generation to the next. This he called, the 'collective unconscious'. The collective unconscious has never been conscious: it arose from primordial experiences, and its images are called archetypes. Mental illness is caused by a disturbance of the inner equilibrium as a result of conflict.

Unlike Freud, Jung had a sincere faith, which seems to have made his teachings more acceptable to religious organisations than the atheistic determinism of Freud. His minute dissection of the personality into a large number of psychological types has little practical importance, and his preoccupation with parapsychology and with much that is speculative and mystical has little relevance to the practice of the present author. Others find his concepts of more value.

Jung was once interviewed 'in depth' on television and was clearly a very kind and charitable man. Such desirable virtues are rare.

Neo-Freudians

Karen Horney

Horney was originally an orthodox Freudian psychoanalyst. In the 1930s, she escaped to the United States from Nazi Germany and was one of several European psychiatrists who modified psychoanalytic thinking, particularly in respect of the effect of the environment on personality. In Freudian terms, a culture is a distillation of the individuals of which it is comprised. It can be changed only if its members change. Horney and the 'neo-Freudians' consider that the reverse is true. They regard individuals as being moulded by the culture of which they were members. They would change if the environment could be changed.

Horney regarded the search for safety and satisfaction, and avoidance of anxiety as the primary motivating forces in behaviour. In anxiety-provoking situations, the individual adopts 'neurotic patterns' in order to cope with them. Like Adler, Horney believed that the personality operated as a whole and rejected Freud's structural and topographic views of the personality.

When the child is valued by his parents and by those around him, he maintains his self-esteem. However, he grows up into a rivalrous, mistrustful, envious and disparaging society which breeds neurosis. It may become necessary for him to *distort* reality in order to make himself feel safe. Safety is the basic need: it represents freedom from fear and anxiety, and may be achieved only by developing a 'neurotic trend'.

If the child's needs are not gratified, he may become hostile towards the anticipated source of satisfaction. But because he is also helpless in the face of his needs, his hostility must be banished. One side of the conflict is, therefore, repressed and a vicious circle is established. The need is exacerbated and the true source of the conflict is forgotten. Neurotic behaviour then becomes rigid and compulsive.

Early life experiences provide the foundation for the adult personality, but Horney believes that the mature personality is flexible, and that in response to appropriate satisfaction, it can continue to develop throughout life.

Therapy is concerned with abandoning the artificial idealised image of the self, and facilitating the emergence of the real self.

Harry Stack Sullivan: Interpersonal Relations

Unlike most other influential psychotherapists, Sullivan did not have a Freudian background, although he reached some parallel conclusions. He did not examine the vicissitudes of childhood sexual behaviour, or regard them as relevant to the development of the adult personality or subsequent psychological illness.

Sullivan's most important contribution is so subtle that it is often forgotten. It is this. The contemplation of an individual in *isolation* is not possible. He can be examined only in the context of his relationship with the person who is 'examining' him. It is as though the isolated 'individual' is a hypothesis: man can exist only insofar as he interacts with other people. They may be real, or the product of his own imagination.

Sullivan adds a fresh dimension to psychotherapy by his insistence that the therapist cannot study a patient unless he acknowledges that he himself is part of the 'phenomena' which he is studying. The *patient* influences the therapist, what he does and what he says. The therapist is an observer, but a 'participant observer'. The therapist studies not the individual, but their *interaction* and thus the patient's interpersonal relations. As an individual, the individual is of no substance.

In formulating his views, Sullivan derives certain 'new' words which seem to cause difficulty to some people. The emergent personality is called the 'self-dynamism'. The word 'dynamism' adds a quality of energy and malleability to the rather static concept of the self. The child's self-dynamism emerges out of its experience of and from the reflected appraisals of those with whom it interacts. The young child has a strong sense of 'empathy'. He interacts with the adults around him in such a way that his reciprocal appraisals preserve his sense of security.

The child has two types of need: for satisfaction and security. Satisfaction is a physical need, and achieved in the state of homeostasis. His bowels, his bladder, his stomach, his skin are in comfortable equilibrium. The approval of significant adults fulfills the need for security. When his security is impaired, he modifies his interaction with the environment and in doing so, learns to control it.

Sullivan defines three 'modes of experience': prototaxic, parataxic and syntaxic. The "prototaxic mode' is idiosyncratic and probably uncommunicable. It is the experience of the very young child, in which the self and the environment are largely undifferentiated. The parataxic mode is acquired by the child as a result of its earliest attempts to organise its experiences. The self is differentiated from the outside world, but in a very egocentric way. The child's first use of language is very concrete, not abstract. Thus, a 'chair' is differentiated from the self, but refers only to one particular object, not to a class of objects.

Eventually the parataxic mode gives way to the adult syntaxic mode. This is characterised by the 'consensual validation' of others. Remnants of the parataxic mode may persist in neurotic or psychotic behaviour. The creaking of the floorboards which is heard at night time, when the house is dark and quiet,is due, syntactically, to their contraction as the temperature falls, or, parataxically, to ghosts!

Sullivan describes a series of developmental stages which roughly parallel those of Freud. They follow the maturing capacity of the 'self-system' and the development of control and socialisation. In Sullivan's view, sexual development is important only in adolescence.

Situations which provoke anxiety are dealt with by dissociation. Dreams and other symbolic experiences permit the discharge of unacceptable behaviour. Actual physical experiences may give clues to the courses of anxiety, and it may then be examined and adjusted. Sullivan postulates an innate 'power motive' which enables the individual to strive for health and perfection.

Sullivan's views on interpersonal relationships are important to all schools of psychotherapy. They remind us that relationships can be modified, both constructively and harmfully by a mutual feed-back mechanism.

His views are especially important as a reminder of the role played by a therapist in the therapeutic interaction. Like two overlapping circles of light, the area of overlap is brighter than its separate parts, and more may be seen in the light of both than in that of either alone.

Behaviour therapy

Disillusionment with psychotherapy grew with its failure to cure everyone, and eventually raised the question of whether it could help anyone. In the 1950s, it came seriously under attack. Its principal opponents were an ingenious and eloquent group, mainly of clinical psychologists, who persuasively espoused the value of behaviour therapy. They had great influence on many therapists who were dis-appointed at the failure of orthodox psychotherapy. These thera-pists, like some of their patients, were sure that someone, somewhere, should be able to do something. In consequence, there was a great upsurge of enthusiasm for behaviour therapy, which soon became a formidable discipline in its own right. Its methods spring from the ideas of Pavlov, and had been favoured in the U.S.S.R. for many years previously.

Many of the tenets of psychoanalysis have taken a firm hold on psychiatry in particular, and on philosophical thought as a whole, but it seemed to offer little to a large number of psychologically dis-turbed people. It was, and remains, very expensive of therapist time, unpredictable in its outcome and, in the present state of knowledge, difficult to evaluate. Several studies suggested that patients who were treated with orthodox analytical therapy were no better off than those who were not. At the same time, the new race of behaviour therapists, often with 'scientific' as opposed to 'medical' training, led to gradual evolution and development of the principles of learn-ing theory.

Learning theory starts with the classical experiments of Pavlov. Pavlov was able to establish 'conditioned' reflexes in dogs. His original observations were due to coincidence. He noted that dogs would salivate not only in the presence of food, but also when inci-dental, non-edible cues such as the dinner gong were presented. Further studies of stimulus and response, and subsequently of 'operant conditioning" led to the discovery of many laws by which behaviour might be encouraged or deterred.

Theoretically, the next step was simple. Behaviour is learned. Some behaviour is maladaptive. If maladaptive behaviour could be 'unlearned' and replaced by adaptive behaviour, the patient would be 'cured'. 'Cure' is a medical concept, and behaviourists do not necessarily accept such concepts as being relevant to the conditions with which they deal.

If behaviour is rewarded, it is reinforced: if it is punished, it is avoided. Behaviour therapy, behaviour psychotherapy or behaviour modification (to avoid confusion, we will speak only of 'behaviour therapy') thus arose out of the simple recipe of 'rewarding' adaptive behaviour and 'punishing' maladaptive behaviour. The next problem was to decide *which* aspects of behaviour were to be reinforced, which were to be punished, and how this was to be achieved.

A crude form of behaviour therapy existed in the 1930s in the treatment of (particularly) alcoholism. The patient was allowed to drink as much as he wanted of whatever he liked. Every time he took a drink, however, he received an injection which would cause him to vomit. The intention was to establish a conditioned response of nausea and vomiting to the thought and sight of alcohol. This primitive form of 'aversion therapy' was successful in a number of cases.

As experience increased, it was demonstrated that behaviour therapy could be effective in the treatment of certain phobias, especially those associated with a single object. Phobias are difficult to treat by traditional methods, although monosymptomatic forms have a better prognosis. The response to behaviour therapy often seemed swift and satisfactory.

A strong movement towards treatment based on behaviourist principles quickly developed, with a parallel loss of interest in psychotherapy. This was destructively analysed, debased and sometimes totally rejected by the behaviourists. Many analytic concepts were rejected as being of little value and were repeatedly condemned because they were not amenable to statistical proof. Their influence was thought to depend heavily on suggestion, and some behaviour therapists dismissed them as being unworthy of any consideration whatsoever. These regarded the *behaviour* as the abnormality and considered that there was nothing to be gained from postulating any hypothetical underlying pathology. In consequence, half a century of careful clinical observation was rejected as being prejudiced and valueless. To add insult to injury, and confusion to their enemies, many behavioural therapists began to describe themselves as behavioural psychotherapists. They wrote of their notable successes, emphasised the speed and simplicity of their treatment, and threw psychoanalytic theories contemptuously out with the bath water.

The inevitable and regrettable consequence of all this was that therapists were split into opposing camps: analytical and behaviourist. However, the mutual criticism and defensive self-examination which followed has probably been valuable for both groups. The experience is not a new one for the analysts. The great psychoanalytic split, to which we have already referred, took place in 1910. Freud, describing Jung in 1910 as a 'psychoanalyst', demoted him in a later (1914) edition of the same work to 'formerly a psychoanalyst'!

Although the techniques used by individual behaviour therapists differ slightly, the basic premises are similar. First, the maladaptive behaviour is carefully analysed — almost to the very reflex arcs of which it is composed! The analysis is focussed on the individual constituents of the maladaptive behaviour, their separate causes, and the factors which increase or decrease them. Information is obtained through very detailed interviews, by personal observation, and from the administration of suitable tests. Therapists may pay particular attention to the individual's susceptibility to 'imaginary', as opposed to actual, stimuli and to situations by which anxiety is precipitated.

When the behavioural analysis has been completed, a suitable therapeutic regime is selected. Crude forms of reward and punishment have given way to the elaboration of many sophisticated techniques. Deep muscle relaxation is sometimes taught for practice in anxiety-provoking situations. Systematic desensitisation combines relaxation with scenes which provoke increasing anxiety. These scenes are organised in a hierarchical sequence, starting with the least distressing and culminating in those which are most distressing.

'Role playing' is used in 'assertive training'. This seeks to free an individual from the *inappropriate* anxiety which he might experience in specific situations. Allied to this is the technique of modelling. Behaviour is modelled by direct instruction, or the behaviour of a normal or admired model is imitated.

In another variation, the usual technique, which is based on *minimising* anxiety, is reversed ('implosion' or 'flooding'). The individual is encouraged to tolerate a strongly anxiety-provoking situation until the anxiety begins to diminish spontaneously. 'Imaginary' rewards and punishments may be used to encourage or discourage behaviour. In the more primitive versions, actual rewards or tokens (like Green Shield stamps) are given or withheld. Real punishments may be used, such as not being allowed to watch television (*sic*). Other 'punishments' include being refused visits, social contacts, being deprived of meals, and being given electric shocks — but only little ones!

When a technique has been selected, the therapist spends much of his time with the patient, discussing its application and rationale, and listening to his doubts and reservations. This discussion, which often occupies a substantial proportion of the time allocated to therapy, is characteristically conducted in a warm, accepting and non-judgemental environment. It is said that it 'conforms strictly to the principles of reality'. Any attempt to discuss, for example, unconscious conflicts or underlying psychopathology, is discouraged.

This aspect of behaviour therapy is the one which is of most interest to the psychotherapist. Behaviourists claim that psychotherapists achieve their successes by using random and unrecognised behaviourist principles. Psychotherapists retort that behaviourists achieve their successes by using random and unrecognised psychotherapeutic principles. The argument is scarcely worthwhile. Presumably both are right.

To many, it appears that the least part of behaviour therapy is the application of the technique itself. Although teaching is detailed, it often passes quickly. The patient is expected to repeat his exercises frequently, in his 'free' time, away from the therapist. Home assignments and diary keeping are important components of the technique.

The response to treatment is often rapid and gratifying. Unfortunately, most doctors, whatever their speciality, have in their professional lives, encountered rapid and gratifying responses to new and elaborate techniques. Follow-up studies of behavioural techniques suggest that the long-term outcome is about the same as it is for patients who have received limited psychotherapy. Behaviour therapy is not a universal panacea, but in experienced hands and with proper techniques, it has an important place in psychiatric treatment.

A small area of anxiety remains in the mind of the author. A substantial number of U.S. soldiers were successfully indoctrinated by 'behavioural techniques' when they were taken prisoners of war in Vietnam. The ultimate potential of behaviour therapy has been sensationalised, although not necessarily exaggerated, in the novel, *Clockwork Orange*.

Needless to say, behaviourists are quick to assert that such 'misuse' of their techniques is inconceivable. Since they are its masters, they must be the first to acknowledge that such misuse is conceivable.

Existential psychotherapy

Existential psychotherapy is a rather metaphysical off-shoot of

Freudian psychology, although much of the parent philosophy has been discarded. To some people, it seems to have a mystical, almost religious quality.

Existential psychotherapy claims kinship with the philosophy of existentialism, and uses some of its vocabulary. However, since the original vocabulary is composed of German hybrid words, the English translations are idiosyncratic and probably less adequate. Thus, the concept of the Dasein, *Being-in-the-World*, means more than being in the world. The individual and his experience constitute a totality which exists in its own right. The hyphens represent an attempt to encompass the full flavour of man's existence. Dasein-analyse is concerned with helping the patient *savour* the whole of his *existence*, whatever that existence might be, including experiences which some people would regard as psychotic.

Abnormalities are due to a breakdown in communication between the patient and the world around him: the aim of therapy is to re-establish the relationship. When this is achieved, the cause of the breakdown may sometimes be revealed, although it is not essential that this should happen.

Since existential psychotherapy has no preconceptions of its own, it is more concerned with the attitude of the therapist than with persuading the patient to conform to a theoretical model. The therapist tries to be non-directive and non-judgemental, understanding, tolerant and encouraging. He offers a safe and trusting relationship in which the patient may learn new ways of relating to people. The therapist is the patient's existential partner.

In practice, many psychotherapeutic techniques are used. Free association is encouraged and dreams are discussed extensively. However, dreams are treated as existential experiences in their own right and are rarely interpreted. They are looked upon as part of the personal experience of the patient. Thus, a dream about snow may reflect the real lack of warmth in the patient's world, perhaps especially in his relationship with other people.

Interpretation is limited, and little mention is made of transference feelings. To the existential therapist, an interpretation of a transference reaction rejects the reality of the experience to the patient, and may lead to a feeling of rejection followed by withdrawal.

For most psychotherapists, the most valuable lesson offered by existential psychotherapy is the importance of accepting the patient's experiences as they are, not as some sort of parable relating to the past. Whilst others interpret, the existential psychotherapist waits with his patient until insight is achieved. There may be little difference in the ultimate approach.

Client centred therapy (non-directive therapy) (Rogers)

Client centred therapy (non-directive therapy) really is client centred, and non-directive. From the outset, everything is decided by the client: the decision to begin; to continue; to conclude; the content of each session and the next step. The 'counsellor' (the word is preferred to 'therapist') treats each 'client' as a unique individual, whose experience of life is also unique. The counsellor even avoids making a diagnosis, lest its implications should distort the attempt to explore the client's world with him. Because he is unique, it is accepted without question that the client is the only person entitled to describe the world in which he lives.

Throughout therapy, the counsellor maintains towards the client an attitude of unconditional positive regard. He accepts his client's account of his experiences, endeavouring to understand and to share them, free from preconception and distortion. He makes no suggestions as to how the client should approach his problems. He may be more *encouraging* than therapists whose orientation is different from his own.

A 'positive drive for growth' is postulated in client centred therapy. In a climate of unconditional positive regard, the client finds the freedom to examine the private view which he has of himself (the 'self concept'). The counsellor is permitted to intervene in order to facilitate this examination.

The client is helped to look at his behaviour with honesty and objectivity, to analyse inconsistencies between it and his self concept, and to examine areas of conflict and incongruity. He is helped to identify the problems which are encountered, to accept the self that emerges, and to face those aspects which were distorted or denied. Thus he develops insight.

The initial consequence of insight is that the self concept is disrupted. It is then restructured, and finally emerges in a new and reorganised form, based on the experiences of the client himself rather than on the opinion of others. By proving itself in action, the new self is esteemed and eventually the client feels sufficiently confident to withdraw from therapy.

Throughout counselling, emphasis is placed on the need to elucidate, clarify, elaborate and especially to *experience* feelings. Thus, most of all, the counsellor attends to and accepts his client.

Client centred therapy goes to an extreme of permitting the

client to dictate the whole course of therapy. For other theoretical schools, an important lesson is the benefit which may occur from allowing therapy to proceed at the speed of, and in the direction indicated by, the patient.

Transactional analysis

This is especially associated with the name of Eric Berne. Berne was a great popularist: a fluent writer and speaker, and has been brought to the notice of a wide public by popular editions of his books.

Transactional analysis begins with a period of structural analysis with a personal therapist. Berne recognises three basic 'ego stages': Parent, Child and Adult. Their names describe their function: they relate to the patient's actual experience. Thus the Child may be small and weak, self-centred and demanding, hoping for magic. The Parent is based on the patient's perception of his own parents: it may be restrictive, controlling, positive. The Adult is oriented towards reality; towards the environment and to the people within it.

The patient is helped to identify the basic ego states, not only of himself, but also of those people with whom he interacts. In the technique known as regression analysis, the patient is allowed to experience the Child state completely. This may be facilitated by role playing, the patient's 'Child' interacting with the therapist's 'Child'.

When structural analysis has been accomplished, the patient proceeds to transactional analysis. This normally takes place in a therapeutic group. The intention is that the patient's 'Adult' should learn to take control of all social interaction.

Behaviour is analysed in terms of 'game playing' and 'script writing'. 'Games' are devices by which certain ulterior motives are concealed within certain types of social interaction. A number of 'games' are described, such as 'uproar', 'rapo' and 'wooden leg'. In 'uproar', an argument develops, which is concluded by one partner walking out. This is a collusive device to avoid intimacy. 'Rapo' refers to sexually provocative behaviour which culminates in outrage when intercourse is suggested. It facilitates sexual gratification in the face of the 'Child's' attitude, which views sex as something which is wrong and dirty. 'Wooden leg' provides an unanswerable explanation for failure to achieve something which might otherwise have been expected.

When the 'games' have been identified, the 'adult' can supplant them by 'gratifying reality experiences'.

'Script writing' involves deciphering lifelong patterns of behaviour which were usually established in childhood. It seems, to correspond roughly to Adler's concept of the life style. When the patient becomes aware of his 'scripts', he can, if he wishes, 'rewrite them'.

The ultimate aim of transactional analysis is to allow the 'Adult' to be in charge of all social situations. The therapist is supposed to be non-directive and non-judgemental, but it is apparent that he superimposes a considerable theoretical substructure to the patient's experiences.

Many people find attraction in Berne's simplistic approach, and enjoy identifying the 'games' which they themselves play. To tell the truth, such 'games' often provide the plots for television soap operas.

The exponents of the method claim speedy success, and speak little of their failures. Many therapists question the diagnostic categories to which patients are allotted. 'Recovery' sometimes suggests a swing from a depressed to a hypomanic stage.

Laymen often find transactional analysis attractive, perhaps because of its naivety, its plausibility and the ease with which they can understand its concepts. It is a reminder to the practitioners of other schools that such is the road to instant popularity.

Rational therapy
This is supposed to be useful in the treatment of people with severe personality disorders. It is based on the rather arbitrary categorisation of emotion as a form of *thought*, which then may itself be used to influence thought.

Its practitioners adopt what they describe as a non-judgemental approach. They embark upon a philosophical discussion with the patient about who is really *suffering* from his behaviour. The rational therapist tries to persuade the patient that it is *he*. It is their view that patients often adopt such irrational attitudes as, everyone must be perfect, everyone must be approved by everyone, and anyone who makes a mistake must be condemned. The therapist 'monitors' such illogical arguments and 'makes the patient face up to things'. Occasionally, the patient varies the monotony by agreeing with what he is told, whereupon the therapist cheers up and speaks of insight.

'Rational therapy' is a pretentious name for an approach of dubious theoretical background. Its practitioners emphasise the high degree of anxiety to which some psychopaths are subjected, and suggest that many of them are dominated by it. In everyday clinical practice, there is a tendency to ignore psychopathic anxiety altogether. It is therefore useful to be reminded that is exists, and that it may be considerable. In view of the widespread hopelessness about psychopathy, some therapists may be interested in learning more about Rational Therapy.

CARDINAL PRINCIPLE: Cardinal principles are not always where you expect them to be.

11

Termination

CARDINAL PRINCIPLE: When all is finished, take care of the conscious, and leave the unconscious to take of itself.

Intensive psychotherapy continues for many months, and the patient comes to assume that whenever a problem arises, he will be able to discuss it with his therapist. He learns that 'just talking' is helpful in clarifying many of the difficulties, even though a solution is not always forthcoming. Thus, in the course of therapy, the patient comes to depend on his therapist. Technically, this dependence is a neurotic one, but it should not therefore be regarded as harmful. The patient shares his decisions. He does not have to accept total and ultimate responsibility for them.

The neurotic dependence of the patient upon his therapist gives him courage to face many of the situations which hitherto he has found difficult. When he meets a new problem, he feels that he has his therapist behind him. Sometimes he 'feels' this, almost literally. It is as though the therapist is actually at his shoulder. He knows that he will be expected to report success or failure at the next meeting, and usually he wishes to report success. Occasionally, the thought comes to him, 'How will I manage when I no longer have a therapist? What will happen when he says that I am to come no more? This may be an uncomfortable thought and the patient tries to put it out of his mind. When things are going badly, and especially if the patient suspects that his therapist is impatient or angry with him, he half expects to be told, 'There is nothing more I can do for you.' This is a frightening thought, and he heaves a sigh of silent relief when, despite, the difficulties, the next appointment is arranged.

How do you know when the patient is better?
This question is asked frequently, both by the patient in the early stages of therapy, and by the therapist in the early stages of his training. We have deferred an answer until this final chapter, because

not only is the question complex, but the answer is subtle and complicated, and requires that we should already have discussed some of the problems which have to be overcome.

Patients who come for psychotherapy suffer from a variety of symptoms. They may, for example, have physical discomfort, irrational fears, unreasonable resentments, difficulty in controlling themselves, sexual problems, chronic states of tension or disagreeable thoughts. They may be unable to do simple things such as leaving the house or travelling by public transport.

Their primary needs, various combinations of feeling and doing, present almost from the moment of birth, can be satisfied only in accordance with the demands of reality and the requirements of society. If they are hungry, their need can be satisfied only if food is present and if it is their's to eat.

In particular, the culture insists that primary needs be tamed, modified or re-moulded. If they cannot be satisfied in a way which is acceptable, they must be struck down, resisted, repressed and denied, by the various mechanisms of defence.

Aggression, for example, must be channelled, limited, formalised. It is permissible to cheer one's team in the institutionalised battle of the football match. It is also acceptable to condemn verbally the irresponsible behaviour of the rival gangs of hooligans who battle with each other afterwards.

This verbal condemnation springs from precisely the same aggressive streak as the fisticuffs. However, in our culture, words are a much more acceptable way of expressing aggression.

Likewise, unacceptable sexual behaviour must be deviated into such socially acceptable channels as artistic creativity or the *appreciation* of artistic creativity. In this we include everything from a child's scribble, the music of a primitive pop group to the most exalted classical works of art; everything that may be created or admired by man, whether it be plebian and popular, pornographic, classical or exalted.

When sexual urges are gratified in these ways, we say they have been sublimated. In Chapter 5, we have referred to some of the other defence mechanisms which are used to modify unacceptable drives.

But some patients encounter stress for which the normal defence mechanisms are inadequate. The stress may be one or many, isolated or repeated, major or minor. For various reasons — they may be biological, psychological or physiological — such patients have found that their normal coping mechanisms are inadequate. Perhaps the stress has been great or the coping mechanism weak. In consequence, they have unconsciously made inappropriate, illogical or abnormal use of *normal* defence mechanisms. Misuse of *normal* mechanisms creates a pathological state, which nevertheless helps the patient to cope with the stress, albeit in an uneconomical and unsatisfactory way.

When he has created a mechanism to cope with stress: a mechanism whereby he can control drives which are socially unacceptable, the patient is often reluctant to abandon it. To reject it will put him at the mercy of his socially unacceptable behaviour. Even though the mechanism itself may cause distress, he is 'safer' with it than without it. The mechanism is called a neurotic symptom.

This raises the major paradox of neurotic illness. If the patient is employing a coping mechanism which helps him face satisfactorily the problems which are imposed upon him by the culture in which he lives, is he ill? Is mental illness a myth? Is the whole thing simply a verbal quibble? Is the 'patient' really super-well? Instead of trying to make him 'better', should we not be trying to emulate him? Such philosophical matters as these have created much agitated, anxious and even angry and emotional discussion. The neurotic patient appears to have no physical or psychological abnormality. It is as though he made ingenious and self-gratifying use of the normal-psychological mechanisms. Neurotic illness has become his way of coping.

However, it is an ineffective and inefficient way of coping. Neither the patient, his friends, his relatives, or the society in which he lives is happy with it. It is fear of his symptom, and the possible consequences to his relationship with other people, that brings the patient to therapy.

Fear is a biological necessity, and the fittest cannot survive without it. Perhaps the common fear of walking close to the edge of a cliff, which is often looked upon as being slightly irrational, is an inheritance from our remote ancestors, who may have survived when their less 'neurotic' brethren succumbed in consequence. We are not asserting that all neurotic fears are the genetically determined results of natural selection!

Fear of the edge of a cliff may spread to other situations, ones which are not dangerous, such as fear of looking from a window or over the side of a bridge. Limited fears such as these may cause little inconvenience, but if they should spread further — for example, to looking out of *any* window or over *any* railing, they may cause considerable handicap and justify medical intervention.

Although patients cannot be freed from fear — it might be harmful if they could — their fear can be brought into proportion and they can be helped to control it realistically.

Realistic fear may proceed to unrealistic elaboration. Fear is also part of superstition. If the salt is spilled, it might be wise to throw a pinch over the shoulder, into the eyes of the devil. If we defy him or deny his existence, he may arrange for a pot of paint to fall on us when next we walk under a ladder.

Although we deal flippantly with the matter, it has a solemn aspect. If we are angry with someone whom we love, and they then die, we may well believe that their death was a punishment for us. This is foolish superstition when it is believed by someone else, but not when we ourselves are involved.

We observed in Chapter 1 that symptoms develop when feelings are suppressed. Now we must ask. to what extent is it safe to express feelings? And to whom? And of what nature? Suppose the feelings are of anger with those whom we love, or of sexual attraction to those to whom we are related by ties of blood?

When his illness started, the patient was often seriously limited in the expression of his feelings, often because of unconscious, superstitious, and childlike dread of the consequences. To what extent is he now able to face situations which he once avoided? Like a parent who must one day let his child cross the road alone, the psychotherapist must eventually let his patient face the world alone. How does he know when he is ready to do so?

This brings the non-judgemental psychotherapist face to face with the judgement of the society which he serves. It is Society which says that the patient is better or not better, not the therapist.

The matter can only be put to the test. One day, the therapist will say, 'now you must manage without me.' Only then will he know whether or not his patient is 'better'. The reader might reflect that precisely the same judgement applies to all medical disorders.

Much will depend upon the care with which he has chosen his patient. Careful selection brings the best hope for a successful outcome. When the assessment has been accurate, the symptoms will gradually diminish in intensity. Occasionally they may flare up, but provided that they are not required as a device to hold on to the therapist, they will eventually be forgotten.

'Better' means stronger. The original selection criteria were designed to identify those patients who had the potential to grow in psychological 'strength' and to eliminate those who were incurably weak. It is important that the criteria for selection should be rigorously applied. Hard, tenacious work deserves a satisfactory reward. It should not be frittered away on sows' ears.

Thus, a time comes when therapy must cease. Sometimes this happens only when the patient or the therapist dies, or when one moves so far away from the other that communication between them becomes impossible. This may be very far away indeed. As the author once discovered to his cost, a patient with a strong positive transference will think nothing of travelling the length of Britain in order to visit his therapist. A colleague who went to work in Australia was greeted with delight by a patient whom he had supposed was safely ensconced in Edinburgh.

Termination of psychotherapy is itself part of psychotherapy, and should be planned and executed with care. The patient must come to terms with the fact that a time is approaching when he will face his problems without help. This fact may be a disagreeable one. For his part, the therapist must accept the paradox that if his efforts have been successful, his patient will sever all the bonds, and he will never know that things have gone well. He will never be able to pronounce the patient 'cured', for if he were to review the case, it would mean that a therapeutic relationship was being continued. In psychotherapy, success is measured by the patient's capacity to manage without his therapist.

Since termination is an integral part of psychotherapy, it cannot be achieved in the course of one session. The patient will require time to work through his feelings about it and to make plans for his future. This will require several sessions.

The author's practice is to reserve about ten per cent of the time allotted to therapy for the process of termination. If therapy has continued for twelve months, he allocates five or six weeks to termination. The procedure is as follows:

Towards the end of a session, preferably when an appropriate theme is under discussion, the therapist reminds the patient that the time is approaching when their meetings must finish. He emphasises his wish to share with his patient the decision about the timing, and asks him to consider the point before their next meeting. Early in the next meeting, he asks the patient for his thoughts on the matter. The patient sometimes suggests that the meetings should stop immediately, or within a very short time. The therapist should not agree to an immediate termination. Sometimes the patient is angry and says that if he is going to finish in six weeks, he might as well stop in five, or in four, three, two or one week, or now. Alternatively, he may suggest a 'natural' finishing date. Perhaps the year is coming to an end, or a holiday is approaching, or it is the anniversary of the commencement of therapy. When these suggestions fall within the ten per cent rule, they can be accepted as appropriate. Thereafter, the therapist should pay careful attention to themes which are concerned with separation, being left alone, being neglected, death, starting a new life, being let down, and so on. It is likely that he will hear expressions of regret and resentment, thoughts of being punished, attempts at 'making up' and expressions of gratitude for benefits received. These matters will usually be reported in respect of incidents from the past, but the therapist will link the latent content with the impending termination. The patient is sorry that therapy is to finish. He is grateful for the help he has received, but resents the fact that he is expected to manage alone.

Occasionally, he will complain that he has derived no benefit from his attendance. Such complaints may be difficult to refute, especially when the therapist himself feels that he has been of little help to his patient. He may feel slightly offended by such allegations, but he must remember that his instructions were that the patient should always put into words what he thought and felt. This is exactly what is happening.

Therefore, the therapist should never protest, try to explain, or endeavour to compromise. The decision has been made, and it must be accepted. Incidentally, if it is true that the patient has not benefited from many months of psychotherapy, it is improbable that he would benefit from more. The fact that he is able to say 'I have not benefited', is evidence that he has benefited!

The patient will often ask if he can return if problems arise, or if things are going badly. The therapist should help the patient to consider the significance of this request. Is it a device to keep the relationship alive? It implies that the patient will encounter situations with which he is unable to cope. It should not be disputed that he will meet situations for which he is not prepared, but it is unlikely that he can be made *more* prepared for unexpected situations by a further period of therapy. Although it is not necessary to give an uncompromising refusal, the therapist should indicate his hope that his patient has the capacity to cope with new problems from his own resources.

The patient sometimes asks about the therapist's expectations for him. The therapist is also interested in the future, but this involves prediction and he must continue to emphasise that he is not a seer. Time alone will show how the patient manages. The therapist himself may *never* know the answer.

The ultimate aim of psychotherapy is to help the patient to 'grow' psychologically: to develop the ability to cope with his problems as a healthy *adult*: to recognise that he is responsible, but not defenceless. It is hoped that he will no longer find it necessary to turn personal problems into disease — indeed doing so is an abrogation of his responsibility for them. If therapy were merely a device to provide an alternative form of neurotic dependence, it would have failed in its purpose. The original contract did not promise independence, but it assured the patient of help in his quest to achieve it. The therapist promised to 'attend' to the patient: he did not promise that all problems would be solved.

Some therapists conclude psychotherapy by a 'weaning' period. If the patient has attended twice a week, the frequency of sessions is reduced to once a week, then to once a fortnight, then to once a month, then to once every three months. When this technique is used, termination is prolonged. The patient continues to attend for several years although he is seen only once every three months. The sessions become little more than a review of what has happened since the previous meeting. Intensive therapy has drifted imperceptibly into supportive therapy, and the patient never experiences the apprehension of facing his problems alone, or the exhilaration of solving them without help. Of course, by maintaining a supportive relationship, the therapist keeps a paternal eye on him. But he deprives him of one of the principal aims of therapy — that of managing by his own efforts.

When it is all over, the patient will sometimes review his treatment. Often he will find that the intensity of the feelings that he once had — feelings of frustration, of affection, sometimes of dissatisfaction, sometimes of terrible fear — have dissipated. Often, he finds that he has forgotten much of what occurred. He realises that much of what he 'discovered' was obvious: that little was really new; that he himself did most of the work. Often he will experience a warm, but now rather remote affection for his therapist. There are moments when he will find himself wanting to get in touch, and sometimes he will think of writing to him. He seldom does so.

In the last minute of the last session, a few patients ask the therapist to say what he 'really thinks' of them. They may ask for a final favour, or for an opinion or for a piece of advice. Such behaviour indicates that to the very end, they have maintained a hope that the therapist is holding some secret, something of wisdom which would be of benefit to them. The request should be interpreted in this light. There is no Santa Claus.

The final moments of therapy are rather nostalgic ones. For the therapist, the last session should be essentially the same as those which have gone before. He should not change his approach in any way. As the patient departs, he may be given a conventional wish of good fortune. In return the patient may press a small gift into the hands of the therapist. Probably he should not accept, but to tell the truth, he usually does.

Despite what has been said, it is likely that the patient will get in touch with his therapist if a crisis occurs. If this happens only very occasionally, in situations of obvious difficulty, the therapist may agree to see the patient for a once-only session. On the other hand, if crises become frequent, they should be interpreted as devices to keep alive a dependent relationship. The problems and fears of breaking the chains of dependency may again be discussed with the patient. The therapist must then make a decision. He may refuse to see the patient again or he may reconcile himself to a situation of chronic dependence, in which occasional supportive attendance is accepted. The therapist should not resume intensive psychotherapy. Although it may be rather trying for the therapist, periodic support is probably better for the patient. Occasionally, when the therapist eventually acknowledges the need for such support, the patient seems to acquire belated independence. This is unusual. Generally, he will require support from someone, and perhaps it is appropriate that the 'someone' should be the therapist who knows him best.

Writing the last few words of a book like this is rather like terminating psychotherapy. The author has a warm, rather nostalgic feeling for the reader he will never meet. He is acutely aware of having written little that was not already obvious. He wonders why some readers have persevered to the end, whilst others could not get past the first page. He wonders what more he should have included, and what he might have omitted. He wonders whether any of it has been useful and how much has been a waste of time. He again hopes that some of his readers will write to tell him.

Suggestions for further reading

Balint M 1957 The doctor, his patient and the illness. Tavistock Publications, London

Berne E 1970 Games people play. Pelican, Harmondsworth

Berne E 1975 What do you say after you say hello? Pelican, Harmondsworth

Boss Medard 1963 Psychoanalysis and Dasein analysis. Trans. Lefebre. Basic Books, New York

Bremner C 1973 An elementary textbook of psychoanalysis. International Universities Press, New York

Brown J A C 1979 Freud and the post Freudians. Penguin, Harmondsworth

Burns L Worsley J (ed) 1970 Behaviour therapy in the 1970s. Wright, Bristol.

Ellis A 1973 Humanistic psychotherapy: the rational-emotive approach. McGraw Hill, New York

Erikson E H 1963 Childhood and society. Penguin, Harmondsworth

Eysenck H J 1966 The effects of psychotherapy. International science, New York

Eysenck H J 1960 Behaviour therapy and the neuroses. Pergamon, Oxford

Freud S 1974 Complete works. Pelican Freud Library, Harmondsworth. Especially: Two short accounts of psychoanalysis. Studies on hysteria (with Breuer). Interpretation of dreams. Three essays on sexuality.

Horney K 1951 Neurosis and human growth. Routledge and Regan Paul, London

Jacobi J 1968 The psychology of C G Jung. Yale University Press, New Haven

Jones E 1974 Life and work of Sigmund Freud. Pelican, Harmondsworth

Kaplan T & S 1974 The new sex therapy: active treatment of sexual dysfunction. Brunnel Mazel, New York

Kasden A E & Wilson, G P 1978 Criteria for evaluating psychotherapy. Arch. Gen. Psych. 35: 407-16.

Laing R D 1960 The divided self. Penguin, Harmondsworth

Malan D H 1979 Individual psychotherapy and the science of psychodynamics. Butterworths, Sevenoaks, Kent

Marks I M 1969 Fears and phobias. Heinemann Medical, London

Masters W, Johnson V 1970 Human sexual inadequacy. Principles of the new sex therapy. Little, Brown & Co, Boston

Masters W Johnson V 1964 Human sexual response. Little, Brown & Co, Boston

Morse & Watson 1977 Psychotherapies. Holt, Rinehart & Winston, New York

Rogers C R 1951 Client centered therapy. Houghton Mifflin, Boston

Rogers C R 1970 On encounter groups. Harper & Row, New York

Rycroft C 1972 A critical dictionary of psychoanalysis. Penguin, Harmondsworth

Sandler J et al 1973 The patient and the analyst. George Allen & Unwin, London

Sullivan H S 1954 The psychiatric interview. Norton, New York

Wolpe J 1958 Psychotherapy by reciprocal inhibition. Stanford University Press, Stanford

Wolpe J 1973 The practice of behaviour therapy. Pergamon, Oxford

Index

Abreaction of emotion, 55, 86, 126
Acting out, 120
Action, course of, 69
Adler, Alfred, 177
Admission to hospital, 117
Advice, 41
Age, importance of, 33
Alcohol, 126 ff
Alcoholics Anonymous, 32
Alcoholism, 139ff
    amnesia in, 141
    tremor in, 142
Ambivalence, 89
Amnesia in alcoholism, 141
Anal stage, 174, 175
Analytical psychology, 178
Analysis, components of, 26ff
    training, 28
Anonymity, 98
Answer, a perfect, 16
Answers to questions, 64
Answers, reserved, 53
Assertive training, 184
Attention, aspects of, 43
Aversion therapy, 183

Bad-tempered people, 156
Behaviour modification, 182
    therapy, 182
Behavioural analysis, 184
Being-in-the-world, 186
Bereavement, 145
Berne, Eric, 188
'Bovarysme, le', 168

Cadence and stress, 63
Case discussions, 130
Castration anxiety, 171, 172
Catharsis, 86
Change, 130
Charcot, 7
Clarification, 51
Cliches, 8ff

Client centered therapy, 187
Client and patient, distinction between,
    18
Coincidence, 84
Colleagues, criticism of, 124
Comments, 54
Communication, doorstop, 67
    forms of, 57
    non-verbal, 13, 58, 60
    telephone, 61
    verbal, 13, 58, 60
'Completely forgotten!', 27
Compulsory 'treatment', 162
Condemnation, 103
Confidentiality, 119, 162
    breach of, 39
Conflict, 21
Confrontation, 97
Conscience, 71, 173
Consulting room, 100
Content, latent, 47
    manifest, 47
'Contract,' the, 38, 108
Contracts, written, 39
Conventional phrases, 66
Conventions, social, 43–4
Couch, 101
Counselling, pastoral, 164
Counselling and psychotherapy,
    distinction between, 17
Counsellor, selection of, 36
Counter-transference, 96
'Course of action', 69
Co-therapy, 116
Criteria for selection of patient, 29
Criticism, 124
Cultural differences, 165

Dasein, 186
Death and dying, 144ff
Deceit, 57
Deductions made by patients, 61
Defence mechanisms, 74ff

Delirium tremens, 142
Denial, 75
  in alcoholism, 140
  in mourning, 145
Depression, 123–4
Diagnosis, the, 68
Diagnosis of neurotic disorders, 155
'Difficult' patients, 152ff
Displacement, 176
'Doing something active', 10
Doorstep communications, 67–8
Dreams, 27, 79
Drugs, abreactive, 126
  effect of, 70
  therapeutic, 125
Dumb insolence, 162

Eccentric, 167
Eclecticism, 170
Ego ideal, 173
Emergencies, 111
Emotion, 54
Emotional retardation, 158
Employment history, 106
Encouragement, 43
Errors, 59
  lies and the truth, 67
  and mistakes, 27–28
Evaluation, 131
Evasions, 58
Existential psychotherapy, 185
Expectations, of the patient, 22
  therapist's of the patient, 29ff
Experience, sharing of, 102
Experts, baffled, 14
Explanation, 42
Extraversion and introversion, 178

Facilitation, 51
Family, history, 106
Family, position in, 177
First interview, 104ff
Fitting someone in, 111
Fixation, 175
'Flight into health', 60
Flirtatious, 167
Flooding (implosion), 184
Free association, 90
Friends and relatives, information from, 118
  psychotherapy for, 35
Frigidity and impotence, 138
Freud, Sigmund, 169ff

Gain, 87ff
  primary, 89
  secondary, 88

Generalisations, patient's, 54
Genital stage, 171
Guilt, 72

Hallucinations, in normal people, 20
Hands, state of, 60
History taking, 46
Homosexuality, 136ff
  Freudian view of, 177
Horney, Karen, 179
Hospital, admission to, 117
Household pets, 148
Hypnotic dependence, treatment of, 129
Hypnotism, 125

Id, 174
'Imaginary' symptoms, 155
Implosion (flooding), 184
Impossible people, 156ff
Impotence and frigidity, 138
Incompatibilities, 114
Individual Psychology, 117
Insight, 50
  in psychotherapy, 148
Inspection, 47
Intelligence, importance of, 33
Interpersonal Relations (Sullivan), 180
Interpretation, 47, 59
Interruption, 54
Interviews, joint, 115ff
Introversion and extraversion, 178
Intuition, 65
Isolation, as a defence mechanism, 78

Joint interviews, 115ff
Jokes, 121
'Just talking', 7–8
  value of, 45
Jung, C.G., 178

Letters, 108ff
  from friends and relatives, 109
  from patients, 60, 109
  from solicitors, 109
  to patients, 60, 109
Libidinal stages, 174
Lies, errors and the truth, 67
Life style, 177, 178
Location of therapy, 98
Logic, 9

Magic, 82
'Masculine protest', 178
Masters and Johnson, 138
Masturbation, 135
Meditation, 126
Mental state, 47

'Mind going blank', 63
Modes of experience (Sullivan), 181
Money, 159
Motivation, deficiency of, 32
    external, 31
    of patient, 30
    suspect, 31
    unconscious, 48
Mourning, 86, 145ff
Multiple determination, 85

Names, use of, 4
Neo-Freudians, 179
'Neurotic' pain, 154
Nightmares, 80
Non-criticism, 103
Non-logic, 81ff
Non sequitur, 56
Normal people, 20

Obsessional thoughts, 86-7
Oedipal conflict, 172
    resolution of, 174
Opening question, 105
Oral-dependent stage, 174
Organic disease, exclusion of, 155
Over-determination, 85

Paediatric case, 11ff
    discussion of, 13ff
Palpation, psychological, 47
Pappenheim, Bertha (Fraulein Annie
    O.), case of, 6-7
'Paranormal', 83
Parents and children, 165
Participant observer, 180
Passive aggression, 162
Pastoral counselling, 164
Patients, addressing, 4
    choice of, 35
    'contract' with, 38
    deductions of, 61
    expectations of, 22
    ideal, 35
    selection of, 29
Patients and clients, distinction
        between, 18
Pavlov, 182
Penis envy, 171
Percussion, 'psychological', 47
Personality disorders, psychotherapy in,
    35
Phobias, 55, 85
Physically ill, 144
Placebo effect, 6
Post-hypnotic suggestion, 7
Prayer, 126

Predictions, astrological, 84
Presents and favours, 112
Probation, 163
Problems between patient and therapist,
    24
Procedure, 46, 104
Projection, 78
Promises, 62
Propositions, turning them round, 55
Psychoanalysis, personal, 25
Psychological types (Jung), 178-9
Psychopathy, fixation in, 176
Psychotherapist, patient's criticisms of,
    37
    personal problems of, 37
Psychotherapy, cliches in, 9-10
    expectations of, 21
    intensive, 18
    its own claims, 21
    supportive, 19
    types of, 18
Psychotherapy and counselling,
        differences between, 17
Psychotic illness, psychotherapy in, 35

Questions, asking, 52
    forcing, 53
    inaudible, 53
    leading, 52
    open-ended, 52
    re-phrasing, 52
Queue jumping, 153

'Rational therapy', 189
Rationalisation, 75-6
Reaction formation, 77
Reassurance, 41
    effects of, 13ff
Receptionist, 103
Regression, 175
Relatives, 166
Relatives and friends, psychotherapy
        for, 35
Repetition-compulsion, 178
Repression, 77
Resistance, 73-74
    conscious, 63
    nature of, 74
Rogers, Carl, 187
Role playing, 184

Scapegoating, 120
Schizophrenia, 123
Second opinions, 121
Secrecy, pledges of, 118
Secretary, 103

Selection of patients, criteria for, 29
Self-awareness, 25ff
Sensitivities, 86
Sessions, duration and frequency, 110
Sexual difficulties, management of, 133
   types of, 135
Sexual history, 106
Shame, 72
Sharing, 49
Sherlock Holmes, 22, 23, 26, 41
Short cuts, 125
Silence, 54, 62, 162
   hostility of, 63
Skin colour, 59
Sleep, 127
Sleeping pills, 127ff
Slips of the pen and tongue, 59
Smoking, 101, 112
'Social suicide', 163
Stereotyped phrases, 66
Stress and cadence, 63
Suggestions and advice, 23, 41
Suicide, 149ff
   impact on the therapist, 37
   'social', 163
Sullivan, H.S., 180
Superego, 173
Superstition, 83
Symbolism, 80
Symptoms, 'imaginary', 154
Systematic desensitisation, 184

'Talking cure', the, 7
Talking, value of, 4
Tape recorder, 101
Technical words, use of, 123

Telepathy, 65–66
Telephone, 61, 110
Termination, 191
Terminology, 17
Themes, recurrent, 45
Therapist, behaviour of, 24
   dress of, 102
   patient's curiosity about, 107
   role of, 43
   selection of, 36
Therapy, inadvertent, with another
      therapist's patient, 34
Titles, use of, 5
To the patient, 19
Transactional analysis, 188
Transference, 92ff
   coping with, 94
   counter-, 96–97
   identification of, 93
   interpretation of, 95
   management of, 95
   negative, 27, 45
Tremor, in alcoholism, 142

Unconscious, the, 72
   interpretation of, 73
   speculations about, 73
   understanding, 44
Untruthfulness, 67
Unwanted people, 156

Verbalisation, 51
Violence, 161

'Weaning' as termination, 197
Wish-fulfillment, 78